Gender, Sickness, and Healing
in Rural Egypt

Conflict and Social Change Series

Series Editors
Scott Whiteford and William Derman
Michigan State University

Gender, Sickness, and Healing in Rural Egypt

Ethnography in Historical Context

Soheir A. Morsy

Westview Press

BOULDER • SAN FRANCISCO • OXFORD

RA
418.3
.E3
M67
1993

Conflict and Social Change Series

All rights reserved. No part of this publication may be reproduced or transmitted in any form or by any means, electronic or mechanical, including photocopy, recording, or any information storage and retrieval system, without permission in writing from the publisher.

Copyright © 1993 by Westview Press, Inc.

Published in 1993 in the United States of America by Westview Press, Inc., 5500 Central Avenue, Boulder, Colorado 80301-2877, and in the United Kingdom by Westview Press, 36 Lonsdale Road, Summertown, Oxford OX2 7EW

Library of Congress Cataloging-in-Publication Data
Morsy, Soheir A.
    Gender, sickness, and healing in rural Egypt : ethnography in historical context / Soheir A. Morsy.
        p.   cm.—(Conflict and social change series)
    Includes bibliographical references.
    ISBN 0-8133-8166-5
    1. Social medicine—Egypt.   2. Medical anthropology—Egypt.
3. Health attitudes—Egypt—Sex differences—Case studies.
4. Health behavior—Egypt—Sex differences—Case studies.
I. Title.   II. Series.
RA418.3.E3M67   1993
362.1'0962—dc20

                                                                        93-9276
                                                                        CIP

Printed and bound in the United States of America

The paper used in this publication meets the requirements
of the American National Standard for Permanence of Paper
for Printed Library Materials Z39.48-1984.

10   9   8   7   6   5   4   3   2   1

27381713

There clearly is not, nor can there be, such a thing as a universally accept-
able account of a living tradition. Any representation of tradition is
contestable. What shape that contestation takes, if it occurs, will be deter-
mined not only by the powers and knowledge each side deploys,
but by the collective life they aspire to—or to whose survival they are quite
indifferent. Moral neutrality, here as always, is no guarantee of political
innocence.

—Talal Asad
The Idea of an Anthropology of Islam

CONTENTS

TABLES

ACKNOWLEDGMENTS

First and foremost my thanks are due to the villagers of the research community for which I have chosen the pseudonym "Fatiha." My visit with them is one of the most significant experiences of my life. To them I shall always be indebted for the opportunity of getting to know my Egyptian homeland from a vantage point that had been obscured by my earlier education.

I am grateful to the Wenner-Gren Foundation for Anthropological Research and the American Research Center in Egypt for supporting the fieldwork on which this book is based.

Many friends, including colleagues, professors, and students at Michigan State University, The American University in Cairo, and the University of California–Berkeley, contributed to the completion of this work with both encouragement and critical insights.

In Egypt support was forthcoming from many researchers, including some affiliates of the National Center for Sociological and Criminological Research, Alexandria University's Faculty of Arts and Letters, and Cairo's Demographic Center.

In the United States the very formulation of the research topic of this book owes much to the activities of the Anthropology Women's Collective at Michigan State and our mentors Judy Brown and Karen Sacks. Randy Donahue gave generously of his time; his computer skills proved indispensable for computations of the raw numerical data. To Lorie Powell, who prepared earlier drafts of this book, I would like to express my appreciation of her word processing skills.

Leonard Kasdan was the first male professor to encourage me to work with historical material on Egyptian women. From Brigitte Jordan I enjoyed the once-novel sisterly support of a woman faculty member and unceasing intellectual challenge. Since as a student I first encountered Professor Arthur Rubel, his support has been continuous, encouraging me to address medical anthropology in light of general disciplinary concerns. For his role in balancing my earlier biomedical bent, among other contributions, I am grateful.

Last, but certainly not least, I am indebted to the members of my family: Ashraf, Gigi, Mona, Fuad, and Amr. I hope that my grandchildren, Cherine, Ziad, Fairouz, and Nadine, will someday include this work in the exploration of their multifaceted cultural heritage.

Soheir A. Morsy

INTRODUCTION

To many Egyptians of my generation the experiences associated with the Nasserist welfare state remain a yardstick against which judgement is passed on more recent changes in the country. Years after the death of Gamal ᶜAbdel Nasser, much debate continues to surround the demise of the Nasserist state doctrine of Arab Socialism in favor of successor policies of economic liberalization, popularly known as the *Infitah*—the opening (e.g. Abdel Khalek 1982a; E. Davis n.d.; A. Hussein 1981; Morsy 1980; Waterbury 1983). Scholarly assessments of Egypt's two major post-colonial political economic orientations prompted the fundamental question of whether socialism was in fact the framework of the country's development strategy during the period between the initiation of republican rule in 1952 and the issuance of the October Paper of 1974, which decreed the state's Open Door Economic Policies (ODEP). It has been argued that Nasser's strategy of "peaceful transition to socialism," with its emphasis on national unity and its consideration of abolition of exploitation as an epiphenomenon of such unity, cannot be equated with socialist transformation based on class struggle (Akhavi 1975; see also Abdel Khalek 1982b; E. Davis 1977; M. Hussein 1973; Lakhdar 1978).

Arguments against the characterization of Nasserist Egypt as socialist addressed the country's continued integration in the global capitalist political economy, as well as the nature of the state and class formation. The result has been the frequent utilization of "state capitalism" as a blanket label for the form of political economy which characterized the Nasserist era. Objection to this designation by anthropologist Mahfoud Bennoune directs our attention to the variability of state policies over the course of Nasserist rule (Bennoune 1991, personal communication). In a collaborative study Bennoune and Hayef differentiate phases of this transformation, which ranged from support for "free enterprise" and "private initiative" to "etatisation" of the management of the economy, the eventual reversal of "socialist transformation" in favor of resurgence of private entrepreneurship, and the "opening" of the country to Arab and international capital in the late 1970s (Bennoune and Hayef 1986; see also Zaalouk 1988).

Aside from being aware of scholarly discourse pointing out the inadequacy of certain labels for illuminating the dynamics of change within Egyptian and other Arab societies (Richards and Waterbury 1990:301), we should note that such labels often do not capture popular perceptions and sentiments. As state ideology, Arab Socialism was regarded by many Egyptians as the framework of a *populist* development strategy which targeted the *masses* as beneficiaries of the efforts of a strong, interventionist state. Promises of wealth redistribution and social equity at home were greeted with great optimism. In addition, the regime's anti-imperialist stance resonated with popular nationalist sentiment.

Today members of the Egyptian nationalist opposition, feminists included, while reassessing the value of the once widely dispensed "promissory notes" (cf. Kruks, Rapp, and Young 1989) and cognizant of the limitations imposed on political participation, nevertheless hold Nasserist populism in a favorable light. This policy orientation is preferred over current development strategies in the era of the "opening," regional oil wealth, and Western domination (Abdel Wahab 1988; El-Baz 1988; Hatem 1992a; Morsi 1976). As observed for other parts of the world, to many of us, the political distance between the sixties and the present seems much greater than the years might indicate (Bookman and Morgen 1988:viii).

Examination of the recent social science literature on Nasser's and Sadat's Egypt reveals a proliferation of macro-analytically focused works which address state policies and their broadly framed societal correlates during the period 1952–1974 and following the "opening" (e.g. Cooper 1982; P. Gran 1987; Hosseinzadeh 1988; Richards and Waterbury 1990:passim; Springborg 1989:passim). By contrast, anthropological studies which document people's lived experiences "on the ground" remain exceptional. This limitation applies to the Nile Delta, the heartland of rural Egypt.

A 1981 review of the multi-language literature of studies on rural Egypt by Hopkins and Mehanna reveals the predominance of a survey orientation which extends back to studies conducted during the Nasser era (Hopkins and Mehanna 1981). Unlike the limited number of prospective studies which address peasant society in the context of political economic transformations of the eighties (e.g. Adams 1986a; Hopkins 1987; Morsy 1985; Saunders and Mehanna 1988), anthropological commentary on rural Egypt during the sixties and seventies is generally retrospective (e.g. Abaza 1987a; Saad 1988; Sabea 1987). Commenting on "the dearth of recent work on peasants," Abu-Lughod observes that with the exception of Hopkins' recent book on agrarian transformation in

Egypt, the only monograph on Arab peasants in current use is a journalistic account which reproduces ahistoricism and colonial stereotypes (Abu-Lughod 1989:299; see also Gran 1987:92; Waterbury 1991:3). In the same vein, the "paucity . . . of theoretical and conceptual debate and analysis" has been the object of caustic remarks by Glavanis and Glavanis (1989:1) in their critique of research on rural societies of the Middle East as a whole.

Commentary on this "dearth" or on the analytical limitations addressed in recent reviews extends to the medical anthropology of Arab and other Middle Eastern societies (Good and Good n.d.; Millar and Lane 1988; Morsy 1981a, 1989). As for gender studies, much intellectual energy has been spent countering the definition of women as "essentially Islamic, and therefore automatically oppressed" (Moors 1989: 195; see also Bybee 1978; Hale 1989), often to the detriment of broader analytical concerns (cf. Kandiyoti 1990; Moore 1988; Ong 1990).

Recently there has occurred a noteworthy shift away from ahistoricism and desocialized cultural abstractions. This development contrasts with the essentialism which has characterized much of the earlier European language academic literature on Arab/Islamic societies (Abaza and Stauth 1988). An increasing number gender studies of these societies now incorporate the type of historical or ethnographic analysis applied to other parts of the world (cf. Abaza 1987b; Bell 1986; Cherif 1989; Glavanis 1984; Hatem 1987; Al-Hibri 1982; Marsot 1978, 1989; Mernissi 1982a, 1982b, 1988; Mohsen 1985; Nash and Fernandez-Kelley 1983; Saunders and Mehanna 1988; Tomiche 1968a; Tucker 1983, 1986). Thus the cultural constructions of gender are integrated into the broader framework of political economic scholarship.

The analytical framework of anthropology's historical political economy (e.g. Nash 1981; Roseberry 1988, 1989; Taussig 1980a) and associated concerns with time and place in ethnographic constructions (e.g. Appadurai 1986; Fabian 1983; Fardon 1990) allow for historical contextualization while retaining anthropology's traditional concern with social and experiential particularities. Regarding Egyptian peasant women specifically, such particularities of social and interpersonal relations are often bypassed even in feminist discourse. As Mona Abaza has remarked, "[Egyptian] feminists allowed themselves to talk on behalf of all women, even if their own 'emancipative' and 'educative' attitude implied serious omissions about the conditions of everyday life which the majority of . . . women face" (Abaza 1987b:2–3; see also Galul 1984).

The present historically informed and ethnographically grounded study of gender, sickness and healing offers a contribution to the scant anthropological literature on contemporary rural Egypt. The empirical data on which this book is based were collected during a year of field work conducted in the Nile Delta village of Fatiha beginning in the summer of 1974.[1] This was the period just prior to the implementation of the state's policies of economic liberalization; Nasserist development policies had been operative for two decades at the time of my arrival in the village.[2] The derivative local-level view focuses on two elements of state populism, gender (Abdel Khader 1987; Hatem 1992b; Hijab 1988) and health (Baker 1979; Hatata 1968; Khalaf 1987). As in the case of urbanites, to many rural inhabitants, the way of life associated with the era addressed in this study remains a baseline against which they continue to evaluate their current situation, whether positively or negatively (Saad 1988; Shahenda Maklad 1992, personal communication).

Ethnography in Historical Context:
The Embeddedness of Culture

In providing documentation of life in rural Egypt, this book draws on historical developments to produce "ethnography in an expanded field" (Koptiuch 1985). It represents an attempt at operationalizing anthropology's "experimental ideal" of taking account of historical political economy as a methodological complement to ethnographic analysis (Marcus and Fischer 1986; cf. Dewalt and Pelto 1985; Roseberry 1988, 1989), extending this orientation to the discipline's medical field (e.g. Frankenberg 1980; Hopper 1975; Morgan 1987; Morsy 1979, 1990a; Onoge 1975; Scheper-Hughes and Lock 1987, 1990; Singer et al. 1988; Young 1982).

The account of rural Egypt which follows focuses on gender differentiation and its reciprocal relation to the cultural and social dimensions of sickness and healing. Informed by Roseberry's conception of community, the one under consideration here is "seen, not as a given society—or culture outside-of-history but as a political association formed through processes of political and cultural creation . . . the generation of meaning of contexts of unequal power" (Roseberry 1989:14). Thus structural relations associated with state development policies, and reproduced in their shadow, are integral to the analysis.

By placing emphasis on the interfacing of historically delineated local-level organizational power and structural power which regulates the political economy (Wolf 1990), this work guards against cultural essentialism, a pronounced tendency in the anthropology of Arab/Islamic societies (Abaza and Stauth 1988). While cognizant of the historical role of religious authority in informing gender differentiation (Kandiyoti 1990; Haddad 1985), and the comparability of elements of contemporary medical knowledge and therapeutic practices to antecedent regional traditions (M.J. Good 1980; Good and Good n.d;

Greenwood 1981; Lane 1987), the accounts of gender differentiation and contemporary medical pluralism which follow are neither studies of the ideological origins of female subjugation nor investigations of medical cultural continuity per se. The primary focus here is on historically delineated social contextualization, not dating (Delphie 1988; see also Eldholm, Harris, and Young 1977). Gender differentiation and medical pluralism are anchored in *historically contingent* social power relations and associated ideological orientations (Hatem 1987; Leacock 1977; Rapp 1977). Thus contextualized, these temporally and spatially bound complex social phenomena are not reducible to textual theological directives pertaining to Muslim women (cf. Antoun 1968; Abu-Zahra 1970), or the literary traditions of Arabic/Islamic medicine (P. Gran 1979a; Gallagher 1985).

In situating sickness and healing in historical context the present work defines power as a primary analytical construct. Far from neglecting cognitive, affective, and behavioral factors, the conceptual framework adopted here maintains the centrality of these traditional anthropological concerns. When "medicine as an ethnographic category" (Glick 1967) is considered, analytical scrutiny is extended to the social relations of sickness and healing as symbols of power (Young 1982:270; see also Fabrega 1990). In short, this study's simultaneous concern with the social production of sickness and the cultural interpretation of suffering guards against replacing the once-dominant idealist socioculturalism of medical anthropology with an equally one-sided materialism wherein culture becomes the missing concept (Worsley 1984:41). In addition to its relevance to "ethno-" medical conceptions, culture is deemed significant as an expression of control, resistance, and defiance (Friedrich 1989). As a mechanism of social reproduction, including socially sanctioned dissent expressed in a medical idiom, culture is linked to material systemic elements, both local and national (Alavi 1973; Fields 1988).[3]

The present study's simultaneous concern with male-female social power relations and the cultural mechanisms of their reproduction is well served by Adams' conception of power. Beyond generally defining power as the "control one party exercises over the (social) environment of another" (Adams 1967:32), he addresses it in terms of control over *culturally meaningful* elements of this environment (Adams 1967, 1975). In addition to taking into account cultural specificity, Adams' formulation accommodates social contextualization. Accordingly, authority is a matter of "performance or evidence of power," not simply a matter of cultural legitimacy or pronouncements about "the way it should be" (Adams 1975:31). We are directed towards "performance" as well as the specific reaction to said culturally informed and socially contextualized behavior. Thus the analysis of power relations brings into focus expressions of both consent and resistance in social discourse (Bookman and Morgen 1988:viii).

Operationally, this study's consideration of the social conditions, material and ideological, surrounding sickness treats individuals *as part of social collectivities*. Medical knowledge, illness experience, social legitimation of sickness, and healing are addressed as sociocultural mechanisms which inform the reproduction of power relations, notably gender-linked differentiation. Given the intimate relationship between definitions of sickness and departures from culturally prescribed role behavior (Stein 1976:117–119; Bryant 1987:55), the accounts of sickness-linked deviations documented here also help illuminate normative cultural constructions of gender. Furthermore, empirically derived accounts of sickness and healing bring into focus intervening variables, notably peasant status, as well as social position within the community and the household.

Organization of Chapters

The point of departure for this study is the historical process of the creation of the community of Fatiha, the ethnographic setting, and the generation of power relations which characterized the "ethnographic present." In light of the above-noted conception of community, Part One takes us well beyond the physical boundaries of the village, its social organization, and the cultural orientations of its inhabitants. We enter the village by way of an account of the historical transformation of Egyptian society as a whole.

In situating rural Egypt in the context of the transformation of national political economy, Chapter 1 presents a historical summary which leads up to the implementation of Nasserist state policies. This account, which begins with nineteenth century state-sponsored modernization, addresses historical developments to the extent that they render comprehensible conditions in Egypt on the eve of the 1952 July army coup and the eventual development of Arab Socialism, the framework of Nasserist agrarian and health policies. The July Revolution, as this transformation is popularly known, marked the termination of the dynasty established by Muhammad Ali, the nineteenth century architect of Egypt's earlier state-centered development project. National political economic transformations of the nineteenth and twentieth centuries, addressed in Chapter 1, provide the historical context for the overview of the village of Fatiha, its social organization, and the cultural construction of gender, all presented in Chapter 2.

Maintaining emphasis on what has been demonstrated as historically derived male-female differentiation, Part Two presents a local-level view of this differentiation as it relates to sickness and healing. The medical system is regarded as a patterned set of ideas, practices, and social relations intended, ideally, to promote health through the prevention, identification, explanation, and treatment of sickness. Beyond defining the structure of the pluralistic medical system and its idealized function, this part of the book emphasizes the embeddedness of medical discourse in social power relations. The medical system is recognized as an avenue of social control, a complex of mechanisms which contribute to the reproduction of the ideological support of gender differentiation.

Part Two also brings into view what Fabrega has described as "the biological (symptomatic) indicators which lead lay individuals to designate a state of compromised health" (Fabrega 1972:213). It presents illustrative accounts of distressed individuals' and their families' variable partaking of culturally inspired conceptions of ill-health, as well as others' contrasting popular and professional definitions of their sufferings. Beyond considering illness as an individualized process (Good 1977), this part of the book emphasizes the *socially* relevant consequences of person-centered symptoms or conditions (Robinson 1971:17). Distanced from the ontological conception of disease,[4] this part of the book traces the process of *socialization* of individual distress, or what Frankenberg (1980) describes as the making social of disease.

Throughout Part Two different dimensions of the medical system are related to gender differentiation. Beginning with Chapter 3, this relationship is elaborated in the course of examination of local knowledge of the body and the relationship between people's physical/mental constitution and their natural and social environment. Ideas pertaining to the body and ranging from those involving conception to those related to death are scrutinized as cultural terrain for the cultivation of gender ideology and the rationalization of adult male-female power asymmetry.

In addition to illuminating the underlying logic of villagers' explanations of ill-health, and their regular implication of emotions and social relations, Chapter 4 reveals the influence of power relations in observed cases of compromised health. Finally, healing is addressed in Chapter 5, which examines illness prevention, negotiations surrounding socially differentiated symptomatic persons' claims to illness, and management of sickness. It covers household care and specialized healing of both the traditional and cosmopolitan professional variety, and their relationship to male-female differentiation.

Supplementary to its emphasis on the relationship between different dimensions of the medical system and gender power relations, Part Two of the book brings attention to how sickness and healing are inserted in local social processes and linked to national power asymmetries by the people of Fatiha *themselves*, albeit in a language different from anthropological "etic" representations.

The concluding segment of the book summarizes the main theoretical issues illuminated by the study. It relates associated conclusions to analytical concerns surrounding the comparative study of gender, and to the anthropological analysis of sickness and healing.

Notes

1. Pseudonyms are used throughout the book.

2. It is important to stress that the period of fieldwork coincided with a phase of Egyptian political economy wherein the state's populist orientation was clearly on the decline. Following the June 1967 military defeat, issues of social justice and "dissolution of class differences" were compromised in favor of "national unity" and "a rightist pragmatic tendency" (Zaalouk 1989:55).

3. Earlier studies which address the interconnectedness of the cultural, political and economic demonstrate that the reproduction of culturally sanctioned power differentials is predicated upon subservient parties' acquiescence to those in positions of political and economic ascendancy. Such recognition of the relevance of culture to political economy dates back to the Khaldunian variant of this analytical orientation. More recently, this relevance has been rendered popular by the successor Gramscian notion of hegemony and the related idea of acceptance of the "conception of the world" belonging to the powerful by the relatively powerless (Salame 1990:32).

4. This conception "holds disease to be an exogenous entity that attacks specific organs and structures of the body" (Kuhnke 1990:1–2).

PART ONE

The National Context in Historical Perspective

1

STATE POLICIES, RURAL TRANSFORMATION, AND MEDICINE

After the expulsion of the French from Egypt, three armies remained in the country: the British, the Turks and the Mamlukes. According to the chronicler Jabarti, they "looted the merchants' shops, made the artisans pay a fourfold tax and raped the women. Upon entering a village they imposed an indemnity on the people, arrested the sheiks, and words cannot be found to describe their behavior to the women." . . . Villages were depopulated and agriculture was abandoned. This fanned the flames of discontent against the occupying forces.
(Lustsky 1969:48)

History, it is said, belongs to the victorious. As is often the case for other parts of the non-Euro-American world, the western civilizational project is often credited with providing the inspiration, if not the opportunities, for "emancipating" Egyptian women and expediting their "integration" into public life. The western mission of enlightment is also often acclaimed for protecting the country as a whole from the scourge of disease. To 1950s Egyptian school children who, like myself, had been "privileged" by being educated at British private schools, this was the history of "our" country. After July 1952 those of us who belong to the "generation of the revolution" gained a different understanding of the protracted historical process of "westernization" and the nationalist resistance to it.

With the demise of the Nasserist development project in favor of Egypt's current "openness," some of us came to remember an earlier "opening" which followed the defeat of Muhammad Ali, the founder of the dynasty which was terminated by the July 1952 army coup. As for the peasant majority population of our country, historical commentary remains the province of those of us who are privileged with the power of the written word. Representations of our rural compatriots have ranged from romanticization of their role in resisting foreign domination to

assertions of their legendary submissiveness in the face of authority
(Brown 1990:10–11, 1991).

Regarding women, historical documentation is very limited, even for
times when their position was undergoing major changes. As recently as
1968 Nada Tomiche noted this limitation for the first half of the nineteenth century, when "there were undoubtedly changes in men-women
relationships which paralleled changes in economic practices, foreign
pressures, and the sudden intrusion of a mechanical civilization." Since
the time when Tomiche wrote that "the position of women is blurred by
the reserved silence of local history," her own work, and more recent
historical research, have contributed to the reconstruction of "the vast
puzzle" of women's lives, drawing on Egyptian works such as Al-Jabarti's,
as well as the observations of foreigners, including members of the
Napoleonic expedition. As a result, light has been shed on "the structural weakening of feminine society under the impact of foreign ways of
life and of economic, technical, and social transformations" (Tomiche
1968:171; see also J. Gran 1979; P. Gran 1979a, b; Tucker 1986).

For this anthropological study, reconstruction of "the puzzle" as it
pertains to the ethnographic setting is not a viable option. As in the
case of other Egyptian rural communities (Hopkins 1991:252; Schulze
1991:172), the village of Fatiha has no recorded history. Whereas knowledge of recent national developments which affected the village is
widely shared among its inhabitants, cognizance of their village's nineteenth century origins is restricted to some older villagers. Oral historical accounts provided by a few of them, including an eighty-four-year-
old woman, Khala Nargis (whose Sudanese slave parents had been
brought to the village by its original Turkish rulers),[1] and the village
headman, El-ᶜumda (a descendant of this elite group), yield the following composite narrative:

> Our village was a vacant wilderness which was taken over by [a] Pasha. It
> was given to him as a gift for his services to the army of the Sultan. . . .
> Later on it was given to a Turk by the name of Tusun. . . . About a hun-
> dred and fifty years ago, Tusun came from Albania with Muhammad Ali.
> He was employed as a ruler in Desuk [a nearby provincial town]. He was
> given our village to settle and bring under cultivation. Tusun gave up his
> administrative post, turned to religion, and settled in Fatiha. He built the
> mosque and a guest house [*madyafa*]. He owned all of the five hundred
> and fifty faddans which were granted to him by the descendants of
> Muhammad Ali Pasha. . . . He retained the village population which had
> been under the tax-farming [*iltizam*] system, and which was doing
> public work. He also distributed land for sharecropping by half. . . . He
> imported peasants fleeing from the hardships of the tax system. . . .
> Under Muhammad Ali, all the land was under the *miri* system. It was

parcelled to families for sharecropping with the landlord, each paying half the expense. . . . Under Isma'il all the land became private property. . . . Under Tawfik land which was not distributed was sold to peasants. Other land owning families—of the village—[a'yan], as the house of Abdel Ahad, Shalash, and Nahas . . . originally came as laborers then accumulated land which the descendants of Touson sold.

Older villagers' historical narrations also suggest that slave labor was employed by Tusun. Khala Nargis describes her ancestors' lives at the time of the Turkish founder of Fatiha thus:

> Tusun brought black and white slaves. Black slaves were not employed as agricultural laborers but as domestic servants since they did not know the ways of the *fallahin.* . . . Tusun arranged marriages of some of the slave women to local peasants as encouragement to work the land. The man was given two feddans and the slave woman a house, and was freed. . . . They [the narrator's ancestors] had no right to leave the Tusun household. . . . They . . . would remain under the authority of the Tusun family.

In 1974, Khala Nargis' descendants were not slaves; some of them were not even peasants. A grandson and a granddaughter had completed their university education. Their grandmother credits Gamal, as Nasser was lovingly called, with providing these hitherto unprecedented opportunities for social mobility among the members of her family. The *'umda*, a proud descendant of Tusun Bey, also interprets the affinal relations forged between his prestigious family of renowned origin (*asl*) and a peasant family as a local expression of changes introduced in the country as a whole in the wake of the July Revolution. He adds,

> In earlier generations we never used to marry from the *fallahin*, and only with few exceptions we did not marry the black slaves. But I have broken this rule. Now . . . education is important. My own daughter married the son of a *fallah*, but he is of course educated [agricultural engineer].

Far from suggesting the demise of social stratification in Fatiha, an account of which appears in the following chapter, Khala Nargis' and El-'umda's commentaries serve to illustrate villagers' own appreciation of "micro-macro linkages." Yet, such "emic" pronouncements do not shed much light on national historical processes covering the period between the arrival of Khala Nargis' ancestors in Fatiha and the marriage of El-'umda's daughter to the son of a peasant. It is this protracted process which renders comprehensible gender relations in this village in light of variables other than those popularized by orientalist traditional wisdom, such as Patai's assertion of the "old, established Muslim views on the God-given inferior nature of women" (Patai 1969 as cited in Morsy 1972:60).

For an appreciation of developments in Egyptian society which lead up to the phased era of Nasserist populism, with both its structural and organizational power relations (Wolf 1991), it is necessary to transcend not only the confines of the village but also the artificial and increasingly blurred boundaries of anthropology's analytical terrain. Recourse to knowledge acquired within other disciplines, notably history, is imperative (Lock 1986:110; Ohnuki-Tierney 1990). This is the charge of the remaining part of this chapter, which provides a detour to the "ethnographic present," thereby underscoring the historical specificity of both the gender and medical systems addressed in the ensuing chapters.[2]

Nineteenth Century Egypt:
From Commercial Revival to Etatism

On the eve of the Free Officers' coup of July 1952, Egypt had been integrated into the world capitalist system for several decades. As early as the second half of the eighteenth century the Bourbons had turned to the lands of the Nile as a source of grain for Southern France. The decades that followed witnessed the erosion of the power of the Mamluke ruling class, the eventual rise of a strong state under Muhammad Ali Pasha, his defeat at the hands of the West, the British occupation of Egypt in 1882, and its incorporation into the global market as a peripheral capitalist formation.

During the reign of Muhammad Ali, between 1805 and 1848 Egypt witnessed a series of administrative, political, economic, military, technical, and educational changes. Centralized control was the essence of the pasha's development agenda, extending to industry, agriculture, and trade. Health development also figured prominently in the state's program of creating a productive and ample labor force. This meant efforts to combat epidemics, as well as reduce infant mortality. Vaccination by trained local paramedics throughout the country resulted in the elimination of smallpox by mid-century (Kuhnke 1990:120).

Muhammad Ali also set out to establish a strong army into which Egyptian peasants were conscripted. Technical support for the army developed on a massive scale and the state became the employer of wage laborers, including women. In trade, the Muhammad Ali period witnessed the strengthening of Egypt's commercial ties to Europe and the increased power of Mediterranean minorities to the detriment of the majority of the indigenous middle class, its women entrepreneurs included. A violent strike by these women was terminated by force (Gran 1979b:33).

The importation of western technical, military, and medical expertise and commodities during the reign of Muhammad Ali is not to be equated with Egypt's "westernization" during the years following his downfall. The pasha's resort to western advisers was part of a well-calculated, "self-conscious policy which balanced the factors favoring greater independence against those militating in favor of dependence" (Ibid:33). Noteworthy in this regard is social historian Eric Hobsbawm's remark that

> in the Islamic world [of the nineteenth century] . . . we observe the first stages of that process by which those conquered by the West have adopted its ideas and techniques to turn the tables on it. (Hobsbawm 1962:20 as cited in Keesing 1981:499)

Under Muhammad Ali, the "turn[ing] of the tables" was clearly in contradiction to western imperial ambitions. His development program had frustrated western economic designs on Egypt and obstructed access to what were to become strategic military bases of the British Empire.

The State, Agrarian Society, and Women

In the agricultural sector Muhammad Ali's development program involved extensive restructuring in administration, property relations, and technology (Abdel Malek 1968; Richards 1982; Abaza 1979a). Although he had abolished the Mamluke-dominated *iltizam* system of tax-farming, promoting revolt by some "women soldiers" (Tomiche 1968:177), his reign was by no means one of demise of privileged access to land by the supporters of the state. The Pasha's land grants to dignitaries extended to the region of Fatiha during the 1830s, when the village itself is said to have been granted to its original Turkish ruler.

Among the important technical developments in agriculture was the replacement of the Delta's basin irrigation by a perennial system. The cultivation and export of a variety of crops, notably long staple cotton, rice, and indigo helped stack the state treasury (Kuhnke 1990:17). This profitable modernization of the economy was underwritten by the sufferings of the underprivileged masses. Popular uprisings, including peasant rebellions, were suppressed with great brutality. Women's labor was subjected to direct appropriation by the state. Moreover, as large numbers of rural males were forcefully drafted into the army,[3] the authorities turned to women to solve the problem of a male labor shortage.

Among other activities, the state's program of irrigation networks also drew women into the construction field. Through their predominance in agricultural production women were also the principal merchants of agricultural products in village markets throughout Egypt. As the state took over control of domestic and guild industry, women also became integrated into the centralized industrial system. During this process of creation of what Mona Hammam describes as an Egyptian "working class-in-embryo," women who were already engaged in commodity production in the towns and villages of Egypt became drawn into the factory system. Here their activities as wage laborers extended to participation in labor revolts (Hammam 1977:34,210,218; Tomiche 1968a).

The intrusion of the state in women's lives did not begin with the reign of Muhammad Ali. But unlike during the Muhammad Ali era, the earlier relationship had involved male intermediaries. By contrast, state authorities of the Muhammad Ali period addressed themselves *directly* to women. Not unexpectedly, the treatment of women differed according to their class position. Financial assistance to the families of the pasha's employees increased and the new civic hospital provided care for women. By contrast, women of the poor, along with other members of their families and communities, paid dearly for "economic progress." As the authority of the old landlords was replaced by the impersonal monopoly of the state, peasants were subjected to forced labor, some of them reaching designated work areas in chains (Tomiche 1968:181).

Muhammad Ali's Reforms:
Medicine and Public Health

When Muhammad Ali came to power in Egypt there were European physicians practicing there. As in the case of other parts of the non-western world of the nineteenth century, the major western imperial powers had exported to Egypt their private enterprise, fee-for-service model (Kuhnke 1990:9). Unlike such private practitioners who came to make a living by healing the sick, those physicians who were *invited* by Muhammad Ali were brought from Europe to *train* Egyptians in the medical sciences within the framework of the pasha's grand scheme of *state sponsored* Egyptianization and development.

A Frenchman, Antoine-Barthelemy Clot, is generally credited with the establishment of Egypt's first medical school, Al Qasr Al-Aini. In addition to receiving ample reward from the pasha himself, this European physician remains well recognized by Egyptian medical professionals for his contributions. Yet, we should not lose sight of an important observation by historian Amira Al-Azhary Sonbol, a descendant of one of the earlier graduates of Egypt's first medical school. Her work serves as a reminder of the role of Clot Bey in *implementing* the pasha's plans of Egyptianization. Aside from his documented arrogance vis-à-vis Egyptians, Clot's commentary is noteworthy in this regard. He states,

Medical institutions, to become durable, must necessarily be national and independent of any foreigners. . . . The teaching of medicine, and consequently medicine itself cannot be perpetuated in Egypt except if it is Arab professors who transmit directly the knowledge to Arab students. Both must be indigenous and therefore share a common language. (Clot 1840:201 as translated and cited in Al-Azhary Sonbol 1981:67–68)

The state's commitment to public health extended well beyond the establishment of professional institutions for human medicine. Egypt's school of veterinary medicine and the development of an academic pharmacy, as well as the institution of a countrywide system of vaccination, had their origins in the Muhammad Ali era. Moreover, the pasha's reign witnessed the development of a system of rural health centers which employed physicians, including women. Throughout the country these were assisted by locally recruited health auxiliaries.

In contrast to the European professional medical model of the time, Egypt's nineteenth century public health program involved the incorporation of traditional medical practitioners. In addition the state established a school for midwifery and created a corps of women health officers known as *hakimas*. In addition to being trained to combat disease in general and to perform surgery, these women were entrusted with maternal and infant health. By 1872, 471 of them served in the country's provincial health service. The image of "the 'doctress' on a donkey" became significant in rural Egypt as state-sponsored health care gained acceptance (Kuhnke 1974).

Although the rural population's anti-state sentiments extended to programs of public health, peasants' acceptance was forthcoming with the demonstrated efficacy of immunization. Far from displacing "traditional" medicine with "modern" forms, the state's promotion and professionalization of allopathic medicine and derivative health services in no way resulted in the obliteration of medical pluralism (P. Gran 1079b:344; cf. Greyghton 1977).

Social Transformation and the Cultural Construction of Medicine

Historical accounts of Muhammad Ali's health programs generally stress the pasha's reliance on European physicians and the translation of European language medical texts by Egyptians sent on education missions to Europe. Yet, these nineteenth century reforms involved something other than importation of pre-packaged western programs of health care. The reform period of Muhammad Ali was basically a continuation of prior trends in indigenous intellectual life of the eighteenth century, trends that extended to medicine.

In the eighteenth century, ideas which were supportive of the contemporary commercial revival in Cairo had appeared in the form of
writings in what are generally considered traditional religious fields.[4]
Such efforts at cultural legitimation involved the *ᶜulama* (scholars) of
al-Azhar. As the lower classes suffered hardships and were beginning to
rebel, these learned men played an important role in cross-class communication. A number of them were instrumental in the revival of Sufi
orders (*turuq*) and related healing traditions. In the nineteenth century,
however, the *turuq* were gradually undermined by the reform institutions of the new bureaucracy (P. Gran 1979b:xiii).

Cultural revivals in the eighteenth and nineteenth centuries reflected
their respective social milieus. The commercial sector of the eighteenth
century, with its need for profits "within an orthodox framework," found
justification in the *ahadith*, the sayings of the Prophet, himself a mer-
chant. As for the philosophical legitimation of Muhammad Ali's reform
policies of the nineteenth century, this was embedded in the study of
kalam (speculative theology), wherein logic, argumentation, medicine,
and the natural sciences were significant. Thus, concern with positivist
medicine involved a local revival which came to *merge* with external
trends in science such as those developing in Europe (Ibid:xiv).

The adaptation of cultural traditions to historically specific political
economic transformations is also evident in the practice of popular
medicine as it pertains to women. In historical studies we are reminded
of non-elite women's political involvement as expressed in healing rituals associated with Sufi orders. Sensing the danger of Western en-
croachment, the members of these orders had developed responses
which were attractive to women, since they were themselves adversely
affected by the new market relations. In spite of the state's attempt to
restrict women's participation, it continued up to contemporary times
(Tucker 1985:109–114; see also Brink 1987; Lapidus 1988:618; Nelson
1971; Saunders 1977). In Fatiha, joining the *zar* remains a significant
expression of culturally sanctioned dissent.

In the latter part of the nineteenth century, as now, professional medical practitioners, by then committed to positivist western allopathic
medicine, looked upon healing regimens beyond their domain as
"quackery." Like their successors in more recent times, some of them
seemed to show interest in identification of the biomedical equivalents
of sociomedically defined sickness categories such as spirit possession.
In a paper delivered at the Institute Egyptien in Cairo in 1860, Dr Shafᶜi
Bey compared the "nervous illnesses which first of all befall women" to
"hysteria, catalepsy, convulsions, and epilepsy" (Shafᶜi 1862 as quoted
in Natvig 1991:179; cf. Okasha 1966). As is usually the case today,
this physician's "explanatory model" did not accommodate the social

production of sickness; he obviously did not appreciate the subtle differences between the healing regimen of exorcism of evil spirits, which dates back to the times of the ancient Egyptians (Dawson 1930:27; Ghalioungui and Dawakhly 1965:9–10) and the protracted process of pacification of the spirits in a *zar* arena. In this regard, it is no wonder that those possessed by spirits saw "no benefit in medicines, and that which cures them is magic, charms, pieces of paper, visiting saints, taking part in *dhikr*, listening to drums with different sounds, and the singer and the tunes and various other things" (Natvig 1991:179).

Not unlike North American biomedical specialists of the nineteenth century who diagnosed the non-conformist women of their societies as "hysterical" (Ehrenreich and English 1973; Smith-Rosenberg and Rosenberg 1973), their Egyptian counterparts operated with a logical scheme insulated from the significant sociopolitical developments of the time. Missing from their consideration is the deterioration in women's position associated with the popularity of the *zar*. They remained oblivious to the fact that "women . . . became increasingly dependent on their families and more vulnerable to inroads by male relatives on their property rights" (Natvig 1991:182).

The State and Colonial Legacy, 1882–1952

Following the military defeat of Muhammad Ali at the hands of the European powers in 1841, his program of industrial development was effectively demolished. By 1879 Egypt had become a debtor nation under the rule of Ismail. This monarch's objections to European control resulted in his dethroning and replacement by his son Tawfiq. With the crushing of the cUrabi revolt, which had encompassed rural Egypt (Schulze 1991:181), the country became part of the British dominion.

The British occupation of 1882 represented but an event in the protracted process of colonialization of Egyptian agrarian society (Schulze 1987). This process was uneven given the variable agricultural potential of different parts of the country. Thus, whereas the cultivation of cotton in parts of the Delta dates back to 1821, for the region closer to Fatiha this did not occur until the period between 1850 and 1860 (Schulze 1991:172,173).

With colonialism holding sway over the Egyptian social formation, it was evident that the classical bourgeois path to capitalist development would remain blocked (S. Amin 1976, 1978; M. Hussein 1973). The growth of the Egyptian bourgeoisie was based not on the expansion of the internal market but rather on the maintenance of external links; profits were exported, not reinvested. The colonial government's economic development scheme meant nothing less than keeping Egypt as "a great cotton farm" (Radwan 1975).

The expansion of the *ᶜezbah* system involved parceling of land to peasants for production of their subsistence crops in exchange for labor in the cotton fields of landlords (Richards 1982:34). Social differentiation now rested on the control of property and cotton cultivation, "determining an individual's material worth and defining his living standard and social position within the village" (Schulze 1991:173, 180). While the inhabitants of Fatiha do not share detailed knowledge of such developments, some of them do recall the wealth accumulated through cotton cultivation by the descendants of the Turkish founders of the village, reinforcing those descendants' sense of social superiority.

In the country as a whole the consolidation of landlords' control over vast areas of land and concomitant decrease of small holdings was accompanied by a growing supply of wage laborers and a consequent rise in rural and urban under/unemployment. While women continued to play a central role in familial household production, and reproduction, it was men who formed the bulk of the wage labor force. Women's and children's entrance into the commercial agricultural sector remained circumscribed and generally limited to times of harvest, with the result of their increasing dependence on male wages (Hammam 1977; Tucker 1976). Under colonial domination, competition to local production from Western industries was also devastating to female artisans and small merchants (J. Gran 1977). Moreover, the colonial era witnessed the interruption of the process of industrial proletarianization of Egyptian women in its incipient stage (Radwan 1976; Hammam 1977).

Under colonial rule the redefinition of Egypt's course of economic development had a counterpart in the public service sector. Consistent with the priorities of British economic policies of extraction of agricultural raw materials, hydraulics and agriculture headed their modernization agenda. This proceeded to the neglect of education and public health (Tignor 1966:319,348–357). Even when pressure from nationalist activists forced attention to these two areas, changes remained compatible with the priorities of colonial economic development. British educational programs for Egypt "had the overall purpose of securing a smooth-running administrative system, a group of Egyptian technicians for subordinate positions, and a modicum of education for the general population" (Ibid:320).

The concord noted for development policies and technical reforms extended to matters of public health. The adverse effects of epidemics on the economy, well recognized by Muhammad Ali, was not lost on either the British or their local wealthy allies. Yet, the fact that concern with the material requirements of agrarian export-oriented production took precedence over the condition of human labor does not come as a surprise. It is understandable in light of the latter's "excess" within the framework of the existing organization of agricultural production.

Informed by the rationality of the dominant mode of production, the colonial state promoted privatization of health care (cf. Noble Tesh 1988). In the earlier days of British domination this strategy even extended to public health services. A British official rationalized the inadequate sanitation system by reference to the fact that the Public Works Ministry, which he headed, "has been trying for years to find capitalists willing to establish water-works in the native cities of Egypt, where the absence of good drinking water is a very fruitful source of disease" (Sir Moncrieff 1891 as quoted in Tucker 1986:116). By 1914, eleven of the "native cities" had water filtration systems and water was distributed by private water companies to the dwellings of those who could afford such a service. As for rural Egypt, sanitation remained neglected (Tignor 1966).

In 1903 Cromer admitted that since 1882 the budget for sanitation and education amounted to less than one percent of the state's total expenditure (Gallagher 1990:9). Additional acknowledgment of the less than praiseworthy colonial public health policy came from the British secretary of state for the colonies, who admitted that "English interest in the matter [of public health] died away" (Ibid:8). Such decline in interest extended to "tropical" disease, the control of which continues to be considered by European exponents of military medicine as a deed which "ennobles" and "justifies" colonialism (Arnold 1988:3).

Contrary to assertions of humanitarian concern for the natives, the case of bilharzia in Egypt reveals the priority of tropical medicine as the welfare of Europeans and their troops. This is well illustrated by the "dying away" of British interest in bilharzia research once Arthur Loos' "skin infection theory" (which erroneously identified "man himself . . . as an intermediary host") was ruled out (Farley 1988:191).

Given the health priorities of British administrators, the role of indigenous medical professionals, particularly women, was greatly undermined. The number of Egyptian graduates of Qasr Al-Aini was severely reduced. Moreover, the social profile of students attending medical school following the British occupation of 1882 differed significantly from those who had been recruited during the time of Muhammad Ali. Most of the relatively limited number of graduated Egyptian physicians came from social strata which could afford the financial burden of now privatized medical education. This form of social differentiation had its counterpart in the provision of services.

Medically modernized hospitals found in the country's major urban areas were designed for the exclusive care of designated national and religious groups, not for the public at large. In such establishments Arab cultural identity, manifest in language or dress, prompted reactions of disdain among the European staff.

Under British rule Arabic was also declared a language unfit for "scientific" study. The anglicization of the curriculum extended to medical education, but not without resistance from nationalist forces. A rationalization for excluding Arabic as a medium of instruction at Qasr Al-Aini came from the famous "radical" European doctor Rudolph Virchow. When this man visited Egypt in the 1880s he was generally impressed by its medical school but expressed reservations about the use of Arabic:

> The whole of the literature of civilized nations is closed to them. They know nothing of the satisfaction to be derived from incessant conflicts in the arena of our sciences by all those who take part in them. The final results become known to them only at a late period in a most summary form. I have known many and can speak highly of their amiability, but have found not one who could be counted on to contribute in a useful manner to the program of the science and art of medicine. (Virchow 1885 as quoted in Tignor 1966:332)

Virchow's and similar rationalizations of anglicization of the medical curriculum on the grounds of promoting "civilized" standards of scholarship are brought into question in light of the fact that such standards were not binding for the *non-Egyptian* physicians who practiced in Egypt. Indeed, the British administration's purposeful restriction of the number of Egyptian physicians stimulated the predominance of foreign-trained doctors, many of whom had *failed* to be licensed for practice in Europe (Ibid:333).

What is also obscured by the above-noted justification of exclusion of Arabic is, among other factors, its oratory significance for the expression of the strong anticolonial sentiment in the ranks of medical and other students.[5] Meanwhile, in typical white man's burden rationality, colonial administrators asserted that British physicians would be instrumental in "spread[ing] the light of Western science throughout the country" (Gallagher 1990:9).

The European ethnocentrism manifested in relation to the agrarian gender division of labor imposed on colonized peoples had its counterpart in medical training in Egypt. The *hakima* system was undermined in favor of the Florence Nightingale model of hospital-based nursing (Kuhnke 1990:133). The indigenous preventive health care promoters/providers who once enjoyed state sponsorship were now barred from the facilities of the medical school, of which their own school had been an extension. Instead, the British imported European nurses and decentralized the system of training, leaving it up to each province to establish

and finance a school for the training of the same types of birth attendants (*dayas*) that had existed prior to Muhammad Ali's public health
reforms (Al-Azhary Sonbol 1981:262).

Whereas the *hakimas* of the Muhammad Ali era had been trained to
address health problems in general, partaking of instructions in hygiene
and surgery in addition to knowledge of obstetrics and gynecology, their
successors under British rule were restricted to midwifery. Furthermore,
the era of British domination witnessed a drastic reduction in the number of women doctors. Egypt was to be brought in line with what Lord
Cromer considered to be the appropriate model of a "civilized world"
where "attendance by medical *men* is still the rule" (quoted in Tucker
1986:122, emphasis added).

Not only were the majority of Egyptian women deprived of the care of
certified female practitioners, they were also the object of blame for
high infant mortality, which the British representative and de facto ruler
of Egypt, Lord Cromer, attributed to "Egyptian mothers (who) do not in
the least understand how to look after their children" (Ibid:117). Meanwhile practitioners of indigenous popular medicine continued to be
indispensable to the populous at large, addressing health problems
conceptualized in both naturalistic and sociomedical terms. As for
health care based on the tenets of western allopathic medicine, this
increasingly came to be channelled through charitable organizations
such as the Lady Cromer Dispensaries, overseen by European ladies
and those of the indigenous upper class (Gallagher 1990 passim). State
commitment to public health was thus reduced to charity.[6]

As the British proceeded to maintain Egypt as a "cotton farm," expansion of perennial irrigation accommodated their development policies.
However, this technological orientation was not without a toll on public
health, resulting in increased waterborne infections. At the 1944 Middle
East Agricultural Conference, the director of the endemic diseases section of the Ministry of Health stated that perennial irrigation increased
the incidence of bilharzia from five to forty-five percent of the population. He added that it also resulted in an increase of malaria "of equally
devastating proportions" (cited in Worthington 1946:73). Health problems were also exacerbated by epidemics associated with widespread
malnutrition resulting from the diversion of staples from the Egyptian
food supply to support British troops (Gallagher 1990:3–19).

Following WWI, a major expression of Egyptian opposition to colonial
rule came in the form of the 1919 Revolution, forcing the British to re-
consider their position and eventually grant Egyptians partial independence in 1922 (Brown 1990:176). Policy revisions resulted in the
Egyptianization of the administration of the Qasr Al-Aini medical school
and the public health bureaucracy. By 1947 the budget for the Ministry

of Public Health reached 6% of the total annual budget of the country (Weir 1948:10).[7]

With the failure of Cromer's British doctors to "spread the light of Western science throughout the country," the state revived some older public health strategies, albeit in compromised form. Around 1900 travelling tent hospitals with trained ophthalmologists were sent out to the rural areas to treat eye disorders and perform surgery (Tignor 1966:356). In 1926–1927 village barbers and midwives were mobilized and retrained to serve the health needs of rural populations (Kuhnke 1990:121). To address the shortage of nurses, the state incorporated traditional birth attendants into the public health structure. By 1932 schools for these *dayas* provided six-month training courses followed by a certification exam (UNICEF 1985:4). The period between 1928 and 1941 witnessed additional public health developments:

> In 1928, a department for endemic diseases in the Public Health Author-ity was established with mobile hospitals. In 1930, village hospitals were spread in rural areas consisting of Outpatient Clinics only without a defi-nite health program. On 7th of April, 1936 a Ministry for Public Health was founded. This new ministry established a "Rural Health Authority." ... In 1939, the Ministry of Social Affairs began to establish "social centers" in rural areas serving 12,000 inhabitants in various health fields. (M.N. Nassar 1986:3)

With the exception of public health quarantines, the villagers of Fatiha generally do not have knowledge of the above-noted rural public health developments. However, they do recall the services of itinerant sanitary barbers who used to come to the village in the past. One of these certified paramedics visited the village in March of 1975, during my presence. Sheik Younis described his training as a village barber thus:

> I inherited the occupation of my father. I worked as an official sanitary barber.... I started with three months training in 1917. I was trained in circumcision, ... surgery, smallpox vaccination, the administration of injections, and the dressing of wounds.... I was authorized to give out permits for burial.

Important as the services of sanitary barbers and certified midwives came to be for rural populations in the nineteen twenties and thirties, the efforts of these local practitioners could not offset the adverse health consequences of colonial domination. These consequences were well recognized by Sheik Younis himself. In addition to being well versed in the microbial causation of what he described as "natural diseases," as well as in spiritual illness, which he, on his own initiative, linked to local organizational power relations, this old sanitary barber's talk took us to the 1919 Revolution. His historical account brought into focus what may be described as the "macroparasitism" of colonialism. Indeed the ancient exploitative relationships described by William McNeill as "macroparasitism in Mediterranean lands" (1977:87) continued to be manifest on the Egyptian southern shore, albeit in a new form (cf. Brown 1987; Scheper-Hughes 1984). As had been the case during the First World War (Schulze 1991:185), local staples were siphoned off in order to feed WWII British troops, to the detriment of the local population (Gallagher 1990:16).

As wartime food shortage and major epidemics threatened the country, public health considerations came to command special attention from the authorities. In this regard an old villager from Fatiha provided a noteworthy explanation of the efficiency of public health officials in enforcing quarantines during the cholera epidemic of the forties. He reasoned that "they did not want . . . [the disease] to spread among the important people of the urban areas [*bandar*]." The village headman also brought attention to the political significance of public health issues during the forties (cf. Ibid), a period of intense struggle for national liberation and class antagonism.

With allopathic medicine upheld by dominant social groups, the charitable "women of society" were instrumental in delivering privatized biomedical care to the impoverished and debilitated masses. In Fatiha older villagers recall the charitable provision of care by the women of the households of the descendants of Tusun. The aunt of the present ᶜ*umda* is said to have provided eye care and dressed the wounds of the peasants of her village. According to older villagers her very possession of disinfectants such as tincture of iodine, and sterile gauze, was considered a mark of high rank in village society.

Egypt Under Nasser:
The Era of Arab Socialism

During the period between 1945 and 1952, Egypt, still occupied by British forces, was threatened with protracted civil disturbances in the urban areas and endemic uprisings in the countryside (Lakhdar 1978). It was under these conditions of intensifying struggle that Gamal ᶜAbdel Nasser came to power through the Free Officers military coup of July 1952, which was led by Muhammad Naguib, soon to become Egypt's first president. With the termination of the monarchy and the departure of British troops from Egyptian soil, the country was set, once again, on the road to state-centered development, albeit in the context of a different world order from that of the time of Muhammad Ali and in light of a different ideological orientation, Arab Socialism.

The new "state bourgeoisie" was formed of the remnants of the old bureaucracy, the aristocracy of the proletariat, the sons of rich peasants and the upper echelons of the old regime itself (M. Hussein 1973). In Fatiha the agrarian bureaucracy at one point included a descendant of the original Turkish rulers in its upper echelons. In addition, the village headman, himself a member of Fatiha's prestigious original ruling family, was well served by his origin (*asl*) in circumventing the state's requirement of landownership as a qualification for holding public office.

The post-1952 agrarian reforms were intended to create a regime of small proprietors rather than a collectivist agrarian structure:

> The size of holdings allotted by land reform authorities was calculated in such a way as to give each beneficiary and his family an annual income just sufficient to meet bare subsistence expenses. (Abdel-Fadil 1975:8, original emphasis)

Far from substantiating assertions of a "non-capitalist" character of agrarian political economy, these small proprietors, including those of Fatiha, usually resorted to wage labor in the process of maintaining their hold over their familial production units.

Although agrarian reforms allowed a large segment of the rural population access to productive resources, imposed favorable tenancy regulations, and limited much of the violence previously inflicted upon the rural poor (cf. Mitchell 1991), these reforms did not terminate the skewed distribution of land. The system of cooperatives that regulated the disposition of the agriculture surplus played an important role in this regard, contributing to the differentiation of the peasantry (Richards 1980). Families of small peasant households, women included, continued to bear a disproportionate share of the burden of the state's program of economic development. Under the banner of "unity, order, and work," they continued to subsidize wage laborers and rich peasants in the rural areas, in addition to the entire urban-biased state program of development.

As the small peasantry, and household production, remained the "backbone" of Egyptian agriculture, this undermined some of the very reforms which were championed by the state. The labor requirements on households of the lower strata of the peasantry, imposed indirectly by state agrarian policies, undermined the state's own protracted attempt to alleviate peasants from "ignorance." Such responsibilities stood in the way of formal education for rural children, whether male or female.

Families in a position to sacrifice the labor of one or another of their children as a form of social investment generally gave preference to boys (Ammar 1966:216; El-Sanabary 1989:ii).

The state's own androcentric bias was manifest in the pattern of land allocation of the agrarian reform program. Eligibility for receipt of land distributed to peasants after its appropriation from the former agrarian aristocracy was defined in terms of status as household head. Coinciding with culturally established definitions of male status, this criterion favored men; it is they who *predominate numerically* as household heads. A male bias on the part of the state was also evident for the wage scale set for rural areas. As Nada Tomiche notes,

A 1956 decree fixed the daily wages of a male agricultural worker at 180 millimes, and that of a female worker at 100 millimes. Thus the woman peasant is discriminated against by law. True, she has been given the right to vote, but as most peasant women are illiterate and thus are ineligible to vote, this right is a very limited one. (1957:43)

Aside from the recognized limitations of certain populist state policies as these pertain to women, and although the dictates of the National Charter were not always operationalized, the very declaration of woman as "man's equal," and protection of her work and legal rights as well as social benefits, provided the authoritative legitimation and protection of girls' rights to education. Educated girls in rural areas became symbols of family prestige. As adults, some young women from families of illiterates received state-supported university educations. Secondary clerical educations were also attained by many young women in rural areas; many of them came to be incorporated into the local agricultural and health bureaucracies. From the ranks of such educated females came some women, including one from Fatiha, who joined local rural chapters of the Arab Socialist Union, the country's unitary party.

In addition to land reform and the "participation" of women in agrarian, industrial, and professional development, an outstanding component of the Nasserist state welfare package was the development of a countrywide system of health care. Not unlike Egypt during the antecedent era, Nasserist Egypt saw the continued development of the professional medical sector and related services, now with intensified vigor (Khalaf 1987:14–17; H. Nassar 1987; M.N. Nassar 1986). The country also witnessed a significant expansion of rural health services, not as privatized charity but as operationalization of the principles of Egyptians' right to free health care (El-Mehairy 1984:19) and the primacy of "the efforts of the state . . . [over] the efforts of individuals" (Hatata 1968:28).

Health services became part of governmental public welfare centers known as combined units. In addition to providing a variety of social services such as the processing of pensions for widows, these units served the rural populations in matters related to formal education, agriculture, schooling, and health (Khalaf 1987:13). Of the different services provided by these combined units, those pertaining to health were most readily acceptable to the *fallahin* (Mayfield 1974:82,83).

Maternal and child health figured prominently in the state's public health program. Centers for maternal and child care, which numbered 216 in 1951–1952 increased to 1,743 by 1968–1969. Concomitantly, mortality among pregnant women dropped by fifty percent over the period between 1948 and 1969 (CAPMAS 1972:27,29 as cited in Hatem 1992a: 15). The Ministry of Health also supervised units which provided peasants with outpatient clinical services for a nominal fee. The payment also covered nutritional supplements for pregnant women and infants as well as medication, now produced in large amounts by Egypt's nationalized pharmaceutical industry and distributed at very low prices (Galal 1983; Handousa 1978). Nursing staff, often but not always female, were drawn from the local rural population (El-Messiri Nadim 1980).

In addition to having responsibility for immunization, maternal and child health services dispensed contraceptive pills and inserted IUDs as part of their family planning programs. To many urban beneficiaries of state feminism, access to contraception was nothing less than a "liberating" experience which allowed them to regulate the size of their families in accordance with their combined public and domestic responsibilities, even when it meant endurance of adverse side effects. In rural Egypt, however, the popularity of state-supplied contraception remained constrained by comparison. For some rural women on the pill, "forgetfulness" or "non-compliance" with physicians' directives of daily consumption expressed a different form of feminism in opposition to the authority of the state.

With the promotion of family planning in rural Egypt, a contradiction was created between the state's demands on small peasant households and its adoption of the ideal of a small family. For the people of Fatiha, as for other peasant communities, a small family means a limited household labor force. It also involves a compromise of women's most significant culturally defined power base of expanding the labor pool and enhancing family standing in the community with the contribution of many sons. Subordinating official concepts of national interest to the requirements of the household labor process and to gender cultural expectations, rural women continued to regulate the size of their families accordingly.

In the village of Fatiha, where women are well aware of the variety of contraceptives available through health centers, the utilization of such contraceptives is minimal. Of a group of 75 women of childbearing age, only three practice contraception. One uses pills, another relies on one of the numerous methods of fertility regulation (ranging from coitus interruptus to use of vaginal inserts) which date back to our ancient Egyptian ancestors (Meinardus 1970:289–290), and the third was surgically sterilized following two caesarean births. As for the remaining 72 women, like others in the village, they shun the state-subsidized and readily accessible pills and IUDs.

As in other parts of Egypt, women in Fatiha also make explicit their worry about "rumors" of adverse health effects (DeClerque 1986 et al.), including cancer and sterility. A more fundamental reason repeated by women is their *need* for children. In short, while appreciative of state welfare programs such as immunization of infants, public education for girls, and nutritional supplements for pregnant women and infants, women take exception to state promotion of contraception. More recent reports of "subaltern women's everyday resistance" (Hammammi and Rieker 1988:105) have their counterparts for the Delta of 1974–1975. Whether in Fatiha or in other parts of rural Egypt, the women concerned, it appears, have long realized what population experts have noted as "accumulating evidence that the demand for children . . . is determining family planning use" (Kelley et al. 1882:25; see also Gadalla 1978).

In spite of state-supported and private cosmopolitan health services, Nasserist Egypt continued to be characterized by medical pluralism. In addition to physical medicine[8] and the spiritual medicine associated with Sufi traditions,[9] the shrines of saints and other holy places (Gilsenan 1973) continued to be involved in healing. Egyptians in rural as well as urban areas continued to rely on a variety of traditional medical practices and practitioners (El-Mehairy 1984: 28–31; El-Messiri Nadim 1980; Khalaf 1987: 79–82). Unlike Egypt during the previous century, Nasserist Egypt did not extend accreditation to the practitioners of popular medicine such as the health barber. Nevertheless, the services of these practitioners continued to be of importance as support for the cosmopolitan health services in rural areas in particular.

While the state did not lend legitimacy to the practitioners of traditional medicine, it did not set out to eradicate their practice of healing. The holding of *zar* in or near mosques, already on the decline in the latter part of the nineteenth century as state regulation of the Sufi orders intensified, was minimal in Nasserist Egypt (Natvig 1991:184; cf. Fakhouri 1968).

In spite of objections by learned sheiks of the Azhar to the deviation of the practitioners of *tibb rawhani* (spiritual medicine) from the teachings of Islam, in general the men and women who practiced this form of healing were not subjected to criminal prosecution. This is understandable given their dealings with personalized, localized problems rather than with matters of national or class relations. The coexistence of a state-regulated modernized productive sector and "traditional" household peasant production had its counterpart in matters of sickness and healing. Positivist biomedicine served as the standard measure of health and sickness among employees of state enterprises, while the state continued to tolerate "unscientific" medicine beyond the boundaries of the public productive sector.

On their part the peasants of Nasserist Egypt, like other Egyptians, "[did] not feel that there is a contradiction between official [health] services and popular [medical] practices" (Khalaf 1987:79). Yet, while even a physician like Dr. Khalaf may regard some practitioners of indigenous popular medicine (specifically those who practice natural medicine) as skilled healers whose work complements the official health services (Ibid), the reverse is not necessarily true.

Rural practitioners of spiritual medicine, like other villagers, do not consider biomedical professionals competent in dealing with socially defined ill-health. In Nasser's Egypt, as today, it was within the framework of popular rather than professional medicine that peasants continued to express different forms of socially meaningful power relations and sufferings, but not to the exclusion of utilization of cosmopolitan health facilities, even when these provided less than satisfactory service.

Contrary to initial intentions of providing rural populations with health services free of change, in practice, peasants often had to pay for public health services. Payment of a private fee to the physician by peasants obtains not only better treatment at the hands of this public servant but also the receipt of the appropriate medication and additional vitamin tonics and drugs provided by the government for public use (anonymous 1976:49).

In 1975 the Ministry of Health started an experimental plan in some parts of the country where payment of private fees was legalized. Of the fee paid by the patients to the health care unit, 20% is officially granted to the physician. The timing of this plan coincides what the late Dr. Abdel Ghaffar Khalaf, a longtime affiliate of the Ministry of Health, describes as "the shrinking of state commitment to the provision of health service" (Khalaf 1987:17).

By the mid-seventies the "shrinking of state commitment," and vigorous promotion of the ideology of "personal initiatives," were evident in other areas of rural life. Notable among the indicators of the demise of Nasserist populism was the declaration in May of 1974 by President Sadat's Highest Court of Appeal of the illegality of confiscation of private property. Accordingly, land which had been expropriated by the Nasser government from big landlords and rented out to peasants was to be cleared of its cultivators and returned to those who controlled it prior to the implementation of the state's program of land reform.

While the beneficiaries of land reform in Fatiha did not express fear of loss of their land (which had been part of a royal estate in the vicinity of the village), as early as 1974–1975 there were signs of retraction of state support. People spoke of the termination of the nutritional supplements which used to be dispensed to pregnant and nursing women. The village headman spoke of the limitations on visits to the village by public health *dayas* and the termination of programs of recruitment of young women for training as paramedics, as well as illiteracy eradication classes. At the time, some villagers were also beginning to consider migration to Iraq following an Egyptian-Iraqi economic cooperation agreement which mandated the permanent settlement of Egyptian peasant families there. Although enticed by the prospect of being land owners, landless people expressed great reluctance to leave their village. People from Fatiha were not among the first to settle in Iraq (El-Solh 1988).

Beyond the altercation surrounding the suitability of the designation "socialist" or "non-capitalist" as description of the Nasserist development course, noted in the introduction, scholars assessing the social impact of this development strategy have utilized a variety of measures. For rural communities evaluations have relied on such indicators as percentage of households beneath the poverty line (Radwan 1977), degree of inequality in income distribution (Korayem 1978), aggregate behavior of crop production and land profitability (Esfahani 1987), expenditure patterns (El-Gindi 1978), and expanded health services (Hatata 1968:103–129). In turn, R.H. Adams, Jr. (1985) utilizes a combination of selected criteria (improvements in income, equality and productivity—land and labor) to conclude a positive impact for the period between 1952 and 1974 (R.H. Adams 1985).

While scholars (including members of today's Egyptian opposition) are well served by explicitly defined measures in their comparison of the overall development patterns of Nasserist Egypt to the antecedent era and the subsequent period of Infitah,[10] this methodology leaves out the reactions of the people who experienced Egypt's failed transition to "socialism."

It is important to recognize that outside of statistically based evaluations and structural analysis and in spite of external pressures and internal contradictions (Abdel-Khalek 1982b; G. Amin 1982), the consequences of Egypt's development trajectory under the banner of Arab Socialism were, for large segments of Egyptian society, nothing less than revolutionary. The pervasive role of the welfare state in regulating access to land, education and public health and as "the employment agency of last resort" (Petras as quoted in Farsoum 1988) was a *welcome* development for many Egyptians. Among the rural population, those of the lower strata of the peasantry came to enjoy hitherto unprecedented security in land tenancy, education for their children, and expanded cosmopolitan health services. These services, although far from efficient, were nevertheless much appreciated as a sign of Gamal's "bias" in favor of ordinary Egyptians, the workers and peasants. In reaction to my own criticism of the poor health services in rural Egypt in 1974, a woman in Fatiha explained to me that "the *fallahin* had never dreamed of seeing a doctor before the revolution."

Although gender-related reforms of the Nasser era were no doubt appreciated by many Egyptian women, they were not necessarily greeted as manifestations of the triumph of feminism by all. This is certainly true for the women of Fatiha. Here, educated daughters are not fixated on personal "emancipation." Like their brothers who have come to enjoy a significant enhancement of power as a result of acquiring attributes of the dominant urban culture, they relish the respect of members of their community. The source of such respect includes members of their families. Education also enhances a young woman's prospects for marriage to a member of one of the distinguished families of the village. More generally, state-supported education provides young women, and men, with opportunities for social mobility beyond the boundaries of their rural community.

The discrepancy between certain forms of "our" feminist logic and that of our peasant compatriots also holds for the issue of access to land. Critical commentary on the regime's male bias in the allocation of land, and promotion of private property over collectivist production, find no support among the peasants of Fatiha. Land ownership, or at least secure contractual relations which regulate access to land, continue to be highly valued. In Fatiha, as in other parts of rural Egypt, through a combination of intensive, self-regulated exploitation of familial labor and reliance on exchange labor, peasant households manage to reproduce themselves (Glavanis and Glavanis 1983). Here, as in the agrarian reform community of Morgani studied by Reem Saad, the idea of the "subsistence ethic" is particularly relevant. This concept offers a perspective on peasant-state relations different from that of the scholarly evaluation based on the criterion of surplus value expropriation. While the latter remains indispensable as a classificatory tool in academic discourse, it is less than adequate as a "guide to the phenomenology of peasant experience." More central in this regard is the question of subsistence, which relates more directly to the "ultimate needs and fears of peasant life" (Scott 1976:4, cited in Saad 1988:9).

It is indeed the question of subsistence which renders comprehensible the incessant attempt on the part of peasants in Fatiha to secure access to land. Like their cohorts in Morgani, they are informed by this cultural orientation in evaluating Nasserist agrarian policies. For the majority of the older peasant inhabitants of Fatiha, the result is the veneration of Gamal. Even as late as 1975, the locally manifest shortcomings of his rule were often attributed to "those surrounding him," to the local bureaucracy, or to exploitation by the people of the *bandar*, the urbanites, but not to ᶜAbdel Nasser himself (see also Shatla 1976:55, 56).

In concluding this account of Egyptian history in relation to issues of agrarian transformation, gender, and medicine, I may deduce that although Nasserist Egypt witnessed a series of reforms aimed at building a society of social equity, as well as attempts to promote gender equality and health, these efforts proved to be less than effective in overcoming historically derived constraints, not the least of which is the colonial legacy (See Kruks et al. 1989:8). The asymmetry characteristic of state-peasant relations, and rural women's subservience to male authority, continued to be manifest in medicine in its cosmopolitan and popular forms. The empirically derived chapters which follow provide a local-level illustration of these power relations as they pertain to gender, sickness, and healing. Thus ethnography complements the methodological emphasis of this chapter.

Notes

1. With the dwindling supply of white slaves from Europe resulting from the establishment of Russian domination during the nineteenth century, the Ottomans turned to Africa. When Muhammad Ali's troops advanced up the Nile they brought back slaves from Sudan (Lewis 1990:72–73).

2. The account which follows represents an integration of information from a number of historical studies including Abdel Malek 1968; Amer 1958; Baer 1969; Brown 1990; Davis 1977; Al-Azhary Sonbol 1982; Gallagher 1990; P. Gran 1979a,b; Kuhnke 1990; Lapidus 1988; Lutsky 1969; Marsot 1984; Richards 1982; Tignor 1966; Tomiche 1968; Tucker 1986. In the description that follows I will specify the source only after quotes, or in cases where a given study upon which I draw is distinguished from other publications by selected descriptive material or analytical insight.

3. It is reported that "often mothers mutilated their children themselves, deprived them of one eye or of the use of one of their limbs, to preserve them from being conscripted" (Clot 1864:334 as quoted in Tomiche 1968:180).

4. In the Middle East the dialogue between religion and medicine operative in Judaism and Christianity extends to Islam. The unification [*tawhid*]

of body and soul is reflected in a statement attributed to the Prophet Muhammad, who said, "science is twofold, the science of religion [theology] and the science of the body [medicine]" (Hamarneh 1967:14).

5. The first martyr of the 1919 revolution was a student by the name of Muhammad ᶜEzat El-Bayoumi (El-Rafᶜi 1968), my father-in-law's older brother. My mother-in-law, a cousin of this martyr and herself a participant in the 1919 popular uprising as a child accompanying her activist aunt, shared with me her recollections of the role of students in the 1919 revolution and the prestige which they enjoyed as standard bearers of nationalist resistance.

6. While it may well be pointed out that the charitable provision of medical care is an established Islamic tradition, private humanitarian service was not a substitute for state-sponsored health services (Rahman 1987:59–79).

7. I am indebted to Professor Nancy Gallagher of the Department of History, UC–Santa Barbara for sharing with me her copy of Weir's work.

8. Physical medicine is an amalgam of elements of the ancient humoral tradition, the bedouin practices which were incorporated in the medicine of the Prophet (*Tibb-al-Nabi*), as well as elements of historically antecedent literate medical traditions, notably those expressed in Tazkaret Daoud, which remains a major reference among herbalists throughout Egypt.

9. The latter part of the nineteenth century (the time of British occupation, the development of the agrarian export sector, and the restructuring of the indigenous commercial sector of petty commodity production) witnessed the proliferation of state-regulated neo-Sufi orders, whose healing transcended the ontological orientation of cosmopolitan medicine to address the psychic and spiritual problems of the time. Much of the support for these orders came from the rural hinterland, where they stood in partial opposition to the landowners. In rural areas, as in the major cities of Egypt, membership in such orders and resort to physicians was, and is, by no means mutually exclusive (Gran 1979a:345,346).

10. During the latter part of the seventies this comparative perspective gained significance in studies by Egyptian scholars. This is well illustrated in the works presented at the annual meetings of the Egyptian Association of Political Economy, Statistics, and Legislation which followed the issuance of the October Paper of 1974.

PART TWO

The Local Context of Gender Differentiation

2

THE VILLAGE OF FATIHA: AN OVERVIEW

Research Setting and Data Collection

The local setting for the present study is the village of Fatiha as I, an upper class compatriot of its inhabitants, came to know it in 1974–1975.[1] This community, the home of some 3,200 inhabitants, is located about 130km northwest of Cairo in the Egyptian Nile Delta. From the nearby district town, trains, state-operated buses and private cabs connect the village to the provincial capital of Kafr-il-Sheik, as well as to Alexandria and Cairo. Like other parts of the Delta, the village climate is characterized by a two-season year. Rainfall is confined to the winter months and amounts to a low average annual precipitation of below six inches. Climatic conditions permit the cultivation of various crops throughout the winter and summer months of the year. Agricultural production involves perennial irrigation with extensive use of canals.

The physical layout of the village partakes of the nucleated settlement pattern characteristic of Nile Delta villages; dwellings are surrounded by fields. In the center of the village stands the mosque, where Friday prayers are held by the males of this totally Muslim community. Women do not pray in the mosque but, like their men, consider themselves "of the religion of Muhammad." Adjacent to the mosque is a shrine (*zawya*) which houses the tomb of the village saint. It was on the day of celebration of the *mulid* of this woman, a member of the village elite (the descendants of the Turkish founder of the village), that I arrived in Fatiha in the summer of 1974. This was the start of my "up close" acquaintance with the lives of the less fortunate members of my Egyptian homeland (Morsy 1988a).

In Fatiha the differentiation between the old masters and the subservient peasants remains evident in the very layout of the village. Close to the mosque and *zawya* locations stands the house of the village headman, and that of a relative, both descendants of the Turkish founder of the community, Tusun Bey. This is considered the central part of the village, which is also the location of the agricultural cooperative, a major symbol of state regulation of the lives of peasants today. Opposite this is an extension to the village headman's house, which serves as an office for a village telephone operator/clerk who remains in touch with the police in the nearby provincial town. The health bureaucracy is in the same location.

Close to the entrance of the village are two grocery stores, a carpenter shop, and a barber shop. With the exception of the homes of the relatively wealthy inhabitants of the village, who occupy less than a handful of houses constructed with red bricks, villagers' dwellings are composed of sunbaked mud. Although less prestigious, the latter are considered more comfortable during the months of summer heat and winter cold.

With occupational specialization at a minimum, almost all the inhabitants of the village are cultivators. Even the few government bureaucrats who reside in the village, as well as the water carrier (*saga*), carpenter, kerosene burner repairman, army draftees, healers, midwives, and students, are involved in agricultural production in one way or another. As shown in Table 2.1, families work land which ranges in size from one-eighth to eight *faddans*.[2] From the figures of this table it is calculated that the majority of households, 43.4%, utilize less than two *faddans*; 42.2% have access to between two and five *faddans*. Less than 1% of village households control six to eight.

Among "landless" peasants, wage labor is a major source of income. However, cases where this form of remuneration is the only source of livelihood are exceptional. Families in this group generally have intermittent control of land through variant forms of sharecropping. Informal agreements rather than formal contracts regulate this form of access, which does not appear in official documentation of land distribution.

TABLE 2.1   Distribution of Land Holdings in Fatiha

Land Area (faddans)	Number of Families	% of Total of 460 Families
8	1	0.2
6	1	0.2
5	11	2.1
4	11	2.1
3.5	6	1.3
2–3	170	36.7
1–1.5	79	17.1
.125–.75	121	26.3
0	60	13.0

In Fatiha the differentiation of the peasantry is relatively limited compared to other Egyptian villages described in the anthropological literature (cf. Abaza 1987b; Hopkins 1991; Morsy 1985; Saad 1988). While the inhabitants of the village are well versed in mass media discussions of the "exploitative classes" of the antecedent royal regime, social stratification as a local phenomenon is not expressed in the language of class (cf. Shehata 1990). This extends to a man who commutes from the village to his industrial job in a nearby province. Although he identifies himself as a member of the working class (*al-tabaka al-ᶜamila*), his behavior within the village, where he expresses great deference towards the ᶜ*umda*, is clearly informed by local elements of social hierarchy. Whereas his status as worker is significant for national political discourse, it has minimal relevance for the local cultural construction of power relations. Here the relevant indicators of social differentiation are social wealth, descent, and public reputation of male and female family members (cf. Hopkins 1977, 1986, 1991).

In addition to taking into account villagers' distinctions between those who are financially "capable" (*ghadrin*) and those who are poor (*ghalaba*), the locally meaningful model of social stratification involves descent (*asl*) and rank (*magam*) as central elements of differentiation. Although these two elements often coincide, recent acquisition of the latter (as through education, bureaucratic employment, or marriage) serves to circumvent limitations pertaining to the former. Indeed, so significant is the effect of education that even some staunch believers in the natural mental inferiority of women are willing to concede that "because of education women became enlightened."

Among the wealthy, as among the less materially endowed, control of land is a primary index of social worth. In accordance with the attitudes of descendants of the Turkish elite who founded the village, villagers consistently rank holders of larger amounts of land and their families higher than they do those who control small areas or no land at all. Although people repeat a proverb which links social position to monetary wealth,[3] cash savings are but a means towards the greater goal of land ownership or, at least, rent. It is this form of property which is considered a durable and reliable support (*sanad*). Similarly, while health is said to be "worth the world," its maintenance is tied not only to monetary wealth but also to access to "the bounty of the land (*kheir el-ard*)." As a woman explained, "people who have land can sleep peacefully because they will always be able to eat."

Regarding family reputation as a significant element in the village system of social differentiation, women shoulder a major responsibility. Even when a man is accused of "forcing himself" upon a woman, other women place the blame on her, citing a proverb which asserts that "if

the rock cracks, it is the fault of the one sitting on it." Women also liken
men to dogs; they are said to come forth when signaled to and to run off
when chased away.

Unlike wealth which, if lost, can be regenerated, at least theoretically,
a woman's honor is likened to a matchstick; once burnt, it can never be
reconstructed. As the proverb goes, "There is no scandal worse than a
woman's." Accordingly, women are expected to be modest in their dress
and their behavior. When this dictum is violated, the family concerned
makes every attempt to keep it a carefully guarded secret. Their efforts
are usually unsuccessful in the limited perimeter of the village, where it
is said that "the walls have ears [and] when a woman becomes pregnant
in Mecca the people next door [in the village] bring the news."

Beyond the verbalization of cultural ideals, living up to them is itself
informed by the status of individual women's families within the community. Thus while observations of some women joking with men other
than their relatives and touching them freely on the street, or in the field,
may substantiate a villager's suggestion that "the face of the countryside
is more exposed compared to the city," it is important to note the position of the family of a woman so involved. It is women of the less prestigious households who are least reserved in their interactions with men.

Since social position and attendant power are defined primarily in
terms of control of agricultural land, I utilized size of landholdings as the
primary selection criterion for a household census. The census population consisted of the occupants of a random stratified sample of 100
households. Derived from the records of the local agricultural cooperative, the percentages of families indicated in Table 2.1 were used as a
guide in the random selection of proportional numbers of households
from each category of size of landholding.

The census population included households which are headed by
persons who (although they may be engaged in agricultural work themselves or have members of their households so involved) are also recipients of a regular stipend as government employees or have income generated by a skill other than agricultural production. For this group of 3
village guards, 1 fireman, 1 fisherman, 3 mosque attendants, 3 tailors, 1
agricultural cooperative mechanic, and 1 *kutab* teacher, it was estimated that their annual income from non-agricultural sources is equivalent to income derived from a *faddan* of land (approximately L.E. 110).
"Landless" families who do not derive such regular income, estimated
by the village headman to constitute approximately 13% of the total
population, were randomly selected with his assistance from the four
named areas of the village. The composition of the census population is
shown in Table 2.2

Census taking proved to be a long drawn out process which took

TABLE 2.2   Household Distribution of Cultivated Land Areas

Land Area Cultivated (faddans)	Number of Households in Census
8	1
6	1
5	3
3.5–4	4
2–3	36
1–1.5	17
.125–.75	25
0	13

more time for pretesting of census categories than I had anticipated. Some categories, such as those related to time allocation for different tasks, proved to be utterly meaningless in the context of village society, where far from negligible variation in work pattern occurs from day to day. My initial concern with getting direct information (about annual crop yields, credit from the agricultural cooperative, debts, loan payments, and income from relatives) neglected the fact that the villagers were not about to disclose to a (then) complete stranger the secretive mechanisms whereby they circumvent authorized regulation of the economy or what has been described as peasants' "every day forms of resistance" (Scott 1986). In some instances in the early days of fieldwork even direct observation proved illusory. For example, when I first asked Gamalat about livestock, unlike other people who simply reduced the number of cows or water buffaloes which they own, she denied having any in her animal shed. This concealed the fact that she, like other villagers, engages in a form of co-ownership of livestock (*shirka*). My direct observation of the absence of any livestock in her dwelling prompted an erroneous conclusion about the accuracy of her answer.

Honest responses to my probing about crop yields, untaxed sources of income, or deliberate postponement of payment of rent (under conditions of state protection of the rights of the tenant over those of the owner) were understandably less than forthcoming during the early days of fieldwork and census taking. At the time, directly communicating with the employees of the agricultural cooperative, and consulting some of their records, proved useful. It was by way of the agriculture cooperative that I found out that certain plots of land were in fact registered under the names of women of households. My interviews with both male and female members had left me with the mistaken impression that the land was held in the names of men. I later came to understand that as men find it demeaning to be dependent on women's property, women in turn believe that marriage to a dependent male is an affront to their own dignity.

Whereas some respondents to the pretesting of the census categories claimed that their land gave particularly low yields, the local cooperative's agriculture engineer pointed out that there are no significant differences between the yields of different plots of the village cultivated area (*zimam*).

Although there were initial difficulties, which also proved to be significant learning experiences, the census of the research population eventually proved important in the collection of quantitative data. Structured interviews related to sickness and healing, conducted at the later stages of fieldwork, complemented participant observation and informal interviews. Both forms of interviewing involved male and female villagers of different ages, as well as practitioners of traditional medicine and medical professionals in the vicinity of the village. Time was also devoted to observations in homes, fields, and a physician's clinic, in the local healers' residence, and in the hospital in the nearby town.

Fieldwork in Fatiha also involved collaboration with a physician who has practiced in the rural areas of the vicinity of the village for about twelve years. In addition to helping in the modification of the Cornell Medical Index (CMI) to render it suitable for local use, he lent his expertise to my attempt at identification of a biomedical equivalent of *ʿuzr* (a local variant of spirit possession). A professor of psychology at Alexandria University provided me with a culturally appropriate psychological test which I administered in the village. She also evaluated the relevant sections of the CMI and commented on drawings which I collected from village school children.

Village Dwellings, Sanitation, and Public Health Services

Village houses usually consist of anywhere from four to eight rooms, including animal sheds. One room is usually reserved for sleeping but may also be used for food preparation and the entertainment of guests, depending on the status and size of the family occupying the house. Members of a nuclear family usually sleep in one room. In extended-family households the mother-in-law sleeps with the children and each couple sleeps in a separate room with infants sharing their bedding. The *khazna* is reserved for the storage of food. It contains large bins made of dried mud mixed with straw, which are used to store wheat or corn for the months between harvests. The stored crops are often laced with pesticides and washed in a village pond prior to consumption.

When a toilet is found in the house, it is simply a small hole which leads to a very large reservoir inside the courtyard. The toilet room always has a small window for ventilation. When no toilet facilities are available inside people's houses, they defecate in the animal sheds or out in the fields.

In all village dwellings, rooms usually have windows for ventilation, and the center of the house (*dahliz*) also has an opening (*manwar*) through which direct sunlight enters the house. The *dahliz* also has stairs which lead to the roof of the house, where straw and dried wood are stored for use in baking. In many houses the area used for baking is not well ventilated; women generally complain of sore eyes and difficulty in breathing, which they attribute to smoke.

No public system of sanitation exists in the village. Individual families assume responsibility for cleaning the surroundings of their dwellings. They obtain water from two sources: the canals and the two public taps, one at each end of the village. About six houses in the village have running water. The water supply from the public tap is intermittent, and villagers often resort to filling their water storage pots (*zir*) directly from canals, adding alum for purification. When available, water from the public taps is used extensively by the women for cooking and drinking, but washing of clothes is usually carried out at the side of canals.

Contaminated water supplies are responsible for schistosomiasis, a disease transmitted by fresh-water mollusks. Repeated infections are difficult to avoid in view of villagers' constant contact with polluted water during the course of daily work in the fields. The use of polluted water for drinking and bathing adds to the spread of infection. The villagers themselves are well aware of the potential hazards of canal water and its effects on their health, but they say that it is their fate as peasants to work in, and drink, dirty water.

As with health conditions, public health services are less than adequate. Aside from the case of child immunization campaigns, which bring public health personnel to the village, the only readily accessible public health services are located in the nearby provincial town, at a distance of about three kilometers. In addition to relying on these services, villagers frequent private physicians in the same town and, when necessary, travel to other locations of cosmopolitan health providers. Villagers also consult a local practitioner of natural medicine, as well as spiritual healers in the village and its vicinity.

Local Government

Fatiha has two village elders (*sheik balad*); each represents one of the two sections (*hisa*) of the village. Both are accountable to the *ᶜumda*, who is also the elected representative of the local chapter of the Arab

Socialist Union. In 1960, the present *ᶜumda,* a member of the village elite of Turkish origin, was the only candidate for the post. In January of 1975, when the Ministry of the Interior was filling 1603 *ᶜumda* posts nation-wide (Al-Ahram, January 7, 1975), once again the present *ᶜumda* was declared victorious by the ministry.

In view of the high esteem in which villagers hold urban mannerisms and personal acquaintances with officials in urban centers, they value the *ᶜumda* as a representative of their village. While many of the villagers believe that the general misery of their life will not be greatly affected by one *ᶜumda* or another and that government officials are primarily concerned with their own interests and not those of the villagers, supporters of the *ᶜumda* take pride in his identity and his descent (*asl*). One such supporter remarked, "We all know that there is no better *ᶜumda* for this village. He is a son of [honorable] origin [*ibn asl*]. He is not like the other *fallahin ᶜumda* who do not know the sky from blindness [*il sama min el ᶜama*]."

The *ᶜumda* performs a variety of local-level administrative duties. In addition to fulfilling the demands of national authorities, whether related to economy, defense, or health, the *ᶜumda* and his assistants spend much time settling local disputes. Only conflicts involving injuries, or those beyond his jurisdiction, are referred to the district (*markaz*) officials, often reluctantly.

Villagers generally prefer locally rendered justice over that of the state courts. In these alien settings the cultural, including linguistic, gap and the social distance between villagers and those who administer justice are immense. Legal codes which inform issues of personal status are by no means commensurate with the emancipatory thrust of state feminism, even in its phase of decline in 1974–1975. The patriarchal statutes regulating marital relations, many of which were originally institutionalized at the turn of the century, remain basically intact (Hatem 1986). However, if a woman commits a "crime of honor," her life is better protected by the state system of justice than by members of her family, who are expected to "wash away" the dishonor. The collective memory of villagers yields a number of cases where the intervention of the police saved the life of a woman, sometimes forcing marriage upon the man who impregnated her out of wedlock. Whether such a marriage is the result of official mediation or other means, its stability depends on the power of the woman's family.

In addition to the *ᶜumda* and his assistants, who are charged with maintaining public order and linking the village to national structures of the Egyptian bureaucracy, ten representatives are elected by the villagers to the Arab Socialist Union. All of these own land, none less than two faddans. Three of them own six or more faddans. Out of the whole village, there are only 55 members of the ASU.

Distanced from the aspirations to public office harbored by the economically more "comfortable," and also well aware of their relative powerlessness vis-à-vis the governorate and national bureaucracies, the majority of villagers often resort to urban patronage. In this regard women play an important role in bringing the requests of village men to the attention of urban patrons through the female members of the latter's household. Village women who were once employed as domestic workers in urban areas often serve in this capacity. It is not unusual that these young women, or even little girls, experience great abuse as they contribute to the reproduction of the rural-urban system of patronage. While women of the urban upper class enjoy the benefits of the state's emancipative projects noted in Chapter 1, for the many poor rural girls and young women, who serve as their servants, "emancipation" is subjected to a different interpretation. It may well mean nothing less than being "rescued" by a relative who would take the exploited villager back home to a life of relative independence, but not necessarily one of greater physical comfort.

Even more limited than men's participation in state-regulated political activities is that of women. Only one "active member" of the ASU is a woman. She is a member of one of the big families of the village and also works as a clerk at the agricultural cooperative. As an educated woman, she is also privileged with the esteem extended to other scholastically certified villagers.

While about 35 women who own land participate in the election of members of the agricultural cooperative council, no women serve on that council. The comparatively high rate of illiteracy among rural women is an outstanding impediment in this regard. In addition to age over 18 years, eligibility requirements include the ability to read and write.

None of the ten representatives to the governorate-level ASU are women. Moreover, some villagers recall that when elections were held in the village in 1972, women's votes were cast for men of their kinsmen's choice. In this regard it is worth noting that this does not constitute a point of contention among men and women. Men's very involvement is not one of clearly articulated ideological contestation but is generally considered to have potential benefits for family members as a whole, at least in terms of enhanced prestige, if nothing else.

Kinship, Marriage, and Friendship

As is typical of the Delta region in general, and understandably so in light of the history of Egypt's land tenure system, kinship units larger than fraternal or extended families have no lasting corporate identity.

Tribal loyalties are non-existent in the village, and terms for large kinship units such as clans (*hamulat* or *qabail*) are alien to the majority of villagers. Genealogies are shallow, and most people cannot recall the names of ancestors beyond great grandparents. Support for distant patrilateral or matrilateral relatives occurs only on ceremonial occasions related to marriage and death. It is also forthcoming with the breakout of such disasters as fire or violent disputes with outsiders, when villagers become unified as "one hand" (*yad wahda*). Sentiments of kinship (*garaba*) are also expressed towards other Muslims and Arabs.

Kinship (*garaba*) is differentiated from affinity (*nassab*). Whereas the former (which derives from the Arabic word for near—*garib*) is linked to a man's body through the *ᶜassab*,[4] the later is associated with the woman's reproductive tract (*maᶜun*). People expect the support of patrilateral relatives as a duty. They are regarded as the group from which an individual derives his/her primary social identity and material possessions. By contrast, maternal relatives are the locus of emotional comfort and sentimental attachment.

The amiable relations between the mother's brother (*khal*) is an extension of the idealized relation of a brother as a protector and comforter of his sister. According to a local proverb, "a brother is like an arm, if it falls off it can never be replaced." However, it is also reasoned that once a brother is married he becomes subject to the control of his wife. Another proverb states, "a brother is the brother [or son] of his wife and the naive one [i.e. his sister] swears by his life."

Marriage is considered a supernaturally ordained means of satisfying what are considered natural human sexual desires, and a preparation for the birth of children. Aside from this general definition, men and women differ in their accounts of additional functions. Some women say that men marry for their self-satisfaction (*mazaj*). As one of them remarked, "They marry us to take their desire [*ghiya*] from us." Others believe that men marry for their comfort. Still others say that, in addition, men marry women to serve their mothers. On their part some men reiterate the description of marriage as a means of satisfying sexual desire. Others bypass this in favor of reference to Islamic custom (*sunna*).

Excluding unions which are considered incestuous,[5] including those between persons who have been suckled by the same woman, preferential village endogamy prevails. In this regard one villager remarked, "In the village we are all kin and affines; brides from outside do not fare well." Indeed the distress of brides from "outside" is often expressed somatically.

Mothers, who play a central culturally sanctioned role in the selection of sons' brides, are particularly opposed to the marriage of their sons to urban women. They explain that if a man marries a woman of equal or lower status, she will obey him, but if he marries one of higher status, she will not make him comfortable and will not obey his mother.

Marriage to close relatives is the ideal. People reason that "those whom you know are better than those whom you do not know." In practice, marriage to close relatives is not the predominant form. Of the 124 marriages recorded in the census, the largest proportion, 86 marriages, occurred between distant relatives or non-kin from the village; 20 father's brother's daughter marriages were recorded. Nine mother's brother's daughter marriages, 2 mother's sister's daughter marriages, and 1 father's sister's daughter marriage were also documented. Village exogamy occurred in only 6 cases of marriage.

Beyond the sample population, 8 cases of polygamous marriages are recorded for the entire village. Taking a second wife occurred among older men who ranged in age from 40 to 66 years. Their first marriages ranged in duration from 3 to 22 years. These males gave a variety of reasons for taking a second wife, including "beauty and love," "arrogance of the first and beauty of the second," "barrenness of the first," "love of change, and incompatibility," "wealth, beauty, and affinal support (ᶜuzuwa)," "love and affection," "beauty and the body," "wealth and some beauty."

In addition to beauty, good nature, domestic skills, and her asl, virginity is defined by villagers as essential for a bride. It is reasoned that a woman who is not capable of living up to the responsibility of upholding her own family's honor is not likely to do so for a husband's family. Only a very poor man will accept marrying a woman who is not a virgin. Such men are recognized as unable to afford the payment of bride wealth (mahr). A man will also knowingly marry a woman who is not a virgin if he loves her very much. In so doing he provides protection (sutra) of her honor and that of her family's.

Older villagers recall the past when a specialist known as mashta used to play an important role in establishing the "bride's family honor" on the wedding night. As a participant in the wedding ceremony known as dukhla, (which literally means "the entry"), this older woman, aside from giving comfort to the bride and confidence to the groom, had the opportunity to resort to methods of covering up the loss of virginity. In so doing she is known to have used blood capsules or leaches. Reflecting on this practice a midwife recalled that

> [in the past] when the family had doubts about their daughter they let the mashta check her out before the marriage and made a deal with her. That is why the mashta always dies blind because of her lying. . . . One time I learned from the mashta how to measure women and people used to come to me to measure their daughters and tell them if they are virgins [bikr].

Today, in the Delta region as a whole, such involvement by an older woman is generally absent. Unlike the situation in urban areas where surgical hymen repair can be obtained for a price, in rural areas women who want to "cover up" their transgression of local edicts require nothing less than the complicity of the groom himself as the wedding night ceremony becomes a more private affair.

The relative devaluation of women who are not virgins (including those who were legally married at one time) is reflected in the differential bride wealth (*mahr*) with which their families are compensated for their labor. For women who are virgins, the standard *mahr* in the village is about 100 L.E. For women who are "loose" (*sayib*), including divorced and widowed women, the groom compensates the woman's family with no more than 30 L.E. In some cases such women will not be provided with a *mahr* at all.

The primary responsibility of a young bride is to produce children for the husband's family. Failure to do so is not only grounds for divorce but also minimizes the potential for remarriage. Moreover, while failure to live up to the primary cultural expectation of motherhood may prompt friends' laments of misfortune or reference to "the will of God," nothing but contempt is likely to be forthcoming from a barren woman's adversaries. Illustrative of such disdain is Zakiya's insistence that her childless sister-in-law (of whose beauty and youth she is known to be jealous) "does not even deserve to have a bowel movement in [her husband's] house." Not even the highly valued attainment of a formal education is an adequate substitute for the culturally valued status of mother. In this regard Maryam, a high school student, wished for her sister to be "a good mother and an educated woman." She went on to explain that "a woman, no matter what she achieves in terms of educational status, is first and foremost a mother."

It is so important for a woman to have children that some villagers claim that a husband may turn a blind eye if his wife commits what would ordinarily be considered a dishonorable act in her pursuit of this culturally valued ambition. Commenting on this issue an older village man stated,

> Women like to have children. If their husbands are unable to have any, the women roam and become pregnant. Even when the man knows that the child is not his, he shuts his mouth because his wife's pregnancy is a proof of his own manhood.

Among barren women of the village, their common agony minimizes any social distance that might set them apart. They develop a close friendship as they meet frequently to share their anguish, accompany each other to healers in the vicinity of the village or the nearby provincial towns, or share the most recent advice from a physician.

More generally, friendship between women is often based on ties developed prior to marriage. They may have been regular partners in exchange labor (*zamala*), shared a field as wage laborers, or formed part of a migrant labor group. A woman may also develop friendship with a relative of hers who lives in the vicinity of the household of her husband's family. Neighbors in the field or on a village street may also become close friends. As such they share secrets and lend each other a listening ear for outpourings of complaints about husbands or in-laws.

Sometimes, particularly when a woman marries up, the close friendship between women may be considered threatening by the husband or his mother. Some women complain that they are prevented from seeing their friends from pre-marriage days. This usually happens in the early days of marriage, when a concerted effort is made by the husband and members of his family to emphasize the bride's new identity. Consequently a woman's relationships with her pre-marriage friends are threatened with decline after marriage. Substitution with amiable relations with co-resident sisters-in-law is considered exceptional. Indeed it is said that "(even) the ship of co-wives (may) stay on course but that of sisters-in-law remains baffled."

Among men, as among women, friendship is not necessarily based on kinship. A bond may develop through cooperating in agricultural work, or, as is the case more recently, through attending school. In the latter case boys, and girls, get together to study after school. Residential or social proximity is not necessarily the basis for this type of association. Although the resulting social bond often involves competition, this is not initiated by the pupils themselves but expresses their parents' conception of education as a significant vehicle of social mobility.

For the village as a whole, although kinship relations are no doubt primary, it is not difficult to take seriously the assertion on the part of some adult residents that they know all the other members of their community. On village streets people often greet each other by name and inquire about the health and welfare of family members, often also by name.

Aside from visitation and hospitality, which predominate among relatives, other members of the community frequent each other's homes on numerous occasions. Among men, and women, visits may also take place outside the home. For men the favorite village spots are the grocer's and barber's shops area or the seating area (*mastaba*) outside one of their homes. Women may meet and converse at the grocer's, the grinding mill, the water filling station, and the market place. So favored is the visit to the weekly market in a nearby village that women of extended family households look forward to their turn to be so privileged.

In general, higher-status villagers host those of lower status. However this pattern of interaction is less rigidly enforced among women and village youth. Men and women of the same household do not usually go out together on visits, except when these are beyond the boundaries of the village. In cases of illness people visit each other a lot, usually without concern about contagion. Villagers feel slighted if they are not visited during times of illness and will often reciprocate the insult. So significant is this social duty that villagers may go as far as Cairo or Alexandria to visit a sick relative or to congratulate a woman's family "on her safety" after giving birth.

The Family, Its Developmental Cycle, and Power Relations

Relatives who reside together in the same household are considered a family. Phases of the developmental cycle of the family are associated with three major types of kinship units: the nuclear, the extended, and the fraternal joint family. Of the 100 households making up the census population (which represents approximately 21% of the village's 460 households), 40 nuclear families headed by males constitute the majority. Other family residence patterns include 4 two-person households,[6] 17 nuclear families with one or more adult relatives, 14 extended families,[7] and 9 fraternal joint families.[8] Of the female-headed households, 8 are occupied by matrifocal families consisting of widowed mothers and their children, and 3 by extended families whose patriarchs are deceased. The remaining 5 households headed by females include 3 two- or three-person units and 2 single occupant dwellings, each inhabited by a widow.

The Arabic terms for household and family (*dar* and *ᶜayla*, respectively) are used interchangeably. Villagers' primary identities derive from their household affiliations. So strong is men's and women's sense of social personhood that I usually had difficulty explaining the concept of individuality to them (cf. R.H. Adams 1986b). People say,

We never think of ourselves as just persons alone. We make ourselves closer and closer to relatives[9]. . . . If a man does not have relatives he picks a wife who will give him good connections. . . . A man stays close to relatives and picks [affines] to make a support group [*ᶜizwa*] for himself. . . . One hand does not clap alone. A lone person never impresses men. . . . The woman who has *ᶜizwa* is supported by her relatives. She is courageous in her relations with women and with men, including her husband and his family.

Among women who do not enjoy family support, or find in their parental households a listening ear and refuge from maltreatment at the hands of husbands or in-laws, there is a conscious effort to "control [the] tongue." Also when such support is shaky, a husband is likely to over-indulge in the exercise of the culturally sanctioned authority with which the local organizational power structure endows him.

Illustrative of the social mediation of male authority is the case of Amna, whom I had originally viewed as the personification of women's success in circumventing male authority. In the early days of my resi-dence in the village I noted how she promptly responded to her hus-band's insults in kind. She also made it clear to him in no uncertain terms that he had no business interfering in what she does with the money she obtains from raising and selling chickens, invoking religious commentary to this effect. A few months later, and in spite of the initial support of her family, she was divorced. When I subsequently spoke with her husband, he said, "She is a woman who does not know her limits, . . . I do not want her back although her father said that she would return and behave like an old shoe. There are some women like that, they do not know their place." When I expressed surprise at the father's alleged characterization of his daughter, other villagers were quick to point out that he did not want to remain saddled with the responsibility of his daughter and her five children. In contrast, women from households of wealthier families expect more sustained support from their relatives.

According to the prevailing pattern of patrilocal residence, young brides are distanced from their natal family residence and incorporated into the husband's household. In this environment the young bride is subjected to a new set of controls above and beyond those pertaining to the power of her spouse. Here she is clearly at the receiving end of the culturally endowed authoritative control of the older men and women of the household, namely the father-in-law or mother-in-law, their sons, or wives of older sons. She is likely to address her father-in-law as *sidi* (master) and her mother-in-law as *seti* (mistress).

The new bride demonstrates great deference to the senior men and attends to the needs of her husband's father promptly and energetically. Not only is it expected that she will wash his clothes, cook his meals, or wait on him as he prepares to go to the Friday noon prayer but she may even wash his feet. In the absence of a father, the senior brother-in-law may expect similar services from a younger brother's wife. Senior men in extended-family households feel perfectly comfortable about exercising authority over wives of sons or younger brothers. Some of them reason that they have paid their *mahr*. In the case of one patriarch of a big fam-ily, whose wife does not live up to the role of authoritative mother-in-law (due to her chronic illness), he is known to check on the cleanliness of the rooms of each of his sons' wives.

As for the young bride's demeanor towards her mother-in-law, it is clearly one of subservience. In this regard, the culturally sanctioned superordinate position of the mother-in-law is expressed symbolically in a wedding ritual. As the older woman stands by the entrance of the bride's new patrilocal residence, she lifts her leg up. The bride passes under her leg. Although this custom is not followed by all village brides, it is still held up as an ideal which is said to be implemented by those who have *asl*. But even such women are resentful of the power of the mother-in-law. As one of them pointed out, starting with a famous proverb,

> "If the wheat is [ever] equivalent to the chaff, the mother-in-law [would] love the son's wife." . . . She thinks that because she has a son she can rule his wife like she rules him. What more [is expected of us]; we have to cross under her leg.

Once in her new extended family "livelihood" (*ma^cisha*), a new bride is conscious of the fact that a mother-in-law's dissatisfaction with her daughter-in-law may terminate the latter's marriage even if she enjoys amiable relations with her husband. Recalling her two-month marriage to her now ex-husband, of whom she continues to speak kindly, Badreya blamed his mother for the divorce:

> Even though I was very obedient to her and even though I used to kiss her hand every morning and let her sleep while I did all the work she was the one who caused my divorce like she caused [his] other divorces. She wanted me to sell my gold and I refused. She told her son to divorce me and since he is a good son he had to listen to his mother.

When a son himself is adversely affected by the actions of a domineering mother, he is likely to take the complaints of his wife more seriously. This is so in the case of Hamida's family. Hamida came to the *^cumda* asking him to mediate a reconciliation between her and her son and his wife, both of whom had left her house and taken up residence at the household of the wife's parents. Hamida showed us her many bruises, which she attributed to her son's merciless beating. In response, the *^cumda* told Hamida that her son and his wife can only take so much. He said that she cannot expect a grown man like her son to be without a penny in his pocket although he is a partner of his father on the job (operator of a mule-drawn cart) and in the field. The *^cumda* added, "You should not force his wife to sell her gold. If you had satisfied him by letting him share in the fruits of his labor he would have remained obedient and would have even forced his wife to sell her jewelry. . . . [Then] you would have bought yourselves a piece of land which would make you [all] secure."

In the extended family a young bride's labor, like that of other members of the household, is managed by the senior women and men of the household. With the birth of children to the incoming daughter-in-law, their labor and its products, like their parents', falls under the control of the senior people. While this phase of the life cycle of the family is generally less stressful for the onetime newcomer, having established the nucleus of her own power base with the birth of children, it is nevertheless tension ridden. As for her husband, he too is likely to experience the stress of subordination to the authority of older brothers, mother, or father. While he may share his wife's frustration at the appropriation of the products of their nuclear family's labor by his culturally authorized kin, expression of dissension is not likely to be forthcoming from him directly. It is often his wife who will express objections to the disproportionality between her nuclear family's contribution to the extended kinship unit's labor pool and the benefits which they receive. A woman who has the backing of members of her family of birth is generally more vocal in expressing such discontent, either directly or through her relatives.

An example of the husband's initiation of withdrawal from the extended family livelihood is illustrated by the case of Osman, a member of one of the village's biggest families. While his father, Sheik Hammam, had originally insisted to me that it is women who are the cause of the breakup in the family, as our friendship developed his assessment of his own family relations took on a more realistic tone. Acknowledging sibling rivalry, Sheik Hammam recalled how Osman had complained about having to work on the family land in addition to contributing his salary as a government employee while his brother Ahmad, who was in the army, contributed nothing when his wife and children continued to be provided for by the sheik. Osman had also pointed out that Ahmad's children go to school and never work on the family land. Failing to respond to his son's charges of unfairness, the sheik simply reminded Osman that, as the oldest son, Ahmad is entitled to certain privileges. Needless to say, Osman was unconvinced. A few days later his wife started asking for the cooking utensils which she had brought to the household as a bride. This was an indicator that her nuclear family would be eating separately. Although Osman and his wife and children continued to occupy his father's household "out of respect" for the older man, they ate separately and spent from Osman's monthly salary and the additional income generated by their children as wage laborers. Other villagers agree that it is Osman's secure reliance on a regular government salary which enabled him to establish a separate livelihood.

Until the actual breakup of the extended family, usually at the behest of couples of the younger generation, the mother of grown sons is at the pinnacle of the household power structure. In this position she enjoys cultural legitimation of her authoritative role over her sons, their wives, and their children. At this phase of the developmental cycle of the family she is liberated from the responsibilities of agricultural labor, and her contribution to domestic work is primarily supervisory. Given the age differential between men and women at the time of marriage, a mother-in-law is generally younger; she is often in better health than her husband. So her authority is backed by an energetic disposition, and she commands respect, illustrating Adams' conception of authority in terms of performance and not simply legitimacy.

Although a mother-in-law is now physically distanced from agricultural labor, her input nevertheless affects decisions pertaining to this productive sector. In consultation with her sons, and with the advice of her own kinsmen, particularly brothers, she coordinates decisions related to the deployment of familial agricultural labor and the management of property. Describing such a situation involving her own mother-in-law, Samira pointed out that

> [the older woman's] opinion is the one which goes for all the interests of the family. If my [older] brother-in-law wants to plant a piece of land with wheat, for example, or if they want to rent more land from another person, they ask their mother. If she says yes, it means yes; and if she says no, it means no. . . . With us women we get up in the morning and say "good morning, *siti*. What will we do today?" She tells me to do such and such and tells my sister-in-law to do so and so. If she assigns to me the rolling out of bread this time and the baking of the bread to my sister-in-law, the next time she changes things around.

Even though the mother-in-law's orders are expected to apply to her sons and their wives, this cultural construction of generational power relations is not always implemented. Some sons' wives *do* defy the orders of mothers-in-law or of wives of older brothers in fraternal family joint households. While some do so "with a strong heart," having assurance of alternate material or moral support, others may do so even at the risk of divorce, as the above-noted case of Badreya shows.

With the death of her husband, a senior woman's power in the extended family is threatened with demise. If she herself controls land, this facilitates her attempt to maintain her privileged position of culturally sanctioned power. To do so she continues to rely on the support of her kinsmen. A senior woman's brother often plays a central role in preventing the fragmentation of family property through inheritance. Past experiences in the village are cited by some mothers-in-law as rationale for not registering their own land in the names of their sons. Older women recall the case of Hajja Tafida, who registered her land in the name of her sons only to be left alone in her old age, taken care of by other "kind hearted" villagers. More recently *khala* Gamalat, who owns two-thirds of a *faddan*, is rumored to have registered her land in the name of her sons but to have kept the deed with a trusted older man in the community, who is to reveal it after her death.

In the absence of incentives for the sons to continue to pool their resources and maintain a single extended-family household, they may demand their individual shares of their father's property. In some cases the mother may take the share of inheritance due her from her husband's estate and choose to live with the son whose wife "makes her the most comfortable."

Now separated in divided living quarters, the constituent nuclear families begin a new phase of the developmental cycle. For the wife in the nuclear family household this represents a new beginning in the protracted establishment of her own power base, wherein sons figure prominently. As for the husband, he enjoys culturally legitimated authority. But as is the case for extended families, wives do not always comply. It is said that the clever woman is the one who agrees with her husband and proceeds to do what she thinks is right. In practice, however, a woman's actions whether in nuclear family settings or otherwise, are never insulated from the power structure of her specific societal context.

With access to culturally valued power bases, even a barren woman in a polygamous household may exert control over other family members, including her husband. This is true for Aziza, who after twenty-five years of marriage was childless. She picked a second wife for her husband so as to beget him "a child to make him happy." The young bride calls the older one mother (*amma*). Bride and husband show great respect towards the older co-wife. Other villagers attribute this unusual relationship to the fact that the older woman "controls the purse from which he trades in cattle."

Family Status, Religiosity, and Education

Of the many households of the village, the one occupied by the family of the ʿ*umda* is by far the most distinguished. Among other manifestations of the significance of this family's *asl* is the annual celebration of the village patron saint day (*mulid*). As a descendant (*khalifa*) of the village patron saint, the ʿ*umda* enjoys the prestige bestowed upon those who are linked to holy people whether by kinship or by following their "way" (*tariqa*). On the day of the patron saint (*mulid*), following the noon prayer, the *ᶜumda*, seated on a horse and dressed in a special attire handed down from one *khalifa* to another, leads a procession through the village streets. He is accompanied by an entourage of sword holders, drummers, and chanters who call out the praises of God and the Prophet (*zikr*).

During the day of the *mulid*, peasants from nearby villages are hosted by the people of Fatiha, who donate food for the entertainment of their guests in the large open space on the outskirts of the village. Those who come to visit the shrine of the Sayida Zebeda do so to fulfill vows to the saint or to ask for her help in the resolution of various misfortunes, including the cure of illness. While the miracles (*karamat*) of the patron saint are the object of marvel, some villagers say that the blessing (*baraka*) of God is above everything else. In practice, however, even villagers who profess Islamic orthodoxy and distance themselves from "the nonsense of the *fallahin*" will, in times of need, pay tribute to the *baraka* of local religiously literate healers or their counterparts beyond the boundaries of the village.

While religious piety, and of course land, are considered significant indicators of social power, formal education, whether religious or secular, is a significant means of social mobility. As one villager noted:

> Families will sacrifice a lot to have an educated son. [For] my grandson, we have given up on his help [in the field] so that he will remain in school. In the past people used to have to pay bribes to keep their children out of school. Now people become jealous from families whose children are getting educated and they try to emulate them.

Villagers recall that in the past, when there were no opportunities for peasants outside the agricultural sector, they considered formal education a waste of time. According to the *ᶜumda*, descent, agricultural wealth and skills, as well as the propagation of the family, had no better substitute, whether for males or females. Literacy in the village was limited primarily to members of the Turkish elite group. They attended school in the nearby towns or were sent off to be educated in Cairo or Alexandria. Other relatively affluent villagers sent their children to the local *kutab*, the traditional school for religious instructions. Here they learned to read and to memorize the Quran.

According to the two teachers in the *kutab*, families who could spare the labor of one or more of their children were rewarded with the prestige gained from having a religious and learned member in the family. The blessing (*baraka*) derived from such training would shadow the whole family. Other attendants of the *kutab* were boys who had a physical handicap, particularly blindness, and whose families had chosen for them the career of reciter of the Quran.

According to Article 19 of the 1923 Egyptian constitution, elementary education (6 years) was mandatory for boys and girls. In accordance with this compulsory (*ilzami*) scheme of education, the school in Fatiha was established in 1934. Children were sent to school occasionally only to avoid the fine for non-compliance with the regulation imposed by the government. Thus, while children were legally registered in the village school, most of them seldom attended. Those who did attend were absent for many days during the periods of heavy agricultural work. Consequently, as revealed by the census data below, many of the (then) children never learned to read or write, although they had been registered in school for a few years.

Today, in spite of the eagerness on the part of village parents to enroll their children in school, the economic constraints on the family often continue to impede the realization of this desire. Only a minority of school-age children ever complete even the elementary level of school education. Fewer still ever complete secondary school. Nevertheless, the opportunities for education among children are greater than they were when their parents were children. Among the adults of the village, the census survey of level of formal education shows that among the 214 adult female and 193 adult male occupants of the sample population of 100 households, 114 males and 171 females are illiterate, having never attended school. Forty-two males and 44 females are illiterate in spite of having been registered in school for periods varying from one to six years during the days of the *ilzami* system. Among younger adults of the sample population, 18 males and six females have completed secondary education. Six males and 2 females have high school certificates, 11 males and only one female have completed intermediate-level education and graduated from technical institutes. One male has attended the university, and a female started university, during my residence in the village. The same male has started graduate training. This man is the object of extraordinary respect from fellow villagers, including his parents. His mother in particular never refers to him by his name but instead uses the honorific title of *ustaz*, a popularized version of the term "professor," which was substituted for the once-popular Turkish titles of the ancien regime.

The relatively limited education of younger adult females reflected in the census data is an extension of a pattern which has been manifest over a number of years. Village records show that enrollment for the school year 1971–1972 was 65 for girls as compared to 181 for boys. In the year 1972–1973 the proportion of girls was even lower, with 51 registered females as opposed to 229 males. Finally, for the academic year 1973–1974, 62 girls and 163 boys were enrolled in the village elementary school. Attendance at the two village *katatib* also reflects a gender bias.

Of the 90 students, ages 5 to 15, who attend in order to partake of instructions in the memorization of the Quran and in reading, writing,
and arithmetic, only 11 are girls. Male bias extends to certain state-sponsored educational programs. During my residence in Fatiha a directive
from a state agency targeted *males* for a program which addresses illiteracy in the village.

Prestige acquired through education or through any other culturally
valued means is important not only to the person directly concerned but to
members of his/her entire family, be they close or distant relatives. People
from Fatiha who attain what other villagers may regard as high positions in
the national or governorate bureaucracy are expected to provide assistance
not only to their families but also to their fellow villagers.

Production, Exchange, and Wealth

As peasants, the majority of the population of Fatiha engage in subsistence activities and produce a stipulated surplus for appropriation by
the state on some 665 faddans, which constitute the cultivated area of
the village (*zimam*). In addition to agricultural products, the state's due
of surplus includes money in the form of taxes. Instead of practicing the
predominant form of household production which characterizes this
peasant community, some people subject village land to capitalist ventures. These are individuals whose families originated in Fatiha but who
now reside in urban areas. As practiced by these descendants of the
Turkish founders of the village, absenteeism involves the regular utilization of wage labor on land left under the guardianship of a local overseer
(nazir), who may also enter into sharecropping arrangements on behalf
of the urban owners.

Descendants of the Turkish founders who continue to live within
proximity of the village also partake of their urban kin's organization of
production. Their agricultural projects are supplementary to their employment as state bureaucrats in the nearby towns. While they share
with the majority peasant population of Fatiha an interest in agriculture,
their life style differs drastically from that of the soil-tilling peasants. The
women who work as domestic servants in their households provide a
vivid illustration of the social and cultural gap which separates the educated and relatively wealthy female beneficiaries of the welfare state
from their less fortunate peasant compatriots.

Access to land in the village takes the form of private ownership or
rent. While state-owned threshing areas are available for common use,
communal landholding is alien to the villagers. It is not traceable to
any period of village history. In fact, as evident from Chapter 1, the village itself was created around the time of the dissolution of communal

lands, when the institution of private ownership of land was initiated by Muhammad Ali and completed by his descendants.

With the implementation of the agrarian reform program, land from royal landholdings in the vicinity of the village was expropriated and allocated to families in Fatiha. Here the distribution of land proceeded according to the general guidelines of the reform program, which allocated plots ranging in size from two to five faddans depending upon the fertility of the soil and the size of the beneficiary's family. As was the intent for rural Egypt as a whole, the majority of peasant beneficiaries in Fatiha came to enjoy no more than bare subsistence. Also in keeping with national guidelines, priority in the distribution of land favored, first, persons who were actually involved in the cultivation of land, whether as tenants or owners, then villagers who had the largest families. In terms of the second category, male household heads with large families were clearly privileged.

All landholders, whether tenants or owners, are members of the agriculture cooperative. Through this institution, state regulation of agricultural production includes crop consolidation and rotation, pest control, pricing, and procurement. For credit, seeds, fertilizers, and pesticides, and sometimes tractors,[10] villagers also turn to this cooperative (*gamᶜiya*). So firm is the grip of the state on the organization of production that the villagers are generally left with no more than the burdensome responsibilities of daily labor.

At the end of each harvest villagers turn in the required amount of crops to the agricultural cooperative. They receive payment for their produce, from which has been deducted loans used to service the land. Interest of 0.47% is charged by the cooperative on the villagers' loans. In the case of a cotton harvest, the total yield of each plot is turned over to the cooperative. By contrast, none of the harvested corn is gathered by the local agents of the state.

In the case of rice, two-thirds of the yield is included in the surplus due the state. Two metric tons are levied on each *faddan*. If a peasant's land provides a poor yield, he/she files a complaint. After assessment of the case, the necessary reduction in the stipulated requirement is adjusted. In any case, after the agricultural cooperative collects the appropriate amount, the peasant is left with between one-half and one ton per *faddan*. Understandably the producers try to maximize the amount of this staple which is retained for household use. As Amin explained,

> Of course if I turn in the rice they will give me its price. But I will find it difficult to buy the rice. You know, now the cost of a *kella* of rice is forty-five piasters, in a month or two it will go up to sixty-five piasters.

About half of the wheat crop is also turned over to the *gam^ciya*. Of the approximately 6 *ardab* harvested from each faddan (which would adequately cover the annual needs of a household of about seven to eight persons), 2–3 are turned over to the cooperative.[11]

Most members of the community work the land themselves, and only a minority of families hire laborers or rent their land to others. Aside from villagers' prescribed obligations to the state, production relations are primarily kinship based. Except for the big families who confine their women's labor to domestic work, members of nuclear, extended, or fraternal joint families collectively cultivate private or rented plots of land. Among families who depend on wage labor, income is derived from the labor of all family members, including children. People seize every opportunity to convert into land any form of accumulated wealth, including women's jewelry.[12]

Aside from private ownership, utilization of land may proceed according to any of three forms of rent or combinations thereof: *naqd* (also known as *khalis*—even), *shirka*, and *zar^ca wahda*. In the cash (*naqd*) arrangement, and in accordance with land reform directives, the state set rent at seven times the tax paid on each *faddan*. The resulting annual payment is approximately 23–26 L.E. per faddan. The tenant is also expected to pay a defense tax, a road tax, and a national security tax, all of which amount to approximately 4 L.E. per faddan per year.

In the cash form of rent, cultivators enjoy legal support. As for the descendants of the Turkish founders from whom land is rented, some of them blame Nasser for having created "pharaohs" out of the peasants. As a member of the Turkish elite group remarked about her tenants, "they might as well own the land." She went on to describe the demise of the inordinate respect and deference which the *fallah* father of her present tenant used to demonstrate in the presence of her now-deceased mother, adding sarcastically that "this was in the past." Like some other members of her privileged group who reside in the city, she has sold part of the land which she inherited from her parents to former tenants. In so doing she reasoned that the "few pounds" which she receives as annual rent are "as good as useless." In need of a lump sum to provide furnishings for her soon-to-be-married daughter, she entered into extended negotiations with the tenant. The cultivator clearly had the upper hand. In addition to de facto possession of the land, he enjoyed legal protection against competition from non-cultivators who might have wanted to buy land for capitalist ventures.

The legal protection afforded peasants within the framework of *naqd* rent does not obtain for cultivation by partnership (*shirka*). Here mutual consent replaces formal contractual arrangements. While it is men who seal the deal with the clasping of hands and recital of the Quranic *Fat'ha*, and also men who witness the oral agreement, the initial "feeling out" of intent often involves women. In the *shirka* tenancy known as *zar^{c}a wahda* (one planting), the duration of the commitment of the land by the owner is more limited than in another variant known as *muzar^{c}a*. The latter is the option of last resort for tenants in their constant striving to have access to land to fulfill the subsistence requirements of their households.

The daily routine of cultivation (which is regulated by the Coptic calendar) involves the expenditure of inordinate amounts of energy, particularly at times of planting and harvesting. A short-lived attempt on my part to help in the wheat harvest was more than enough to convince me that when it comes to agricultural production, the "observation" part of "participant observation" is a more realistic endeavor. As for those who make their living by doing agricultural work rather than by observing it, the production of their meager needs involves nothing less than hours of back-breaking work. This often lasts from sunrise to sunset, with a short break for lunch in the fields. It is no wonder that villagers usually complain of pains in their backs, legs and wrists. Many of them use woolen wraps as belts or props for wrists and ankles to minimize pain and "give support to the bones."

While the months of planting and harvesting are the busiest, agricultural production generally involves unceasing year-round efforts centering around the preparation of the soil, planting the seeds, irrigating the sprouts to maturity, harvesting, weeding, and processing the varied yields. In Fatiha of 1974–1975 cotton, still a significant export and a national industry–destined agricultural product, is generally considered the most labor intensive crop. As the peasants put it, cotton needs a lot of servicing (*khidma*).

During the season of its cultivation, cotton covers a third of the village cultivated area. Preparation for planting involves ploughing the land three times. Although ploughing is generally a male responsibility, some women, particularly widows with no grown sons, do undertake this project. As for the planting of the cotton seeds, women are much more involved in this phase of cultivation. Along with male and female children they place the seeds in locations designated by a male supervisor.

In September, six months after its planting and after repeated spraying with pesticides, which Egypt is known to use in tremendous amounts, the cotton is ready for harvesting. The assurance of a high yield of this nationally significant agricultural product requires nothing less than a relentless effort on the part of peasants of both sexes, and almost all ages, to keep the cotton plants pest free. Assistance from the agricultural cooperative comes in the form of a cash advance of 15 L.E. per *faddan* for individual holders to recruit the additional requisite labor. Whether

as owners or as wage laborers, and at great risk to their own health, peasants come in prolonged contact with the pesticide-laced cotton plants
as they handpick pests at different phases of their growth cycle. For this
monotonous, strenuous, and unhealthy task, as for the harvesting of cotton, the daily wage is increased from the usual 0.25 L.E. to no more than
0.40 L.E.

Following its harvesting from an area of land, and in accordance with
the agricultural cooperative's crop consolidation scheme, cotton is not
replanted in the same area until two years later. Instead, the area is
planted with wheat. The associated gender division of labor involves the
assignment to men of the responsibility for spreading the wheat seeds.
At harvest time in May the labor of all household members is harnessed.
In Fatiha, where agricultural mechanization is minimal, the processing
of wheat is one of the few occasions on which peasants resort to ma-
chines. They rent threshers from (an increasing number of) private owners or from the agricultural cooperative.

The cultivation of rice follows the wheat harvest. The initial preparation of the sprouts (*shitla*) begins at home. These are then transferred to
the field and placed in a small area from which they are spread throughout the entire field. This involves the labor of men, women, and children. While no doubt a time-consuming and arduous task which involves hours of standing knee deep in mud, the planting of rice by
moonlight is enjoyed by village youth and remembered with nostalgia
by many of the younger married couples. As a young married woman
remarked, "lucky is she who gets to place the sprouts when she is near
her beloved." As is the case at weddings, this is one of the few occasions
when women chant songs with well-recognized sexual implications. For
a few months to come, the labor of all household members is applied to
the seemingly endless task of weeding until the rice harvest time in
October. As is the case for other agricultural tasks, it is only older persons,
along with relatively affluent villagers, who are exempt from participation.

Rice is in turn replaced by alfalfa, which is harvested four times. During the winter months the cattle are fattened. Depending on household
income, women either sell the large supply of milk obtainable during
this season or use it for household consumption, including turning it
into butter and cheese. The planting of corn then completes the agricultural cycle. As for cultivation of vegetables for daily household consumption, this is a year-round endeavor. Peasants utilize every grain
of soil within their reach, interspersing a variety of vegetables between
the major crops which they cultivate. Village ponds provide some fish,
which are sold on the village streets.

In Fatiha expressions of peasants' "subsistence ethic," and associated
efforts at reproduction of the household as a productive entity, go well

beyond the sphere of production, extending to the realm of exchange. Transcending the formalized sharing associated with *shirka* tenancy is a form of exchange labor known as *zamala* (partnership). This partnership is considered poor people's substitute for hiring wage laborers. Indeed, villagers say that "the person whose arms are wide [i.e. affluent] does not become a partner, he hires laborers." Within the framework of this non-contractual form of cooperation, villagers help each other with a variety of work. Far from restricted to kin relations, this form of mutual aid extends to friends, neighbors, as well as others who reside or work in the vicinity of the village. In agriculture, assistance may comprise the digging of cotton and the harvesting of wheat or corn. *Zamala* also extends to ploughing, where the borrowing of draft animals may also be part of the exchange.

Specific to women is *zamala* surrounding baking and, to a certain extent, child care. The relatively balanced reciprocity associated with baking is minimized in child care by the generalized sense of responsibility which all village adults are supposed to have towards children, whether their own or not. This collective obligation extends to the sharing in major disasters befalling co-villagers. An outstanding expression of the collective shouldering of major misfortunes is evident when cattle are slaughtered if their imminent demise appears to be inevitable. Villagers willingly buy meat from the owner of the animal as a way of compensating for his/her major loss.[13] Other disastrous occasions when cooperation among villagers is expected include deaths and extended illness.

Mutual aid includes the borrowing of a variety of belongings ranging from animals to food. Member of households of close physical and social proximity exchange the latter frequently. In cases where significant amounts of rice, corn, or wheat are given to members of households who have not harvested their own, it is expected that equivalent amounts will be returned when such items are acquired either from the borrower's field or through market purchases. Women also use each other's ovens. If one has no time to bake, she borrows a stipulated number of loaves from her neighbor and returns the same number when she bakes.

Women and men join or initiate revolving credit associations. Since the establishment of the agricultural cooperatives with their credit system, villagers no longer have to resort to money lenders. Older villagers recall that in the past such lenders used to charge the peasants exorbitant interest rates, sometimes reaching as high as ten percent.[14]

Barter involves such items as salt, rice, corn or other agricultural products. Services may also be paid for in kind rather than in cash. Instead of exchanging labor as in he *zamala* arrangement, women who help others in baking without expectation of reciprocal assistance are rewarded with some of the baked bread they helped prepare. During harvests agricultural products are exchanged for a variety of goods and services ranging from children's sweets to the payment for field laborers to help in baking to the circumcision of a child or the recitation of the Quran at funeral services.

Whether help is sought for agriculture or architecture, villagers try to minimize the amount of cash paid out for services rendered. In building raw brick structures, women prepare the mixture of dirt, ashes, straw and other available items such as chicken feathers. Some may also become involved in the "baking" of the bricks. The actual laying of the bricks, and the measurements, are done by a man. When the widow Madiha built her house, even her children were involved. As she explained, "the more my daughters and I do, the less I have to pay [the male builders]."

Attempts at accumulation extend to spiritual wealth as "investment in the after life." Most people do not make a public production of the giving of alms. As a regular recipient remarked, "I was given many things by people whom I do not even know. They simply give to the people of God [ahl Allah]." In contrast to this woman's expressing appreciation, some poorer villagers voice resentment of their wealthier neighbors. While acknowledging that "during the mulid the poor take from the rich," a poor villager added that

> the rich are kind only during the mulid, [otherwise] they act like non-believers [in God]. The rich are always suspicious of the poor, if they lose something they always accuse us, if they become ill they say that we envied them.

Differing opinions aside, and whether by design or otherwise, some villagers enjoy a privileged reputation as generous donors to those in need; others are known, and disliked, for their stinginess.

According to Islamic tradition, the "capable" donate to the poorer members of their community on occasions other than the mulid. Around harvest time the alms of the land (zakat il ard) take the form of corn, wheat, and rice. On other occasions the fulfillment of vows may involve donations of either food or cash. Money may be placed in the contribution box of the zawya by those seeking divine interventions, including the healing of a loved one.

In addition to accepting religiously sanctioned alms from other villagers, some residents of Fatiha regularly receive state aid. The Ministry of Social Welfare provides pensions to widows, disabled men, and orphans. Aid is provided in two major forms: either monthly stipends for the very poor or bi-annual support for those who are temporarily incapacitated, including those suffering from long-term sickness. An irregular form of financial aid is given to students for the purchase of books and supplies.

While the sharing of material wealth is socially valued as intimation of kindness or piety, this in no way surpasses the importance which villagers attribute to thrift and saving, often towards the ultimate shared goal of accumulating agricultural land. Among women the effort to acquire "mud" proceeds with a well-defined phased strategy. This surpasses women's constant attempts to acquire cash for purchasing such items as tea, sugar, clothes, or medicine through the sale of agricultural products either in the village itself or in the weekly market of a nearby village.

The realization of a woman's dream to acquire land may begin when she makes an investment of a few pounds of accumulated savings to purchase some chicks. After these grow into chickens, fattened on dried out pieces of leftover bread, peels of vegetables, and broken pieces of corn or the chaff from wheat, she sells the eggs or the chickens themselves. When enough cash is accumulated from such a venture (which, finances permitting, may be undertaken simultaneously with other projects of income generation), the woman may be in a position to invest a larger sum of money. Under such circumstances she may purchase a goat on her own or find a friend or a relative, or even a member of the wealthier households of the village, willing to be a co-owner. This means sharing in the maintenance of the animal and the profits from its products. In turn the goat's kids may be sold for about ten pounds each, a large sum of money by village standards. Additionally, milk derived from the mother goat may be consumed by members of the woman's household, turned into cheese, or sold for cash.

This pattern of investment and reinvestment may be repeated, graduating up to cows or water buffaloes, and eventually to land. When land is finally attainable a woman willingly sells her jewelry. In some cases a woman makes her husband a co-owner in return for his acceptance of the responsibility for cultivating the land.

Women who can afford to undertake such accumulation of wealth do not start from scratch. They are the relatively fortunate ones who have a "starter" (*khamira*—yeast), minuscule though it might be. Yet, although necessary, the mere availability of the initial asset is not sufficient for a woman to build up her savings. She needs the support of her family to overcome pressure from her husband and/or older affines who urge income pooling and collective consumption of field and animal products within the household.

Deprived of investment opportunities or support of a trusted friend or relative, a woman may wrap her cash savings in a rag which she then puts in a wall of her house, covering it with mud. She is constantly assured of the safety of her cache as she fulfills her responsibility of maintenance of the physical structure of the family residence. Between the layers of wall the cash remains until the opportune moment.

For men, as for women, accumulated savings are readily invested in land whenever the opportunity arises; acquisition of land is the ultimate goal. Even those who buy jewelry do so only as an intermediate step towards buying, or at least renting, land. They buy gold when it is cheap and sell it when it is expensive.

Aspirations aside, the opportunities for wealth accumulation in Fatiha are minimal. Rather than finding accumulation of wealth, one finds the fragmentation of property through its division upon inheritance. In view of the significant economic constraints under which the villagers operate, they are generally reluctant to invest their savings in any project which is not considered fail proof. Purchase of land and its cultivation with the standard crops of cotton, wheat, and corn is thus the most rational choice. Innovations such as the cultivation of aromatic plants for the international market, and potatoes for urban consumers, have been undertaken by relatively rich cultivators from a nearby village. The family whose members introduced aromatic vegetation was the same one which experimented with the planting of potatoes as a cash crop. Villagers say that it is only the well-to-do who can take the risk of experimenting with new crops.

In 1974–1975 some villagers were contemplating a new set of risks, and rewards, which would involve departure to Iraq. According to village officials who have been in contact with employees of the "work offices" (*makatib ʿamal*) which are currently reviewing requests, the Iraqi government is offering Egyptian peasants Iraqi citizenship. The financial incentive is considered immense by local standards: 8 *faddan* of land per family and even more, up to 20 *faddan* for larger families, in addition to food and lodging. Hassan, a member of an extended-family household which operates about 3 *faddan*, is preparing to go to Iraq. Although excited about the prospect of having a member of the family own as much land as does the biggest household in Fatiha, Hassan's family decided that he should go to Iraq on his own at first, to check out the situation for the others. His wife, Nargess, has no desire to leave the village. She prefers to "eat bread and salt," adding, "How will I see my father and my mother when I am in the end of the world?" Many other villagers agree with her. In fact even when the pursuit of "eating bread," not to mention accumulating wealth, involves *internal* migration, similar resistance is sometimes expressed.

When wealth is accumulated through one means or another, or in one form or another (e.g. cash, houses, land, farm animals, furnishings, or jewelry), it is passed from one generation to the next, ideally, in keeping with Islamic traditions. Accordingly, when a man dies, his wife and children inherit his property. His daughters are entitled to half the share of their brothers. The female is said to receive a pile (*kum*) and the males two piles (*kumin*). As for the wife of the deceased, she is entitled to one-eighth of the total property (*timin*).[15] In practice, however, Islamic edicts pertaining to a woman's inheritance are often violated, leaving sons as the only beneficiaries of their father's wealth. This contributes to the skewed distribution of land and to the attendant asymmetry in power relations.

To avoid implementation of religiously sanctioned prescription for wealth distribution among siblings, fathers resort to secular mechanisms of property transfer; they register land in the names of sons through legal sales. This is rationalized by the assertion that whatever land is acquired by a daughter ends up belonging to her husband's kin. It is also reasoned that the restriction of land inheritance to sons is an indirect way of protecting daughters from greedy men who are only too eager to marry a woman who "has mud on her" (i.e. owns land).

In practice, villagers' rationalizations for depriving daughters of their religiously sanctioned share of parental property are not valid. For one, the registration of land in the names of sons only is not always a matter of public knowledge. It may come as a total surprise even to members of the same household after the death of a father. Even the sons themselves may not be aware of their status as exclusive beneficiaries until after the father's death. This is the case for the household of Hajj Saber where the patriarch, wanting to ensure proper treatment at the hands of his sons until his death, had in fact registered the land in their names and kept the documentation with a trusted friend.

Another affront to the rationalization for barring a daughter from inheritance relates to the fact that the land is not necessarily held at the disposal of the family of her husband. Among women who inherit land, some *willingly* turn it over to their brothers for cultivation. In this situation women are the beneficiaries of derivative power in their dealings with their husbands' families. Far from deprived of the bounty of the land, they are usually the recipients of part of the harvest. As a contribution to the collective livelihood of the extended family, a woman's share of the harvest prompts reward to the woman concerned and her children, taking the form of favoritism in the distribution of food or reduction of work load. She and her children are likely to be favored over other female members of the household whose economic dependence on males is more pronounced. As for revocation of the brother's privileged access to his sister's land, this does not usually occur until a time when she is no longer threatened with divorce and enjoys a sense of security as her own children, particularly sons, grow up. This usually coincides with the withdrawal of her nuclear family from the livelihood (*ma^{c}isha*) of the extended family, leaving the woman and her children and husband, *not* his family, as the primary beneficiaries of the maternal grandparents' inherited wealth.

Of the village's total of 453 land plots, 325 are controlled by men as compared to 125 by women, who constitute no more than 10% of the village's landowners. Contributory to this lopsided distribution is the fact that when a woman dies, her husband usually inherits her wealth, including land which he shares with their children. He also takes her jewelry, leaving her clothes to the members of her parental household, who may well give them to charity. If the deceased woman is childless, her husband and her siblings inherit from her, the former receiving half of her estate and the latter sharing the other half.

Gender Differentiation

Gender differentiation is manifest at all phases of life, beginning with birth. On this occasion the delivery of a girl prompts conspicuous expressions of disappointment among members of the extended family, especially if the mother has no sons. The mother's father and her brother are absolved of their obligation to provide her with a large pan full of food, contribute to the celebration of the seventh day after birth (*sebou^c*), and place money in the newborn's clasped fist. Yet preparation for "manhood" is not without its toll for the child concerned. While children in general may be subjected to physical punishment during the early years of life, there is a noticeable severity for boys. They are expected not to indulge in "womanly" behavior, which is promptly held in check by fathers in particular.

Neither girls nor boys are spared the burden of laboring.[16] Variation only pertains to the weight of the burden. From the earliest years of his/her life, a village child is a source of productive labor which contributes not only to the local community but also, indirectly, to the national economy. By no means an uncommon sight in the village is that of a little boy or girl, probably no older than four or five, helping load a donkey and then leading the animal to the field. The scene is repeated with such a child guiding the cows and water buffaloes to and from the field or directing the ducks or geese away from the pond towards the house around sunset.

Children under ten years of age help plant seeds, weed, or carry lunch to the field. At this early age some girls are taken away from the village to work in the households of urbanites. Those who are spared this traumatic experience practice their domestic skills in their own families' households; a few help out in the households of the village headman and his relatives of Turkish origin. In their own households girls perform chores ranging from baking to washing to force-feeding the ducks and caring for younger siblings.

A male child may also help care for younger siblings or cousins, especially if he has no older sisters. By his early teen years, however, he is reluctant to engage in domestic work. His reluctance or refusal to comply with some of his mother's requests stand in sharp contrast to his obedience to his father. At a phase of the developmental cycle of the family when the father is contemplating withdrawing from the integrated livelihood (*ma'isha*) of the extended family, he finds in the son the nucleus for establishing his own domain apart from the authority of older brothers and parents.

In her early teens a girl's labor targets both field and household. With her mother and other female household members she sweeps, bakes, fetches water, takes care of younger children in the household, or carries on her head a load of cooking pots to the canal. There, in the company of others of her age or older, she scrubs the utensils to a glittering shine while catching up on the latest developments in the village, arranging for *zamala*, or getting a lead on wage labor. As for work in the field, she is no less skilful than her brother, accompanying animals and their loads to the fields, planting, weeding, and harvesting, whether on her own family's land or as a wage laborer.

Children's own sense of gender identity is highly developed from a very early age. They demonstrate clear appreciation of gender role cultural expectations and definite, shared ideas about power relations between males and females. This is reflected in the statements of seven girls and seven boys, ages 8 to 13,[17] who responded to a story completion test which I conducted in the village. In conjunction with unstructured interviews and direct observation, these children's responses reveal emphasis on the role of males, particularly fathers, as disciplinarians and on fathers' special strictness with boys. The authoritarian role of the father stands in contrast to the imagery of the mother as relatively passive, protective, and tolerant. While formal education is valued by the children themselves, when confronted with a fictitious narrative which forced them to choose between formal education and locally prescribed gender roles, they defined female roles as primarily domestic and maternal. Additionally, village children hold in high esteem symbols of urbanism. This mirrors the sentiments of adult villagers who also express their aspirations for their children in terms of acquisition of symbols of urbanism. In so doing they are more likely to refer to their male children.

Beyond childhood to early adult life in the mid-teens, young men and women take on expanded shares of familial responsibilities. While young men work in the field, young women (except for those in secondary school, or members of the households of the big families) are involved in both agricultural and domestic labor. At this stage of life their contribution is considered more than simply "helping out." They shoulder major duties pertaining to the daily operation of the household, alleviating their mothers' burdens.

Not only is there an established valorization of male over female labor in the reproduction of the household, but parents differ in the appreciation of their daughters' contributions. For example, Fatma's father tells her "you are better than any man Fatma . . . may God bless you with two daughters who would take care of you as you have taken care of me." In contrast, Bahiga's father admonishes her ingratitude and lack of appreciation of his role in enriching her with "house and field." He adds that while she neglects him, she is obsessed with sex with her economically dependent husband, the flesh of whose shoulders is said to be from the sweat of the old man's brow.

Married adult men are primarily involved in agricultural production. The primary elements of their cultural role expectations are those of provider and propagator of the family. Given the centrality of procreative capacities and the attendant reproduction of the household labor pool, a man's sexual impotence or sterility, like a woman's barrenness, is grounds for divorce. As for married women, and aside from the idealized definition of their duties as domestic, by far the majority also share their husbands' responsibility for agricultural work. Under certain circumstances, such as a husband's extended illness, a woman may even take on the male task of ploughing.

Domestically women assume full responsibility for a variety of tasks. Significant among these are child care, cooking, washing, baking, processing of field products, milking the cattle, making dung cakes, repairing the walls of the house, and fetching water.

To fulfill her responsibilities, whether domestic, maternal, or agricultural, a married woman's day usually begins before the sunrise prayer call. She starts by cleaning the animal shed, feeding the animals, either hauling water for them to drink or leading them to water. Upon her return home she feeds the animals again, then ties them up. While the rest of the family is still asleep, she starts to sweep, then goes out again to fetch water for the drinking and washing of the day. She then fuels the kerosene lamps and fills pots for drinking water. About two hours after she wakes up, she prepares breakfast and then takes water for her husband and children to wash in. Then they all sit down to breakfast, at which time the husband, after drinking his tea, may also smoke his water pipe (*goza*). The wife then loosens the animals, hands them to him, and he leaves for the field. The children also leave; they either accompany their father to the field or, if they are students, go to school.

On the day of baking, and in addition to doing other domestic chores such as child care and washing the dishes and clothes, a woman starts preparation as soon as her husband leaves. Having assembled all the ingredients the day before, she makes the dough. Taking full advantage that the oven is going to be hot for some time, she prepares other foods. For this she picks out the dirt from large amounts of rice and washes and peels vegetables, all in preparation for baking. Around noon she fixes lunch and, depending on the socioeconomic status of the household to which she belongs, either sends lunch to the field with a child or takes it to her husband herself. If her family's status permits, she stays on, returning home before her husband in time to take her fowl inside and prepare food for the animals once more, taking them from her husband as he arrives by sunset. As he washes up, she milks the cattle and puts out the food for supper.

Not unlike national statistics which minimize women's work in rural Egypt, ignoring the significance of non-remunerated labor, the males of Fatiha generally undermine women's work contribution and do not associate it with a monetary value. In response to a woman's complaint of being tired, her spouse may well respond sarcastically, saying, "Why, what have you been doing all day?" or "If people were to see the way you are acting, they would think that you have been in the field all day." More generally, some men, informed by the popular language of industrial development of the hegemonic urban society, argue that "houses have no factories to produce; our factory here is the field."

Even when women's work in the fields cannot be denied, men generally tend to underestimate its significance; some may even claim that women only get in the way. Such ideas stand in contrast to the testimony of some older villagers. Like older women, some older men emphasize the *complementarity* of women's and men's work, citing the famous proverb "Man is a river, woman a dam." Illustrating the joint efforts by man and woman, an older man pointed to the fact that

the woman drives the water wheel while the man controls the water and spreads it throughout the fields. He may load dirt for the animal shed and she will pull the donkey and lead him home or whereever. He works in the fields and she takes his lunch to him. She collects firewood and loads it onto the camel and he stacks it on the roof of the house. Take the feeding of the cattle in the home, either one can do it, also leading the animals to drink. He ploughs for the corn and she spreads the corn line. She helps in the weeding of cotton and picking the worm from the cotton plant. In the planting of rice, both plant the rice. Both also work at weeding of the rice plants and in the harvesting of cotton and storage of the crops.

Older villagers also stress the importance of a "blessed life," which they associate with familial, including matrimonial, harmony. In contrast to older villagers, who are concerned with *baraka*, their younger relatives and neighbors are more likely to make explicit the material worth of the contributions of each family member, expressing differential valuation of male and female labor.

Whereas a monetary value is readily designated for the substitution of a male's labor in cases of illness, extended sojourn from the village, or death, discussions of the replacement of women's labor make no similar reference to remuneration.[18] A woman's work is generally considered replaceable by any other female relative or neighbour:

> When a man is ill, if his relatives are busy and in case he has no sons to take over his work, his family will hire a man to do his work. . . . A man's [wage] per day is known; it is 25 to 30 piasters plus breakfast and lunch. A man does not go to the doctor until he is beat because he cannot afford to stay out of the fields. He may take an aspirin, or a Novalgine; he fools himself and persists in working. . . . If the man falls ill his wife leaves the house and neglects the children and their needs and works in the field because the bounty [*kheir*] all comes from the field. . . . The woman can never do these [field] tasks as well as a man.

By contrast, substitution for a woman is judged as

> not cost[ing] anything. Because every household has friends and relatives who can fill in for the woman and maybe do her work even better . . . women come over and it is a tribute to the family. It is only a cooperative effort which the woman may eventually reciprocate. . . . The closest [female] relative comes to do the work. If a substitute is hired she gets a cup of rice, a few loafs, but not money. If we bring the woman's neighbour, her sister, or any relative, she does not take anything. [The sick woman] stays in the bedding and her relatives help her and give her all sorts of home remedies.

Women themselves generally attest to the authority of men over them and acknowledge the physical and moral superiority of males. This is expressed in statements such as "I am lower than him, he is a man, isn't he?"; "God also said that man is preferred over woman"; "A man is better because he runs after our bread. . . . He protects [the woman] from hunger and nakedness. . . . He protects her honor"; "We do not have the same strength as men"; "Some women are stronger in character than men but most women must obey men."

Apart from shared ideas regarding women's physical, mental, and moral inferiority, their acceptance is far from universal when they implicate women personally. Some women argue that beliefs related to the presumed religious inferiority of women are made up by men who use them to boss women around. Similarly, a man's opinion about "the place" of women in general is not necessarily operationalized when it comes to women of his own household. Thus, while wife beating is a male prerogative, and while the *cumda* may respond to a woman's complaint by saying, "What do you expect when you insult your [older] sister-in-law in front of your husband," he himself would not approve if his daughter, or another woman from a big family, were to be subjected to the same battering.

In some cases a woman herself may "extend her hand" on her husband. One such act occurred during my residence in the village.[19] A follow-up of this case revealed that the woman involved was not only subjected to public ridicule but ended up divorced upon the demise of her agnates' support.

To other villagers, it was not the woman's transgression of male authority which was the focus of discussions of her divorce. Instead, the termination of her marriage is attributed to her misjudgement of the support that would be forthcoming from her kin. Needless to say, villagers are well aware that women, like men, do deviate from the path of cultural prescriptions. What is worth stressing is their awareness of the fact that the consequences of transgression of cultural authority are not uniform. As a reminder to the anthropologist, villagers repeatedly cite the proverb "Your fingers are not all alike." Indeed, as the implications of this proverb suggest, the cultural construction of gender differentiation is mediated by social context involving differential access to alternate, effective, culturally valued power bases.

In sum, women's as well as men's everyday actions and choices are no doubt subject to historically derived cultural constraints. Nevertheless, gender identity and the restrictions that it implies are also mediated by a woman's control of or access to one or another culturally valued power base, be it the contribution of sons to the extended family, religious piety, ownership of land, sustained agnatic support, or her physical beauty.[20]

Both the cultural construction of gender and its social mediation find expression in different facets of social life extending to the medical domain. As the next part of the book is intended to demonstrate, this tension, or what the late Robert Murphy (1971) described as "the dialectics of social life," is manifest in relation to the human body, sickness, and healing.

Notes

1. Although the present description of Fatiha relates to this specific time period, I have opted for the linguistic convenience of the ethnographic present.

2. One *faddan* is equivalent to 1.04 acres.

3. The proverb states, "If you have a *millim* (penny), you are worth a *millim*, if you have a pound, you are worth a pound."

4. This refers to the lower back of the man, from which the semen is believed to descend and cause pregnancy.

5. These are unions between members of a nuclear family other than the parents, between children and siblings of parents, and between sons and daughters-in-law and the parents of their spouses.

6. Of these, three are occupied by childless couples and one by a couple whose female children had all married out.

7. These consist of parents or parent substitutes, married sons with their wives and children, and unmarried siblings.

8. These households are occupied by brothers, their wives and children, as well as unmarried siblings, one parent (mother), and, sometimes, an older relative.

9. This even seems to hold for villagers' hours of sleep. The majority of their dreams involve relatives, whether kin or affine.

10. By 1974–1975 a few tractors were owned by villagers who rented them out at the hourly rate of 1 L.E.

11. With the introduction of the high-yield variety Mexican wheat, the co-operative's share increased. The peasants were less than pleased with this Mexican variety, preferring the Indian variety which they are "used to." In addition to their dislike of the "ugly black color of bread" made with the new variety, cultivators complain of its very low yield of chaff (*tibn*). Whereas no more that 15–17 *himl* (approximately 156 Kg) of *tibn* is derived from the wheat yield of a *faddan* planted with Mexican wheat, as much as 25 *himl* are extractable from a similar acreage of the Indian variety. The *tibn* is indispensable for the peasants. When not consumed within the household, as in the feeding of animals, it is sold for approximately 4–8 L.E./*himl*, depending on season.

12. When a husband or significant members of his family make demands on his wife to sell her jewelry, she is likely to refuse unless she is forced under the threat of divorce or made co-owner.

13. As for concern over adverse health consequences, an older village woman responded to my own concern by pointing out that we know nothing of the health condition of the cattle that are slaughtered under government supervision.

14. Disguised forms of exacting interest are currently operative in the village. This proceeds through the pre-harvest sales of crops, grocery purchases

by the month (*ʿala ishahr*), and credit sales by itinerant vendors. When such practices are brought to the attention of some older villagers, they continue to insist that the present situation is better than the past, when deeds "against religion" involved the foreign money lenders. As for the many other vices imputed to these foreigners, these include their adeptness at luring the cotton-enriched rural dwellers to their taverns and stripping them of their fortunes with the help of alcohol and "naked women." By contrast, Nasser is believed to have brought respectability and "Islam" to the land of the *fallahin*.

15. A woman engaged in a consensual union (*ʿurfi*) is not entitled to any inheritance. Men are likely to enter into such unions when they are already married and have children to whom they prefer to leave their inheritance. Whereas Egyptian women are known to enter into such unions on their own initiatives, thereby retaining the right to repudiate their husbands, I did not come across any such cases in the village.

16. This includes school children. Captions of drawings which I collected from school children include "the pupil milking the water buffalo."

17. Villagers believe that girls mature at an earlier age than boys. A similar conclusion is drawn by the psychologist, based on her evaluation of drawings which I collected from a group of village school children. Apart from individual manifestations of "high IQ" and "mental retardation," she found that in general girls' drawings reflect greater intellectual maturity than those of boys of the same grade.

18. Men's work in the field is considered so important, and unsubstitutable by women, that even the most energetic of widows who are known to undertake a variety of male tasks, including ploughing, are accused of using their charm and sexuality to lure men into helping them out with their work in the fields under the guise that these "strangers" are wage laborers.

19. Initially this case seemed to provide a vivid illustration of the anthropological emphasis on women's informal power, agency, and choice, which was popular in academic discourse at the time of this field work (Rosaldo and Lamphere 1974).

20. A beautiful woman who leaves her huband's household as a result of a quarrel with him, or with another member of his family, is likely to "hold out" for a long time. When asked whether her husband has tried to make up with her, her reply may well come in the form of the proverb "leave the handsome one to his ways until he comes with his tail up against the back of his head." When the husband does come for reconciliation, he is expected to expend not only a great effort to redress the insult extended to the wife's family but also to express his regret materially by giving gifts.

PART THREE

Sickness and Healing:
Male-Female Differentiation

3

BODY CONCEPTS: CULTURAL CONSTRUCTION AND SOCIAL MEDIATION

The centrality of social personhood in villagers' lives, manifest on a daily basis and celebrated in popular proverbs, also informs their conception of the human body. Although they are well aware of a given body as a separate, complex entity of differentiated parts, their evaluation of its condition entails much more than physical constitution. In addition to displaying similarity to earlier Arab/Islamic medical traditions which regard the body as a unity of soma and psyche, villagers' body concepts partake of earlier traditions which attend to social communication between bodies (Devisch and Vervaeck 1986:543,550).[1]

Far from holding body concepts associated with ontological definitions of disease, villagers attribute general functions to only a few anatomical structures. Instead, as parts of this chapter and the next will show, they regard as central the body's articulation with the social, natural, and supernatural realms. The body's condition and secretions are linked to these spheres. Informed by an integrative concept of the body, villagers view compromised health not simply as disruption of the function of designated body parts but, more importantly, in terms of meaningful social events. So central is the relation between the social and psycho-somatic dimensions of human existence that villagers' ideas about the human body are readily recognized as a significant intellectual domain for the reproduction of social ideology, notably the naturalization of gender cultural constructs.

Body Formation

Villagers consider male-female differences as originating with God's creation of humankind: "God created Adam first and then made Eve [Hawwa] from his left side. That is why the man is stronger." Some

79

people add that "women were created from the crooked rib." Aside from
the latter claim, there is unanimity regarding the role of divine power in
the process of conception.[2] In their attempt to beget a healthy and
blessed child, villagers assign to the husband responsibility for invoking
the name of the Almighty during sexual intercourse. However, it is coun-
selled that a clever woman will not depend on her husband's memory in
this regard and will whisper the appropriate Quranic invocation herself.
Evidently, paternal responsibility is not a substitute for the prescribed
maternal duty of safeguarding the offspring's welfare. The centrality of
maternal affect is in no way indicative of female subservience to male
authority. Indeed, pregnancy and child rearing are central elements
constituting the core of a woman's power base, whether in Fatiha and its
rural environs or in urban Egypt[3] (cf. Dwyer 1978:170; Ortner 1974).

Villagers who are familiar with the Quranic account of conception describe the process thus:

> It says in the Quran that the human body is created from *ᶜalag*, which
> means something hanging. This is from the man; the woman has noth-
> ing but blood of menstruation which comes from the vein of her back.[4] If
> the house of child [*bit il wild*] is clear, the woman becomes pregnant
> from the *ᶜalag* of the man.

The very circumstances under which conception occurs are noted retrospectively to account for a given child's nature (*tabᶜ*). Just as a greater
significance is attributed to the male seed (*bizra*) than to female menstrual blood (or egg, according to some villagers), priority is assigned to
the character of the father. As for how this can be reconciled with the
birth of females, responses only refer to "God's knowledge." Similar invocation of the supernatural serves to lend legitimacy to the assertion
that gender differences are implanted at conception. The essence of
males and females is thus naturalized.

During pregnancy, the nature of the foetus is generally described
in terms of its sex, which is believed to be evidenced by the mother's
health. Whether during pregnancy or during the post-partum period,
girls are considered more taxing on their mothers' bodies, causing
greater discomfort during pregnancy and inducing excessive bleeding
after delivery.

In contradiction to the importance which is attributed to the male
seed, it is the wife who is held responsible for the birth of a daughter.
Retrospective rationalizations include reference to the predominance of
females in a woman's own family of birth, a factor which may influence
the choice of brides by young men and members of their families. After
the birth of a female a disappointed husband, although conceding that

"it is the will of God," may add, "[the mother] is the one who is carrying." Older villagers frown on such ingratitude to God and some of them reprimand those who attempt to tamper with what is regarded as the divine process of conception.[5]

As is conception, embryonic development is generally regarded as "only in the knowledge of God." Such rhetorical characterization of gestation conceals the variety of ideas which villagers have about the process of foetal development. For example, whereas those who are informed by Quranic knowledge explain that the bones are formed first, then covered with flesh, others claim a reverse order. Another assertion is that light-skinned infants are those conceived before menstruation and darker-skinned ones are those conceived after. But regardless of the mechanism involved, lighter skin color is considered more appropriate for females than for males: "A strong man has black hair . . . fair men are like girls. . . . If [a man's] face is very white, we say that he is like a girl."

In general, villagers consider both the physical and the emotional states of a mother to be significant influences on the outcome of her pregnancy. From abstract shared knowledge to implementable wisdom, this belief is mediated by the familial status of any given woman. Accordingly, while pregnancy may entitle a daughter of one of the big families (*bint al akabir*) to preferential treatment, whether in terms of access to choice foods, frequent visits to her parental household, or reduced work load, less fortunate women do not enjoy similar pampering or dispensation from their numerous responsibilities in production and social reproduction. For example, Samya, a young bride, complained of how her mother-in-law continued to make her wash the family clothes daily, in addition to doing her field chores and other housework. After she gave birth her happiness with her new twin sons did not last long. She attributed their subsequent death, and her own illness, to her mother-in-law's "stinginess" and "cruelty."

Body Structure and Function

Local terms used to denote the body are *gita*, *badan*, and *gism*. In contrast to the internal body, external body parts are well differentiated, labelled, and assigned specific functions. Given the emphasis on the interconnectedness of the external and internal body, safeguarding health involves care for both. The positive effect of external bodily cleanliness is rationalized in terms of allowing the skin to perform its function of "breathing" by removal of the dirt which obstructs this process.

Contrary to the ideal of cleanliness, in practice washing and bathing are constrained by the absence of a readily available supply of water. Other factors come into play. Significant among these is the limited supply of clothes. Villagers generally limit the purchase of new clothing to annual festive occasions or cotton harvest time, when they receive cash from the agricultural cooperative. As a result of the limited supply of clothes, even those who manage to wash their bodies often may continue to wear the same clothes for several days. Fleas, and in some cases body lice, continue to live in garments and produce itching and eczema all over the body. Less than adequate nutrition is also manifest on the skin. Discoloration of the facial skin is prevalent among children and young adults.

For adults, bathing is a weekly ritual involving the use of soap and a *lufa*. This is in addition to the usual bathing after sexual intercourse, which may be daily, particularly for those who pray and must purify their bodies. In the warm months males use the pond for bathing. Young boys bathe in the river almost every day of the summer months. The mosque has running water; this is often used for bathing by men during the summer.

Generally the cleanliness of children is not given the same attention as that of adults. Whereas women will regularly wash up after returning from the fields, they are less likely to impose on children the same regimen. Women who leave their children dirty may be scorned by their husbands and mothers-in-law and told "cleanliness is from piety and filth is from women" (*al-nazafa min al-iman wal wasakha min al-niswan*). In some cases, and particularly for boys, mothers' "neglect" may be purposeful, intended to avert the covetous Evil Eye (cf. Foster 1972). Children in their early teens take care of their own cleanliness; their appearance often represents a sharp contrast to that of their younger siblings. Consequently, while it is possible to distinguish between the older children of poorer villagers and those of their more affluent neighbors as they are dressed in their clean outfits in the evenings, it is difficult to differentiate the socioeconomic level of children under age five.

Personal cleanliness and general appearance, while recommended and idealized by such statements as "cleanliness is from piety" (*al-nazafa min al-iman*), are not without social regulation:

> When people see a woman whose husband is away taking care of her appearance they always accuse her of trying to tempt another man. But my mother-in-law doesn't care. In spite of the fact that she is a widow, she is very clean and takes good care of her face and eye brows and always bathes and wears clean clothes. Now that my husband is in the army, sometimes I am reluctant to take care of my appearance. Women whose men are far away are expected to leave themselves filthy and ugly so that no one will look at them. But my mother-in-law doesn't care; she says, get up and bathe and change [clothes].

The external body is the object of a variety of adornments. In addition to expecting adornment to produce a psychological uplift (*na*ᶜ*nasha*), villagers consider certain forms of personal adornment to be medically efficacious, inducing relief from specific forms of corporal aberrations. Accordingly, tattooing[6] is performed on protruding forehead veins. This is expected to relieve the pressure which accompanies the frequent hauling of heavy loads. Tattooing is also performed on people suffering from poor eyesight. It is imprinted on the side of the head near the weak eye to relieve pressure which causes the "clouding" of vision.

Mothers resort to tattooing their children to prevent the death of siblings born after them. The idea is that an unweaned child's temperament is out of balance when his/her mother is pregnant. He/she is described as "knocking with head and kicking" (*rafas wi tahan*). As a result of communication between the bodies of the older child and his/her yet to be born sibling, this impulse is transmitted to the latter. Consequently he/she is born weak and may die. Tattooing is believed to suppress the impulse of knocking and kicking, thereby ensuring a healthy life for the unborn sibling. Aside from the adverse impact of frequent pregnancies on unweaned children, repeated births are also considered taxing to the mother's body.

As medical anthropologists have reported for other parts of the Delta, *kuhl* is used in Fatiha both as an eye makeup and as a medicine.[7] Using any available applicator, whether a thin twig or their own fingers, women smear the inner parts of their lower lids with the *kuhl*. Among the majority of married women, this is part of their daily personal care routine, which follows the washing of their faces in the morning. Among unmarried women the use of *kuhl* is much more restricted and usually confined to special occasions or the treatment of eye problems. Whether used by women on themselves, on their infants at birth, or on their older children, the therapeutic properties of *kuhl* are cherished. Although rarely, men also apply *kuhl*, but only as medication.

Ear piercing is another practice which has ornamental/medicinal uses. For personal decoration, only the ears of girls are pierced. For illness, the upper ear of either a boy or girl is pierced "to allow the fever in a child's body to escape through this hole." Blue bead earrings are also used to guard against illnesses precipitated by the Evil Eye of a covetous barren woman or a family adversary. The local bedouin medical practitioner of natural medicine may also cut a notch from the upper ear of the child of a mother who has been losing many children. The idea is to disfigure the child's body so that he/she will be spared from harm inflicted by supernatural spirits.

The external sexual organs of both males and females are also the object of ritual surgery. Boys are circumcised at any age. The operation,

known as *tahara* (purification), may be planned to coincide with significant celebrations such as a *mulid*, either in the village or in adjacent
towns. Whether performed in the village or elsewhere, the child involved
is in a state of great fear, screaming and crying out for help from mother
or father. Once he is overpowered and held with his legs parted by adults
who may include his own father or mother, the "cutting" (*ass*) is done
by a barber who operates with a pair of scissors and then dresses the
wound with Mercurochrome and gauze.

For girls, genital surgery takes the form of a variant of clitoridectomy,
which is also referred to as *tahara*. Although the term applied to the
male operation is used to describe the female ritual, the stressing of reli-
gious/medicinal significance for the former is replaced by a social explanation for the latter. Girls are usually circumcised at around twelve
years of age, "because they are too small before that." In spite of the fact
that (unlike male circumcision) the practice is outlawed in Egypt, gypsy
women continue to travel in the Delta to perform this operation.

As is the case among their male counterparts, young girls boast of the
fact that they have been circumcised, a sign of their imminent womanhood. As is the case for the males, little girls are full of fear of the pain
accompanying the operation. Its performance entails the use of a long
shaving blade. The legs of the screaming girl may also be held apart by
close kin. Her female relatives or neighbors also restrain the upper part
of her body. To stop the bleeding and enhance the healing of the wound,
the gypsy applies a heavily salted onion to the wounded area.

As in other parts of Egypt where female circumcision is considered a
ritual preparation for marriage (Ammar 1961:121; Assaad 1980; Berque
1957:44), in Fatiha the practice is deemed necessary to safeguard a
woman's honor by ensuring her chastity at marriage. Since the clitoris is
identified as the locus of sexual excitement, and given women's entitle-
ment to sexual gratification within marriage, the gypsy who performs
the operation is always cautioned against its complete excision. The relatives of the "bride" shout out to her, "go easy on her, sister."

Although clitoridectomy predates Islam and no Quranic reference to
the practice can be found, the villagers of Fatiha justify the custom
by reference to the Islamic *sunna* (see also Blackman 1920:280–316;
Meinardus 1970:322, 325). In this respect, it is similar to male circumcision, which is also explained in terms of Islamic teachings. However,
for the latter, there is no concept of genital surgery as a way of con-
trolling sexuality. For males, who, unlike women are not considered
"lacking in mind and religion," it is the hygienic function of circumcision that is emphasized.

Villagers, including healers, provide minimal differentiation of the
internal body's structures and few elaborations on their functions (cf.

Shiloh 1961, 1962). They reason that "every part (of the internal body) is important," adding that "God Almighty put every part there with a purpose." "Whatever is inside us" is said to be essential for survival. Such sweeping statements aside, there is general agreement on defining the heart as the most important part of the body (cf. Good 1977):

> The heart makes us breathe. . . . If the heart stops for a second, the person dies. The heart is the most important part of the body; it makes the body move. . . . If the blood from the heart stops flowing the whole body stops.

Derived from the heart, blood is considered the lifeline of the body. Pulsation (*nabd*) is attributed to "breathing and the moving of the blood in the body." The pumping action of the heart is also considered significant. Informed by examples of natural processes in their environment, villagers use an agricultural analogy to describe the action of the heart:

> The heart irrigates [*yisgi*] the whole body and the veins are the canals [*ganawat*] which lead to all the parts of the body. . . . Our substance is the heart.

Rate of heartbeat is not distinguished for males and females as such but related to the size of the body. Villagers remark that

> the heart beats faster and works better for people who are not very fat; if a fat person becomes sad his heart may stop working right away.

While people in the village generally agree that the heart is the most important organ of the body, some of them designate the head to be "as important as the heart." As a local healer put it,

> The head with the brain is the most important part of the body. If the head is not well, the person cannot walk or think anything; the father of the body is the head, the brain makes the other parts of the body work.

For the inhabitants of the village as a whole, the importance of the head is explained by reference to its function as a structure for housing the brain (which is believed to be located in a vaguely defined part of the upper head). As for the brain itself, "it expresses everything" and is responsible for "thinking and evaluation of different situations." Additional attributes of the brain are "power of concentration" and "making the other body parts move." Just as women are believed to be lacking in piety, they are believed to be "lacking in brain," a condition considered of natural origin.

Regarding the bones, these are said to "carry the person and make him move." The bones are "the ceiling of the flesh" or "the support of the flesh." The flesh in turn "protects the bones." "Soft" bones are associated with youth. Thus, young children who fall without injury are said to be capable of sustaining these shocks due to the "softness" (i.e. malleability) of their bones. Older persons, however, are endowed with brittle bones, hence their susceptibility to permanent handicaps resulting from injuries to their bones.

Muscles are differentiated from bones. Whereas bones are considered "only the structure of the body," muscles "enable the person to do hard work." The strength of men's bodies is attributed to their having more muscle than women, and their bones are also said to be bigger and stronger. Again this differential is considered natural.

Other named body parts include the stomach with its intestines, both of which are associated with the function of digestion. The proper functioning of the stomach is affected by the kinds of foods which are ingested. Men who contradict the religious prohibition of consumption of alcoholic beverages justify the imbibing of beer on grounds of its medicinal properties. They say, "It is good for the digestion, it is like coca-cola. . . . We drink it after a heavy meal."

As is the case with other structures of the internal body, villagers' accounts reflect minimal differentiation of the constituent parts of the reproductive system. This extends to midwives, who say,

> The house of child [*bit il wild*] is inside us under the area where menstrual blood comes from and under this is the opening for the water [urine] and then under it is the thing [i.e., the vagina].

Further differentiation of body parts isolates the chest (*sidr*), the liver (*kabid*), the kidney (*kila*), the gall bladder (*marara*), and the spleen (*tohal*). Of all these, only the function of the chest is elaborated. Villagers link the lungs (*ri'a*) with breathing and associate their malfunction with the "sickness of the chest" (T.B.). The other organs are vaguely connected to the digestion of food. In this regard, the function of tasting is attributed to the tongue, which is also associated with speech. Finally, hearing is attributed to the ears, again with minimal elaboration of the mechanism involved. The processes of hearing, seeing, smelling, and feeling are all attributed to the power of God. Villagers, including the practitioners of natural and spiritual medicine, consistently concede to physicians superior knowledge of the functioning of internal body parts.

Proper functioning of the body and, by extension, proper psychological "disposition" are generally considered to be greatly influenced by nutrition. Good nutrition is usually described in terms of amount of food consumed. This is not to say that different qualities of food are not recognized. The emphasis on quantity reflects villagers' pattern of consumption of standard staples with minimal variation.

The body's production of natural substances, ranging from nursing milk to semen to menstrual blood, is linked to nutritional status. Among menstruating women, a "good" flow of menstrual blood is attributed to heat in the body, which is in turn linked to good eating and physical strength. Menopause is considered a sign of the weakness of old age. Good food is also considered essential when "strong medicine," such as oral contraceptives, is ingested.

Food is also considered necessary for any activity involving the expenditure of energy ranging from work in the fields to childbirth to sexual intercourse. When taking her husband's lunch to the field at noon, a woman says, "I'll take him a bite to support his heart." If we follow the same logic, ideally a woman should be well fed after giving birth. The consumption of meat and chicken prescribed for women at this time is explained in light of the enormous amount of energy expended by the mother during birth. Similarly, a new groom who is expected to be expending a large amount of energy in sexual intercourse is advised to eat well. A new bride, by contrast, is not considered to particularly need good nourishment. People say jokingly, "she is well fed." Thus, energy is viewed as supplied to the body in forms other than ingested food. In this regard, "peace of mind" is believed to have the same positive effect on the body as good nutrition.

Choice foods (e.g., meat, cream, baked rice, milk and eggs), when available, are saved and offered first to male members of the household. Preferential treatment of men in the allocation of food is rationalized in part by the natural differential body size between men and women, as well as in reference to the greater amount of energy expended by men in the field.

Privileged access to food by males may well begin in childhood. It is rationalized that boys need greater nourishment to expedite their growth so that they will fulfill their prescribed role as helpers of their fathers in agricultural work and, when the time comes, succeed them as "breadwinners," household heads, and guardians of their sisters' and mothers' welfare.

Young women complain of the discriminatory practices of their mothers. It is known that mothers secretly give valued foods such as eggs, butter, and cream to their sons. Older women rationalize this differential treatment, explaining that "a woman does this because she knows that in the end she will live with [her son], and under his mercy." When such "mercy" is not expressed, mothers complain of maltreatment by their sons, referring to the latter's ingratitude, "in spite of [mothers'] sacrifices in food and drink."

Consideration of specific instances of the operationalization of cultural constructs pertaining to nutrition discloses the significance of power asymmetry, which includes but transcends gender differentiation. Thus whereas, ideally, men should eat the better foods, and in larger amounts than women, in households where women are independent of supervision by older female affines, some of them admit that they eat better than their husbands "because they nibble a lot" during food preparation. In extended family households, however, the mother-in-law and adult male members eat first. They are then followed by junior women and their children.

In some extended-family households, two types of bread are baked. The "better" quality type made with "good white flour" is served to the mother-in-law and her sons. The less-valued bread containing whole wheat, corn flour, or ground fenugreek (*hilba*) is served to the junior daughters-in-law and their children. In such an extended family setting, the valued food is served by the mother-in-law, who passes out shares. In doing so, she may discriminate openly between males and females and between favored and not so favored daughters-in-law and their children. Women say that when they complain to their husbands about this blatant mistreatment, the husbands defend their mothers and say, "If you don't like it here, why don't you go and eat somewhere else."

Women who can find a sympathetic generous relative may in fact go and "fill [their] stomachs" at his/her house. People in the village often joke about mothers-in-law's control over food distribution. They comfort a daughter-in-law, telling her "never mind, tomorrow [i.e. someday in the future] you will be with your husband and children [in a separate livelihood]." In this phase of the developmental cycle, food sharing is more egalitarian, but the distribution of high quality food is assigned to the husband in the nuclear family. This privileged task passes on to the woman at a later phase, when she in turn acquires the honored status of mother of married sons.

In addition to attributing importance to food as a way of maintaining a healthy body, the villagers of Fatiha rely on certain natural substances to maintain a "healthy disposition" (*mazaj*). Tea and cigarettes, and to a lesser degree *hashish*, are used, particularly by men, for the purpose of "straightening the head" (*ᶜadl il dimagh*). Among men, *miᶜassil* (tobacco saturated with molasses) is used in the water pipe (*guza*); *hashish* is also used in this contraption. A woman may prepare the *guza*, taking the first puff (allegedly "to ensure that it is in working order") and then passing it on to her husband. *Nishug* (ground spiced tobacco) is also used for "proper disposition." Sniffing of this mixture stimulates the nasal linings and causes sneezing. The sniffing of *nishug* by females is usually restricted to older women. Sometimes they also use cigarettes, justifying their habit by reference to the medicinal efficacy of these substances in the treatment of such ailments as headaches and watery eyes. Men do not find it necessary to put forth such justification.

As with conception, the cultural construction of death involves reference to supernatural power. In addition, villagers' repeated use of analogies related to agriculture inform discussions of death:

> This is all in the hand of God. The soul [*ruh*] of the human being comes from God. God sends an angel to take a person's *ruh* when the time comes. Everything is in the hands of God. We are like plants, the one which ripens is cut off. The person whose leaves fall off, dies.

An elaboration on this analogy states that "all the names of people are in a big tree in heaven, the ones whose leaves fall die forty days later." After death, the soul departs from the body, and from that instant on the earthly characteristics of the body are lost.

As with birth registration, nationally operative bureaucratic controls regulate the termination of life in Fatiha. Regarding infant mortality, the disadvantage to girls documented in national statistics (Valaoras and Farag 1972:34) is manifest locally. As shown in Table 3.1, for infants under one year of age the average death rate is 103.2/1000 births for males, as compared to 121.6/1000 for females. Villagers' general impression that more girls die in the early years of life, which some attribute to their inherent weakness, is given credence by official village documentation of mortality. As indicated in Table 3.2, females represent a higher percentage of total deaths (58.2) than do boys (41.8).

Statistics on causes of infant and child deaths, like all other official health statistics, are based on biomedical indicators. With the exception

TABLE 3.1   Male-Female Mortality: Infants Under One Year

Year	Males		Females	
	Births	Deaths	Births	Deaths
1970	49	6	73	7
1971	64	6	63	5
1972	52	9	65	16
1973	65	3	70	5
1974	51	5	58	7
Average	56.2	5.8	65.8	8
Death rate	103.2/1000 births		121.6/1000	

TABLE 3.2 Male-Female Mortality: Children Under Five

Year	Total Deaths	Males	Females
1969	18	6	12
1970	20	6	14
1971	18	11	7
1972	35	13	22
1973	22	8	14
1974	26	14	12
Average	23.2	9.7	13.5
% of total deaths		41.8	58.2

of the occasional mention of burning, accidental poisoning, and "neglect of [child] care," environmental correlates, not to mention social conditions, generally have no place in official registries. Instead one finds the repeated implication of "respiratory attack" (*nazla shuᶜabia*) or "intestinal attack" (*nazla maᶜawiya*). In addition to these "master" causes, which sometimes appear with added superlatives, cause of death found in official documentation may also include blaming the victim, which is implicit in the shorthand reference to "neglect." Other causes of death registered for children under five include anemia/ Pellagra, pneumonia, general weakness, severe cough, "usual diseases," pneumonia/measles, severe cough/measles, weakness from birth, weakness of the mother, measles, and diarrhea.

For children and adults, as for infants, relatives of the deceased are required to obtain a certificate of death prior to burial. Biomedical measures, which also serve to determine other facets of villagers' lives (e.g. induction in the army, sick leaves for bureaucratic employees, qualification for pensions) serve as standards in official certification of death. Villagers' own holistic conception of the human body is supplanted by the desocialized, curt, technical language of professional medicine.

In addition to old age, causes of death for villagers ages 10 to 105 registered during the years 1969–1974, during which time there was an annual average of 21 deaths, include heart attack, spleen (disease), ascites, rheumatic fever, liver and ascites, liver (disease), stroke, intestinal cancer, fever, nerves, heart (disease), plague, protracted illness, heart (disease) and asthma. This sanitized official record leaves out the complex process of social production of compromised health, of which the villagers themselves are all too well aware when they lament their misfortune of being *fallahin*.

Official documentation leaves unaddressed the social conditions under which death came to a number of male villagers whose ages ranged between 10 and 60 as a result of "plague," to four males ages 11, 12, 14, and 17 as a result of "rheumatic fever in the heart," and to two village women, ages 29 and 35, whose death is officially linked to "nerves." As for the repeated documentation of liver (disease), ascites, and spleen (disease) in death certificates, although these deaths remain unconnected officially, the villagers themselves attribute them collectively to bilharzia. Clinically, the more severe consequences of schistosomiasis include cirrhosis, which results from the passage of eggs into the liver's venous system. Subsequently, the spleen enlarges significantly and the combination of liver and spleen dysfunction results in complications of the disease such as anemia, jaundice, and ascites (Isselbached et al. 1980:908).

While some villagers are well aware of the life cycle of the parasite (sketches of which are brought home from school by some pupils), the majority frame their explanation of infection in terms of their own "*fallah* cycle," as one literate peasant once put it to me. Indeed, noteworthy is villagers' sensitivity to what may be regarded as issues of "occupational health." In addition to many villagers repeatedly referring to the polluted water with which they are in constant contact, the unhealthy conditions under which women bake, and increased pesticide use, some villagers note the connection between working in the agricultural cooperative's pesticide store and death from cancer.

After a family member dies from one cause or another, some family members go out to secure the required documents for burial, and others make the necessary arrangements for preparation of the corpse. There are no specialists who perform this religious ritual, but some people are known to be experienced in this procedure and may be asked by the family of the dead person to help. In expressing the deep respect for the dead, a man explained, "I would never refuse such a request. It would be sacrilegious (*haram*), even if the dead person were my biggest enemy."

The procedures for preparing male and female corpses for burial are identical. The only difference is that males are washed by men, while females are washed by women. The preparation of the body for burial is as follows:

> After death the man is given ablution then they wash his right arm with his right side. The same thing is repeated for the left side. Next his anus is washed. Then the whole body is washed. He is then picked up to a sitting position and told, "this is the day of the meeting, servant of God." Then the body is purified with water and sprayed with cologne [if available]. Now he is considered ready to meet the angels in this clean state.

Next, they stuff all the openings of the body, the eyes, ears, everything and clasp his hand on a kerchief. They then wrap him in cloth and dress him in undershirt and an under short. They then cover all his face. If the family of the dead cannot afford to buy these needs, the whole village forms a cooperative. Then he is wrapped in the *kafan*. If he is rich the *kafan* is made of *shahi* [satin-like material] and silk. If he is poor, it is only the white cloth which is the *sunna*. The *kafan* has a belt which is tied by the son; if he has no sons, it is tied by the daughter.

The action of tying *by a son* is a blessing that both men and women request from God throughout their lives. People wishing well to others sometimes say, "May God grant you a son and he would tie your *kafan*." Villagers pity a person whose *kafan* is tied by a daughter. In lamenting the life of a dead person they may say, "Not even a son to tie his *kafan*."

After the ritual preparation of the body, the corpse is placed on the wood (*khashaba*), which is then transferred to the mosque or placed in an open area where prayers are performed. With limited exceptions, women do not join the all-male procession which follows the *khashaba* to the graveyards. If the dead person's family are relatively well off, they set up a tent where the Quran is recited and food is served. In any case, recital of the Quran always takes place at the time of burial.

As in the beginning of life, when divine protection is invoked, its end also involves religious remembrance. As men and women of the village (and beyond, depending on the status of the dead person) come to the household of the deceased to console his/her family, they remind its members that all people are destined by the will of God. They say, "Just as He creates us, He takes us."

With the termination of men's and women's lives in the world of mortals there is a suspension of cultural prescriptions regulating their spatial proximity and differential valuation. Unlike the case of their upper class urban compatriots, the dead men and women of this peasant community are buried in the same graveyard.

Body-Environment Articulation

By analogy to plants, villagers say that too much heat from the sun and too much moisture may cause debility of the human body. Similarly, social experience and emotional trauma are believed to affect the condition of the body. Such beliefs are given linguistic expression in the sayings "[He/she] bursts my gall bladder [causes me frustration]"; "My blood was drained [due to fright]"; "My blood disappeared [on being startled]."

As extensions of the underlying logic of connecting social experience, emotional state, and physical well-being, both social behavior and psychological disposition are described in terms of bodily states. It is said of a wicked person that his "heart is like a rock" or that "his heart is black." A kind person, by contrast, is said to have a white heart. The expressions "his eye cannot be filled" and "his hand is long" are used to refer to a greedy person and to a thief, respectively. Of an insensitive person it is said that "he has no blood." As for one whose habit cannot be changed, reference is made to the essence of his/her character "in the blood."

Idiomatic expressions referring to body parts are used to describe social relations and feelings. A person is said to be "feeling the pulse" of another when trying to sense his/her opinion or intentions. The expressions "inside my heart" and "the hearts are with each other," as well as "I love him like the pupil of my eye," are laudatory statements which villagers exchange regularly. Expressions of hatred such as "a strike in his heart" and "may his body be poisoned" are also used frequently. In addition, intimate relations based on kinship ties are expressed in terms of the body or exchanges between bodies. Of those who are of "one's flesh and blood," it is said that they will always be dear, no matter what differences arise, since "blood can never turn into water." Of their offsprings, mothers say, "The pain that they feel, I feel." The underlying logic of this statement also finds expression among pregnant women. In the effort to beget an infant of certain desirable qualities they "eye" someone who enjoys these very attributes. A number of village women say they used to stare at "the children of the Turks" so that their children would "turn out to be as beautiful."

Just as the body is affected by the natural environment and social interactions, bodily substances are expected to have a reciprocal effect on the natural environment, and on culturally significant social events. Attributes of the body itself either in the form of natural substances (e.g., semen, blood, or sweat) or powers (e.g., the evil eye) are also believed to affect elements of the natural and social environments which surround the human body. Thus, women's state of infertility during menstruation is transmitted to plants in the fields. These, in turn, are expected to wither away and die. Similarly, a menstruating woman coming in contact with bread dough will prevent it from rising.

Since bodily substances, including human excreta, are considered potent in their effects on social relations, they are put to use in the practice of sorcery. Women therefore guard their menstrual blood lest it may harm others or lest others may use it to harm them. The placenta is also believed to be infused with supernatural powers which may be harnessed to harm its owner, and by extension, his/her family. Similarly, semen from a man may be collected by his wife and given to a sorcerer who would ensure the husband's impotence with women other than herself.

The social value of maternity finds expression in the healing power attributed to nursing milk. This milk, a powerful symbol of life, is recommended to barren women to help reverse their state of infertility. Belief in the healing power of this milk is also manifest when a woman squirts a few drops of her breast milk into the infected eyes of a co-villager, who may well be an adult non-kin male. In matters of health the prescribed modesty of women is temporarily suspended in favor of their culturally sanctioned responsibility for protecting and nurturing human life. In the same vein, while women uphold local codes of modesty by covering their arms, legs, and head, public exposure of their breasts during nursing is practiced without the slightest inhibition.

Some bodily substances are recognized as particularly dangerous to elements of the social environment. The idea of ritual pollution (*nagasa* or *zafara*) attaches to social interactions after sexual intercourse, during menstruation, and after childbirth. In the case of sexual intercourse, both males and females are considered polluting; bathing is necessary to rid the couple of this state. In this regard it must be emphasized that the state of pollution of a man after sexual intercourse is not attributed to his contact with his wife as such. A man is also considered polluting if he ejaculates without engaging in sexual intercourse. Also worth noting is the fact that the pollution associated with sexual intercourse is not harmful to the individuals involved. Their state of pollution gains significance only in a social context.

Both men and women must purify themselves before prayer, before fasting, and before engaging in any social activity which their state of pollution may affect. As reported by Granquist (1947:60) for Palestinian Arabs, a woman who is impure from sexual intercourse is believed to prolong the labor of another woman and to delay the birth of her child. When actual accusations occur, the culprit implicated is inevitably an antagonist. Recalling her experience in such a situation, Kamla remarked,

> My labor pains had already started and I had eaten two eggs to increase the contractions [*talg*], I felt the head of the child. But when my mother-in-law came in, the child went in again because she was polluting [*nigisa*]. But as soon as she left the room the child fell out.[8]

Pollution (*nagasa*) associated with menstruation is also considered potentially harmful. Menstrual blood may be used as a poison which brings about gradual death to both men and women when ingested. The effect of menstrual blood on humans is no less damaging than its effect on plants. Intercourse during menstruation or during the postpartum period when a woman is still bleeding is also expected to cause a man blindness and/or severe pains in the back. According to some villagers, a man may also suffer severe pains in the stomach. As reported for other parts of the Arab world and adjacent areas, in Fatiha the harmful effect of menstrual blood is believed to extend to bleeding in the postpartum period, when a woman is also considered polluting (Blackman 1927; Delaney 1988; Fuller 1961; Granquist 1947; Shiloh 1962). As a woman explained,

> After delivery the woman is impure [*nigisa*] because she bleeds. The blood smells bad and it has left overs from delivery. Men here are not like those of urban areas. They have sexual intercourse with their wives during menstruation and some also have intercourse with their wives after childbirth. In both cases he himself gets back pains and his smell is like that of bad blood and it lasts with him for forty days [the same period as the bleeding of women after birth is expected to last]. The smell [*zafara*] of the woman is transferred through his sexual organ [*ʿura*] to the man's body.[9]

Bleeding, like ejaculation during sexual intercourse or during males' "dreaming," is regarded as a natural attribute of the human body. As Faithorn (1975) has remarked for the Kafe of Highland New Guinea, the body's substances are regarded by the people of Fatiha as symbolic of life-producing forces, the misuse of which is deemed harmful. Bodily substances are seen as the charge of those from whose body they derive. Therefore men and women alike are held responsible for protecting society from the harmful effects of their misplacement.

In addition to recognizing the significance of the body as a medium for the reproduction of gender ideology, we should not lose sight of the mediation of related medical ideology in social discourse, and the health promotion function of certain cultural elaborations of the body. Postpartum confinement is noteworthy in this regard (see also Ammar 1961; Browner and Sargent 1990). Recommendations of women's confinement for a period of forty days after birth express an ideal which is seldom realized among the poor peasants of Fatiha. In fact, even at the level of belief, differences are correlated with the status of the family to which a given woman belongs. This is evident in the results of structured interviews conducted with female adults of the census households. As shown in Table 3.3, the extent to which they recommend menstrual and postpartum isolation, rated on a scale of 1–3, is commensurate with the socioeconomic status (SES) of their household (HH). On the isolation scale, 1 indicates the highest degree of isolation, involving abstention from sexual intercourse, baking, and getting in contact with plants; isolation degree 2 indicates avoidance of sexual intercourse and plants; isolation degree 3 expresses belief in avoidance of sexual intercourse only. As for SES, a rating of 1 indicates the highest landholding, SES 6 indicates the lowest, including "landless" households.

TABLE 3.3   Percentage Frequency Distribution of
Recommended Isolation

HH SES	N	Isolation	% Frequency Distribution
1	16	1	56.2
		2	18.7
		3	25.0
2	11	1	36.6
		2	27.2
		3	36.6
3	85	1	7.0
		2	51.7
		3	41.2
4	20	1	5.0
		2	30.0
		3	65.0
5	38	1	0
		2	10.5
		3	89.5
6	16	1	0
		2	0
		3	100.0

From cultural ideal to social practice, the concern with confining bleeding women transcends the concern with protecting others (including women who have just given birth and who are considered particularly susceptible to harm) from these women's *nagasa*. Indeed, in relation to birth, the practice is revealed to be primarily a way of protecting the woman herself and her newborn baby, both of whom are considered particularly susceptible to the evil eye. As one woman put it, "People love children and they give the evil eye to the woman who has them, and to her child."

When realized, confinement of women after birth is also practiced as a preventive measure intended to protect them from the potential of sterility as they come in contact with others who have just given birth and who are themselves bleeding. Ideally, a new mother is entitled to rest and good food, as well as protection from drafts and chills. After giving birth she is cautioned by her mother, relatives, and neighbors to keep away from the cold and moisture, to which her "tender" body is considered particularly sensitive.

In practice, it is only the women of the households of the big families who can abandon, and only temporarily, the multifaceted responsibilities of production and social reproduction. More generally, mothers-in-law who advise their own daughters to take the necessary precautions after birth are not likely to demonstrate the same enthusiasm for preventive care with regard to their daughters-in-law who have recently given birth, especially if the infant is a female.

Presenting a contrast to her affine's faking (*dalaᶜ*), the older woman might refer to the case of a relative, neighbor, or acquaintance who kept on working in the field after stopping long enough to deliver her infant by herself, cut the umbilical cord, and at the end of the day put her new-born in a basket which she carried home on her head as she pulled the water buffalo behind her. While the junior woman is likely to cry over her mother-in-law's "lack of mercy in [the] heart," the older woman herself may lament her misfortune in having such a "lazy" son's wife.

Whereas the implementation of the ideal of postpartum isolation does not alter the local organizational power structure as it pertains to the household, it does provide a culturally sanctioned dispensation from the multitude of responsibilities with which peasant women are burdened as they contribute to the reproduction of their community and to national development.

For women themselves, the practice of the ideal of postpartum isolation is most welcome. For those to whom its implementation is denied, it remains a much-coveted correlate of the privatization of women's labor, a significant status symbol to which members of the community as a whole aspire. Whether in relation to menstruation, birth, or age, the confinement of women's labor to household-based reproductive activities prevails in families whose members accumulate sufficient surplus to make female labor dispensable. In this case material surplus derived from familial labor is converted into the culturally meaningful power base of family honor.

Notes

1. As ethnomedical studies have documented for other parts of the Middle East, many of villagers' body concepts (including those which attest to natural differences between males and females), as well as their beliefs about illness causation and therapeutic practices, are traceable to earlier regional medical traditions (Ahmed 1989; M.J. Good 1980; Good and Good n.d.; Rahman 1987). The villagers themselves are not knowledgeable of specific linkages between their understanding of the human body and antecedent medical traditions. They only point out that many of their medical beliefs and practices have been passed "to father from grandfather."

2. For a detailed account of beliefs surrounding conception and pregnancy, as well as documentation of observed cases of birth, see Morsy 1981b.

3. The perseverance of women in this regard is illustrated by a "crime" reported in a national newspaper during the time of my residency in Fatiha. A barren woman living near a town close to the village, in her desperate attempt to reverse her state of sterility, opened up the tomb of a recently deceased little girl, washed the lifeless infant's body, then used the bath water to wash her own body (Al-Ahram Dec. 9, 1974).

4. Menstrual blood is generally believed to originate in the back of the woman. The Arabic word for menstruation used in Fatiha literally means "my back" (*dahri*).

5. In this regard a midwife disapprovingly recalls a time when "[women] thought that they could interfere with God's will by smearing themselves from the inside (i.e. in their vaginas) with lemon juice so that they would become pregnant with a son."

6. This practice, once considered a distinctive indicator of peasant status, is generally on the decline in the village. However it is still valued by some older villagers who also recommend it to younger members of their households.

7. For an account of the use of *kuhl* and its composition (including the active ingredient to which its therapeutic properties are attributed) see Inhorn Millar and Lane 1988.

8. When I asked women if a male who is polluting from sexual intercourse would have the same effect, they replied, "what would bring a man to a place where a woman is delivering?" When pressed to answer the question on the assumption of a hypothetical situation where a man's presence was actualized, they responded, "pollution is pollution."

9. Women themselves complain of back pains and pressure around the eyes during menstruation. Menstruation is also believed to affect the emotional state of women adversely.

4

MEDICAL TAXONOMY[1]:
THE CENTRALITY OF EMOTIONS
AND SOCIAL CAUSATION

Villagers report a variety of illness conditions, examples of which are presented in the census data of Table 4.1. Retrospective evaluation of this data discloses the underreporting of certain forms of compromised health in the earlier period of fieldwork. For example, in spite of the fact that eye disease represents a serious health problem, only two cases of eye irritation were reported. It is also significant to note the underreporting of illnesses such as *tarba* (fright), *ᶜuzr* (spirit possession), *hassad* (evil eye) , and *ᶜamal bil marad* [sickness of sorcery]. In time it became clear that eye inflammations are so common that respondents did not consider them worthy of the label "illness." As for the remaining underreporting, this probably expresses villagers' reluctance to disclose the "nonsense of the *fallahin*."

Even the earliest days of fieldwork disclosed villagers' tendency to define the ultimate cause of health and illness in terms of social relations and emotions. Even some of the natural causes of illness documented in the census survey (see Table 4.2) are linked to the "lifestyle of the peasants" (*ᶜishit il fallahin*) by the villagers themselves. This is not to say that biomedically defined compromised abilities are excluded from serious consideration as indicators of ill-health. As suggested by Table 4.1, villagers do recognize (and attend to) such forms of impaired health, as well as accidents and a variety of ailments (e.g., wounds, fractures, insect bites, tooth-aches, and strained muscles from overwork). Reference is also made to physical symptoms which are gross and diffuse, including such complaints as headaches, weakness, dizziness, aches all over, trembling, hot-cold spells, chills, nausea, weight loss, pains in joints, and swelling.

Diagnostic Indices

When someone falls ill in Fatiha, diagnosis focuses on causation rather than underlying pathology. Most generally, illness causation is considered

99

TABLE 4.1   Illness Reporting in Census Survey

Illness	*Number of Reported Cases*
Rheumatism	4
Heartburn	1
Allergy	3
Headache	14
Tonsillitis	5
Weakness	20
Back pain	6
Fever	31
Stomachache	6
Cold	4
Asthma	2
Diabetes	1
Kidney	3
Bilharzia	2
Malaria	2
Paralysis	1
Pain in joints	7
Pain in reproductive organs	1
Heart	7
Dizziness	1
Chest pains	8
Shortness of breath	2
Spleen	2
Nausea	1
Menstrual cramps	2
Dysentery	1
Eye irritation	1
Appendicitis	1
Liver	1
Psychological shock	1
ᶜuzr	10
Tarba	1

in light of villagers' conviction that all misfortune is under supernatural regulation. Further probing exposes a repertoire of illness causes, notably emotional distress. More fundamentally, whether manifest in physical discomfort, altered disposition, or deviation from cultural role expectation, diagnosis of illness ultimately implicates social relations. This is the case even for illnesses of named body organs such as "heart disease" (*marad il galb*) and "stone in the kidney" (*haswa fil kila*). Well beyond focusing on the anatomical structure specified by these labels,

TABLE 4.2 Census Survey of Illness Causation

Cause	Number of Reported Cases
God's will	22
Hassad (evil eye)	5
ᶜamal (sorcery)	1
Smoking	2
Sexual intercourse	2
Overwork	8
Living creatures	4
Sadness	12
Fright	3
Blow	2
Contraceptives	2
Poverty	1
Natural environment	36
Smoke inhalation	1
Old age	5
Chemicals	3
Fever	4
Pregnancy	5

villagers seek precipitating factors such as emotional distress and interpersonal conflict. These may even cause death, as in the case of a husband who "died from sadness which caused swelling in his stomach." His demise is described as the outcome of his wife's infidelity.

Structured interviews focused on locally significant named illness states underscore the importance of emotional distress. Fifty-five adult males and females were asked to link specific causes to the four illnesses of *tarba* (fright), *hassad* (evil eye), *ᶜuzr* (spirit possession), and *ᶜamal bil marad* (the illness of sorcery). The results, documented in Table 4.3, show that physical causation was selected less frequently. Scrutiny of the percentages recorded in this table reveals that they do not add up to

TABLE 4.3 Somatic Versus Psychosocial Causes of Illness (percent of respondents; N = 55)

Illness	Somatic Causes	Psychosocial Causes
Tarba	25.0	96.4
Hassad	0	98.2
ᶜuzr	3.6	94.6
ᶜamal	0	92.7

100%. This results from the multiple, and multi-level, causes assigned to a given compromised state of health (Glick 1963).[2] As for the limited and minor implication of somatic causes for *tarba* and *ᶜuzr*, respectively, this relates to belief in the natural predisposition to fright among women, whose "nerves" (*aᶜssab*) are considered weaker than men's.

The cultural construction of congenital infirmities represents a departure from the general tendency to de-emphasize physical constitution and physical processes in favor of social causation. For infirmity which is designated hereditary (*wiratha*), or "inborn" (*khilga*), physical constitution is accorded primary consideration in the explanation of compromised health. Inborn physical defects ("from God") are implicated in cases of idiocy (*habal*) and insanity (*jinan*). It is believed that "the person's brain may be small from birth and as [he/she] grows up it does not grow proportionally to the rest of [his/her] body."

While some villagers argue that congenital defects are not to be equated with illness, others add that the infant never becomes ill when in the mother's womb, or when nursing. Still others suggest that "inheritance" (*wiratha*) is responsible for *sukar* (sugar illness or diabetes), *azma* (asthma), *uraᶜ* (hair loss), and *shalal* (paralysis).

As for congenital mental deficiency, this is generally believed to be inherited from the father during conception. Consequently, although mentally deficient persons in Fatiha (as in other Egyptian villages, see El Sendiouny 1972:23–26) are treated kindly by fellow villagers and may even be considered in possession of *baraka* (supernatural blessing power), they are nevertheless a source of shame to their families.

Aside from the prominence of what Fabrega has described as the "region of the person" (Fabrega 1976) in relation to inherited infirmity, the centrality of psychosocial causation in diagnosis generally prevails. It is causation with its multiple levels (Glick 1967), rather than precise physiological processes or anatomical changes underlying illness symptomatology, which is the foundation of medical taxonomy (cf. Glick 1963).

For analytical purposes illness causes may be differentiated into two broad etiological categories of natural and supernatural. This differentiation conveys some healers' distinction between physical illness (*marad gussmani*) and spiritual illness (*marad rawhani*), a distinction indicative of their respective specializations. Yet, for either category, diagnosis ultimately implicates one or both of the core elements of emotions and social relations.

Natural Causes

Illness is attributed to such causes as bad food, bad water, worms, insect bites, sunstroke, and humidity. Unsanitary living conditions associated with dirty water and flies are implicated in cases of bilharzia and eye infections, respectively. Villagers also attribute the former to their condition as peasants whose livelihood depends on the continued contact with the earth and water.

Mosquito bites are linked to malaria, which is believed to cause miscarriages, and even death, if not treated by a physician. Fever is attributed to both sunstroke and moisture (*rutuba*) in the air. Extended exposure to moisture is said to induce hot-cold spells, which cause weakness, increased susceptibility to additional illness, and reduction of appetite for food. Additional outcomes include *duzentaria* (dysentery) and *rumatizm* (rheumatism).[3]

Other naturalistic causes offered as explanations of illness include excessive indulgence related to food, work, and sex. Such excesses are said to exhaust the body and cause discomforts and weakness. Overeating is believed to cause "crowding" (*ziham*) and thus brings about the discomforts of indigestion. Overindulgence in sexual activity by a man, particularly with a woman other than his wife, is also given as a cause of illness. A man is said to become very sick as a result of such encounters because he ejaculates in fear and guilt and, as a result, without much sexual pleasure.

The idea of contagion is also reflected in villagers' beliefs of natural causes of illness. It is stated that

> fever is contagious [*mu'diya*]. . . . The heat from one body transfers to the body of the other who sits near him. . . . Influenza is contagious, it has bad air which goes to other people through inhaling. . . . The illness of the chest [TB] is contagious and the doctor must treat the people who have *marad il sadr* [the illness of the chest] immediately or else they make all those around them sick. . . . Dirt can also cause illness and if I drink after a person who is sick . . .

In addition to specifying *direct* natural causes of illness, villagers identify the natural environment as an *indirect* cause of illness. Thus, the darkness which falls upon the village at night, the roaring winds and swaying tree branches, or the dark low clouds are believed to cause severe frights which induce the illness of *tarba* (fright).[4] The various dimensions of this illness, including cause, symptoms, severity, age relatedness, and sex relatedness, are recorded in Table 4.4, which also indicates the degree of consensus (presented in percentage) among a sample of 55 respondents who were instructed to associate this illness with various illness dimensions.[5]

In turn, *tarba* resulting from contact with the perilous natural environment may predispose a person to the more severe illness of *'uzr*

TABLE 4.4   Illness Dimensions Associations: *Tarba, Hassad, ᶜAmal*

Illness Dimensions	% Positive Association Tarba	% Positive Association Hassad	% Positive Association ᶜAmal
Cause			
Instrumental			
1. Nat. envir. & subs.	16	0	2
2. Phys. constitution	25	0	0
3. Spirit intrusion (*malbus*)	0	2	0
4. Hassad (gaze)	0	98	0
5. *ᶜAmal* (sorcery)	0	0	96
Efficient			
1. God	20	7	4
2. *Hassid* (witch)	2	96	0
3. *Assyad* (spirits)	0	2	2
4. *Sahir* (sorcerer)	0	0	93
Ultimate			
1. Sadness	2	0	0
2. Anger	4	11	47
3. Jealousy	0	100	91
4. Hatred	2	96	95
5. Punishment by God	4	0	0
6. Fear	96	0	0
Symptoms			
Behavioral			
1. Sleeps more	9	18	49
2. Insomnia	93	85	82
3. Eats less	76	80	91
4. Loss of consciousness	9	7	42
5. *Tayih* (in a daze)	42	29	80
6. Cannot bear self	80	80	93
7. Makes no sense talking	15	13	45
8. Disrespect to superiors	5	5	44
9. Does not socialize	27	15	44
10. Depressed and unhappy	84	65	45
11. Cries	38	38	73
12. Cannot run after bread	15	11	84
13. Cannot discipline children	2	2	58
14. Cannot unite with wife	9	7	93
15. Cannot pray	2	4	38

(continues)

TABLE 4.4 (continued)

Illness Dimensions	*% Positive Association* Tarba	*% Positive Association* Hassad	*% Positive Association* ᶜAmal
16. Cannot fulfill maternal responsibilities	0	4	60
17. Cannot fulfill duty as wife	2	2	76
18. Cannot do housework	5	7	75
19. Yawns often	9	96	33
20. Does not speak much	36	35	45
Physical			
1. Weakness	95	98	95
2. Headache	91	100	95
3. Aches all over	87	96	95
4. Trembles	64	49	60
5. Hot-cold spells	18	22	35
6. Cough	9	7	4
7. Chills	13	16	9
8. Nausea	5	16	22
9. Weight loss	42	31	78
10. Vomiting	13	2	35
11. Swelling	5	9	29
12. Loss of balance	40	38	73
13. Difficulty in breathing	31	44	55
14. Lump in throat	13	18	35
15. Diarrhea	27	29	24
16. Fever	13	40	29
17. Pain in joints	53	55	67
18. Earache	11	20	36
19. Watery eyes	20	42	44
20. Rash	4	7	7
21. Back pain	45	40	65
22. Dizziness	75	18	87
23. Chest pains	15	18	23
24. Stomachache	16	18	38
25. Excess blood in body	2	4	18
26. Excess water in body	2	2	0
27. Drying of blood in body parts	76	60	55
Severity			
1. Minor illness	80	60	13
2. Significant illness	33	47	9

(continues)

TABLE 4.4   (continued)

Illness Dimensions	% Positive Association Tarba	% Positive Association Hassad	% Positive Association ᶜAmal
3. Heavy illness	36	69	91
4. Fatal	0	73	82
Age Relatedness			
1. Children only	0	4	0
2. Children mostly	61	91	2
3. Adults only	0	2	2
4. Adults mostly	61	36	89
5. Older people only	0	0	0
6. Older people mostly	16	11	7
Sex relatedness			
1. Females only	2	0	0
2. Females mostly	40	4	25
3. Males only	0	2	2
4. Males mostly	15	29	13
5. Both males and females	40	64	53

(described below). In this regard villagers also believe that the turbulent waters of the Nile and the dark desolate fields harbor supernatural creatures. Through a touch (*lamsa*) these may gain access to the human body and precipitate ill-health. Illnesses thus inflicted are considered the consequences of stressful emotional experiences and/or conflict-ridden social relations, including experiences associated with powerlessness. Under these conditions emotional distress *predisposes* the individual to attacks by supernatural beings whose presence in the natural environment is believed to be pervasive.

Supernatural Causes

Ideas about illness, its cause, prevention, and cure, are closely tied to beliefs regarding the supernatural and religious rituals. Most generally, explanation of illness in terms of supernatural causation entails reference to "His Will." As He is the source of life, He also determines its crises and its termination point. It is said that no one lives beyond the time that is "written" (*maktub*) for him/her.

Villagers, including the local healer/"carrier of the Quran," believe in the *jinn*. These supernatural subterranean beings are referred to by various names, including ᶜ*afarit* (ghosts), *assyad* (masters), *awlad il ard* (children of the ground), *karin/karina* (male/female relative), *ikwatna* (our siblings), and *ahl il ard* (people of the ground). Under the command of sorcerers such creatures are considered instrumental in precipitating harm, including illness. Under the appropriate command they are also effectual in bringing about cure.

A local literate diagnostician who has studied the Quran describes the community of subterranean supernatural beings as follows:

> Just as there is the life of the *inss* [adamites], there is also the world of the *jinn.* This is stated in the Quran and the *Hadith.* Our *kara'in* [relatives] are not all Muslim. Some are Christian. Some heard the word of God and became Muslims and some did not. . . . They live everywhere. They do everything we do. They have sexual intercourse, they eat, sleep, but they live longer. They can also do superhuman acts. They can cause illness or cure it. . . . *ʿUzr* [spirit possession] is spontaneous . . . but *sihr* [sorcery] is by use of *jinn* in causing illness, this is of course different. In *sihr*, the *jinn* is prepared [i.e. summoned] by a *sahir* [sorcerer]. There are good *sahara* [sorcerers] who for example remedy situations between lovers and if someone is ill he is cured. This *sahir* [sorcerer] is called *ʿilwi* [from above]. This means that he uses *khudam* [supernatural servants—jinn] from above. These are angels. He is a good person who prays. He reads the oath which says "in the name of God the compassionate and the merciful, may prayer and peace descend on the most honorable of messengers [The Prophet], our master Muhammad. I swear on you oh Simamil [the name of the *jinn*] to be present this hour and to do for me such and such by the right of what is written on the forehead of *ʿazrail* [the jinn of death]. I beg your speed this hour. God's blessing in you and on you." *Il jinn il sufli* [lower jinn] is used [commanded] for evil deeds, including the causing of illness, e.g., blindness and hemorrhage, and discord, like divorce.

According to this healer, whereas good jinns are all males, among the *sufli* (lower) jinn, some are males and some are females.[6]

Another healer also refers to the supernatural relatives (*karin/karina*) in the explanation of illness:

> I was called by *halag il siha* to see his two year old son. He had been very ill, he would not eat. They had been with him to the doctor several times. When I saw him, I threw the rosary and found that he had fallen. I asked them why they did not come to me sooner. I found that there is no use because he had been hit by his *karina* [supernatural relative] because she was taking revenge on his mother through him. I knew that he was going to die but I did not tell them.

Such punitive actions by the supernatural *karin/karina* are explained as emanating from the subterranean beings' concern for the welfare of their earthly relatives. The *karin/karina* act promptly to remedy imbalances or distorted priorities in people's lives, as when they neglect their children, overexert themselves in work, or become sad to the detriment of their health.

Initially the *karin/karina* may give warning signals, such as illness. If these are left unheeded, they act more ferociously and may even cause the death of unheeding mothers' beloved children. This action is illustrated by the experience of a woman who recalled the death of her child. She said, "My son died when I left him in the room by himself; his sister bit him." When I pointed out that she had just told me that she has no daughters, she said,

> It's his sister from the ground who killed him. . . . [She] bit him because I did not spread any salt [to appease the supernatural beings]. A woman should not leave her infant alone[7] when he is a week old and she should spread the salt in the house.

As she related this account, the woman lamented her bad luck of living with her husband's family. She complained of their constant demands "in house and field," which forced her to leave her child unattended. The family's "stinginess" was also noted as preventing her from spreading the protective salt.

While villagers generally interpret the punitive action of *awlad il ard* to be in the best interest of the affected person or significant others in his/her family, some, including healers, remark that not all subterranean beings are so motivated. They also describe a more elaborate classification among "the inhabitants of the ground" (*sukan il ard*) and associate the action of inflicting illness among differentiated groups with specific triggering behavior on the part of human beings:

> When a woman is pregnant and she is upset with her husband, and doesn't eat [thereby depriving the foetus of nourishment], the *karina* of *ahl il ard* strikes the foetus. The *karina* is from beneath the earth, she comes in the shape of a farm animal and hits the woman and forces the foetus down.[8] *Assyad* [masters] come under fright or sadness or sorcery, but the *karina* [sister] only comes to a woman when she is upset with her husband or his mother, when the sadness is minor.

Core Diagnostic Elements: Emotions and Social Causation

Although both the natural and social environments are implicated in illness causation, the social dimension of the environment is generally accorded greater significance. Thus, the villagers may attribute an illness to a sunstroke, chills, bad food, or worms, in typical holistic posture, but they also refer to the social identity of the peasants, which forces them to be exposed to natural elements with little protection to their bodies, either externally (by proper clothing) or internally (through proper feeding). Similarly, while a woman's poor health during pregnancy is attributed to her poor nutrition, people are often quick to note the social essence of this condition by pointing to her husband's poverty, her mother-in-law's stinginess, or her condition as a *fallaha* (peasant woman). Similarly, illnesses attributed to supernatural beings and powers (e.g., spirit intrusion, sorcery, and the Evil Eye) have ultimate social causes.

Illness explanations in terms of the social dimension of the worldly environment involve retrospective diagnosis. This is the case for three important forms of illness: *ᶜuzr,* literally "excuse" (caused by *nazra ardiya*—supernatural gaze from the ground),[9] *hassad,* or the Evil Eye (caused by *nazra insaniya*—a covetous human gaze) and *tarba* (caused by a frightening experience). As shown in Table 4.4, all these illnesses are associated with emotional etiologies. The first is precipitated by distress, the second involves feelings of jealousy and envy towards others, and the third illness is caused by fright.[10]

Elaborating the idea "a healthy mind [exists] in a healthy body," people identify emotional experiences as causes of different types of afflictions ranging from the falling out of hair to heart trouble and diabetes, to impotency in men and barrenness in women. Such afflictions may be attributed to fright, precipitating the illness *tarba,* and predisposing a person to other more serious illness.

Emotionally distressful experiences are said to "shake the body," thereby reducing the person's defense against illness or precipitating certain specific types of illnesses which result from the "boiling of blood." Distress is implicated in the illness of *haswa fil kila* (stone in the kidney). Sadness and rage cause *fawran dam* (boiling over of the blood), and as the blood settles it causes "sand" (sedimentation) to settle in the kidney and gradually a stone is formed. *Brostata* (illness of the prostate gland) is also believed to be caused by excitement resulting from frequent sexual intercourse.

Emotional restraint is also linked to illness. As one woman noted, "If a person tells others of what is bothering him, he gets relief." In any case the severity of illness precipitated by emotional distress is mediated by the (*tab*ᶜ) of the affected person.

Since women are believed to have half the nerves (*aᶜsab*) of men, an identical emotional blow is expected to have a more deleterious effect on a woman than on a man. Similarly, children are particularly susceptible to emotional distress. These beliefs are reflected in Table 4.4, where 15% of respondents associated the illness of *tarba* with the category "males mostly," while 40% and 61% linked the affliction to "females mostly" and "children mostly," respectively.

Hassad

The significance of feelings of jealousy and envy are elaborated in the illness of *hassad* (the evil eye).[11] Table 4.4 summarizes various dimensions of this illness state.

Belief in *hassad*, which predates Islam, is legitimized by reference to Quranic descriptions of the malevolent power of the *hassid* (possessor of the evil eye). The power of a gaze is a great source of danger to humans, animals, plants, and even inanimate objects. The "eye" (*ᶜayn*) is by far the most common reason advanced to explain almost any type of misfortune, including illness and even death. The malevolent power of a covetous gaze brings about sure destruction to the object of that gaze, be it a human body, another living creature, or an inanimate object. In fact, villagers emphasize the danger of the eye by reference to Islamic narrations which describe the destruction of rock by an envious glance.

As indicated in Table 4.4, manifestations of *hassad*, whether behavioral or physical, are generalized indicators of ill-health. These are not unique to *hassad* (compare symptoms of *hassad* in Table 4.4 to those of *tarba*, for example). In fact, with the exception of yawning, which is associated with the illness by the majority of villagers, symptoms of *hassad* overlap with indicators of other afflictions. Neither is the severity of the illness a principal diagnostic indicator. "The eye" may cause illness ranging in severity from slight to fatal. In short, cause (defined in terms of interpersonal relations) is the single most important factor in the diagnosis of *hassad*. As shown in Table 4.4, this is evident when one compares the degree of consensus among villagers linking the cause, *nazra* (covetous gaze), to the illness *hassad* (96%) with those linking this etiological element to other illnesses (2% for *tarba* and 0% for *ᶜamal bil marad*).[12]

Those who possess the evil eye are described in terms of their insatiable desire to possess whatever others have. Moreover, they make no attempt to hide their envy of others' good fortune. This is indicated by their constant self-pitying sighs and their lingering, longing gazes at desirable objects. While relatively powerless people who do not control culturally valued resources may be accused of *hassad*, it is generally agreed that anyone can have the evil eye: "Some men are known for their evil eye, some women are this way too." As for those who trigger *hassad*, they are likely to possess culturally valued attributes ranging from beauty to *asl*. This is the case for children, especially males:

The youngest one that I lost was only ten days old. . . . Of course he was given the eye. He was a boy after two girls. The next child that I lost was almost three years old. . . . [W]hen [a woman] saw him she said, "How beautiful, how can the son of black people have such beautiful hair?" And that was that. He died less than a week later. He fell sick. I followed the advice of older people and gave him rice water instead of my milk. But he had diarrhea and he remained this way and then died.

Educated children are considered particularly vulnerable. As a mother explained,

People never leave us alone, they always say, "Look, they have their children in school and they also have land." There is no month that passes without one of us being sick.

As with other illnesses, explanations of *hassad* reveal distinguishable levels of causation. The ultimate cause, envy, lies in the social sphere of interpersonal relations; the efficient cause is the person who possesses the power of envy not as an individual but as a social entity in a particular relationship to the affected person or his/her family. As for the instrumental cause, this takes the form of a longing gaze, operative not mechanically but as an extension of a social person in a particular social context.

Accusations of the evil eye are significant not only in revealing the underlying logic of medical taxonomy but for identifying one or another culturally valued power base, be this male status, possession of land, or education. The significance of male status and related differential valuation of males and females is reflected in Table 4.4. This is indicated by the greater consensus among respondents that males are the more likely objects of envy (29% of respondents) than females (4% of respondents). Whereas Table 4.4 suggests that older people are not generally considered the object of *hassad*, some villagers point out that older persons may be affected because they are usually richer and have many children.

ᶜAmal bil Marad

Supernatural causation of illness by subterranean beings may be differentiated into two broad categories: direct and indirect. Direct causation involves these supernatural creatures as efficient causes of illness. This is illustrated in cases of spirit possession (ᶜ*uzr*). Disturbing emotional experiences, including those associated with relative powerlessness, are identified by villagers as the ultimate cause of this affliction. As for indirect action on the part of subterranean creatures, this is manifest when they are controlled and manipulated by other efficient causes of illness, namely sorcerers. The resulting illness is known as "deed for illness" (*ᶜamal bil marad*). Several dimensions of this illness category and respondents' degree of consensus about linking each of these dimensions to the illness are summarized in Table 4.4.

The efficient causes of *ᶜamal bil marad* are humans who, through their religious knowledge, control the actions of supernatural beings and direct them to execute specified commands, including the infliction of illness.[13] In the village itself, sorcery is practiced only by men. More generally, the sorcerers who are located elsewhere in the governorate (and frequented by villagers) are also most likely to be males who have knowledge of the Quran. Their status as males, who are more likely to be literate than females, predisposes them to control yet another form of power, that which derives from religious knowledge.

While some females may be literate in Quranic knowledge, this is a necessary but not sufficient condition to practice sorcery. Proper manipulation and ultimate command over supernatural beings requires knowledge of specific command passages. As in the case of another culturally valued power base, land, knowledge of sorcery is more likely to be passed on to a son than to a daughter. To the extent that females have limited or no knowledge of the Quran, and to the extent that male sorcerers are more likely to be the beneficiaries of their elders' secret knowledge, women's renown as sorcerers is limited. Exceptions do exist: Some villagers of Fatiha are known to take their complaints to a female sorcerer in a nearby village. This woman has memorized the Quran. She has also been on a pilgrimage to Mecca more than once.

The instrumental cause of *ᶜamal bil marad* is the supernatural power of the *khudam* (supernatural servant) commmanded by the sorcerer. This manifests as physical discomfort, as well as altered social behavior and psychological disposition. Sorcery is said to be effective through a variety of supernatural acts known only to sorcerers themselves. As a woman described her own experience,

> *Sihr* can be made on an egg on which [Quranic passages] are read. . . . [Then] . . . a hole is pierced in the egg. It keeps dripping and the person keeps bleeding and bleeding, sometimes even to death. It was made for me; I think it was my neighbor. Once I kept bleeding for two months, and once for a month. The doctor said I had a miscarriage, but I know I was not pregnant. I know it was a *ᶜamal* and after this my period never came again.

The sorcerer's deed, for which he or she receives monetary compensation, may also be performed on the intended victim's *atar*. This may be anything which came in touch with the targeted body or derived from it.

Atar may take the form of an article of clothing, hair, a fingernail, or a rag used to wipe a person's sweat, blood, semen, or excreta. Any of these items is acquired by the sorcerer through the person(s) on whose behalf harm, including illness, is to be inflicted on a specified adversary. The sorcerer's "reading" is focused on the *atar*, thereby summoning the *khadim*, who receives the command and acts accordingly.

Sorcery accusations reflect strained social relations, and *ᶜamal bil marad* is considered a form of revenge. Mariam recounted how the people who had originally wanted to marry their daughter to her cousin's bridegroom "tied" the groom (i.e., rendered him sexually impotent through sorcery) on his wedding night. He was "untied" (*infak*) after three whole days of constant Quranic readings. Mariam also spoke of the case of a man who was known to engage in extra-marital sexual activities. His wife had him "tied" for other women, but not for herself. Recognizing the social control consequences of sorcery and its impact on the man's disposition, Mariam added that the husband stopped frequenting other women when he heard what his wife had done to him, "for fear that he would be embarrassed in front of [his lovers]."

Another case where sorcery is implicated in male impotency is that of a husband who had been taken from his wife by another woman whom he later married. The new wife described his sexual impotence as follows:

Fifteen days ago he was tied, then Sheikh Muhammed released him. But now Said is tied [*marbut*] again. He says that his first wife wrote for him. He knows this from seeing his *atar* with Sheikh Muhammed. The Sheikh wrote Quranic words in two ceramic plates and made Said drink water from these plates. After drinking from the second plate, he said he felt numbness coming down through his body and it went out from his toe. He was cured. Then he was tied again, he would get an erection but as soon as he approached me, he would lose his erection. . . . [two weeks later] . . . He told Sheikh Muhammed about his condition. Sheikh Muhammed attributed it to excessive consumption of *hashish* and advised him to abstain from *hashish* and his wife for two days. He did as he was advised and when Fawzeya came to see me today in the morning, she found me bathing [i.e., after engaging in sexual intercourse].

The results of sorcerers' magic may be nothing less than total breakdown for the intended victim:

First Nawal was married to Mahmud Mubarak's brother and then fell in love with a man called Sheikh Ismaᶜil Zaki who wrote for her [performed sorcery] to be divorced from her husband. After this, she went to him and told him to marry her. He married her and her first husband started to write for her. . . . She became crazy and they sent her to the palace in Hilwan [a mental hospital outside of Cairo].

Still another case of sorcery is that of Rasya, the daughter of Murad Khalil, who opposed her father's marriage to his cousin:

> Murad Khalil's cousin wanted to marry him. But Rasya objected since her [sick] mother was still living. The father's bride wrote for Rasya and she became ill. She lost all her hair, she had very severe knee pains and eventually she could not walk. She remained this way for four months until they found a Sheikh in a nearby village who could untie the deed [*ᶜamal*].

Finally, Fahima's experience of *ᶜamal bil marad* illustrates the grave physical debility which results from sorcery:

> She used to be fat and beautiful. Now she is skinny and ugly. She looks like a shadow. She is pale and weak. She drank *sihr* [magic] . . . probably from her husband's relatives. She had a big fight with them. . . . They tricked her and made her drink the *sihr*.

ᶜUzr

This local variant of spirit illness is attributed to supernatural etiology. But, as in the case of other illnesses, this only defines one level of causation. In addition to having a social ultimate cause, *ᶜuzr* is known to be induced by a variety of negative emotional experiences, including those associated with subordination, sadness, fright, quarrels, and anger. As shown in Table 4.5, the affliction is associated with non-specific physical symptoms and impaired social behavior. The latter is described in terms of interpersonal relations and deviations from culturally designated role behavior. The patterned opposition between the sexes is reflected in the fact that females become possessed by male spirits, while males are "touched" by female spirits.

As noted for children, the *assyad's* action is interpreted as concern for the well-being of earthly adults. This was evident when a *sayid* "arrived" to Um Fahmy in my presence. She stopped talking suddenly and said, "I feel heavy, I feel he is coming now." Her voice changed and sounded masculine. The new voice said:

> I have been coming to Um Fahmy for fifteen years because she was screaming. . . . We make her ill so that she can tell them that she cannot go to the doctor. . . . When she is not happy we make her whole body blue and when she regains her consciousness we make our demands which are for her. We ask for perfume. When she is unhappy we become unhappy too and so we punish her by making her ill . . . because we love her.

TABLE 4.5   The Illness of *ᶜUzr* : Illness Dimensions Associations

Illness Dimension	% Positive Association
Cause	
Instrumental	
1. Nat. envir. & subs.	2
2. Phys. constitution	4
3. Spirit intrusion (*malbus*)	95
4. hassad (gaze)	20
5. *ᶜamal* (sorcery)	0
Efficient	
1. God	20
2. *Hassid* (witch)	20
3. *Assyad* (spirits)	87
4. *Sahir* (sorcerer)	5
Ultimate	
1. Sadness	87
2. Anger	89
3. Jealousy	7
4. Hatred	9
5. Punishment by God	2
6. Fear	82
Symptoms	
Behavioral	
1. Sleeps more	56
2. Insomnia	73
3. Eats less	84
4. Loss of consciousness	85
5. *Tayih* (in a daze)	85
6. Cannot bear self	85
7. Makes no sense talking	82
8. Disrespect to superiors	71
9. Does not socialize	80
10. Depressed & unhappy	89
11. Cries	91
12. Cannot run after bread	89
13. Cannot discipline children	69
14. Cannot unite with wife	80
15. Cannot pray	71
16. Cannot fulfill maternal responsibility	75
17. Cannot fulfill duty as wife	76
18. Cannot do housework	93

(continues)

TABLE 4.5   (continued)

Illness Dimension	% Positive Association
19. Yawns often	45
20. Does not speak much	45
Physical	
1. Weakness	93
2. Headache	95
3. Aches all over	95
4. Trembles	62
5. Hot-cold spells	20
6. Cough	20
7. Chills	24
8. Nausea	36
9. Weight loss	69
10. Vomiting	27
11. Swelling	31
12. Loss of balance	73
13. Difficulty in breathing	75
14. Lump in throat	58
15. Diarrhea	20
16. Fever	38
17. Pain in joints	78
18. Earache	56
19. Watery eyes	54
20. Rash	11
21. Back pain	71
22. Dizziness	87
23. Chest pains	51
24. Stomachache	45
25. Excess blood in body	7
26. Excess water in body	2
27. Drying of blood in body parts	58
Severity	
1. Minor illness	9
2. Significant illness	7
3. Heavy illness	80
4. Fatal	67
Age Relatedness	
1. Children only	0
2. Children mostly	7

(continues)

TABLE 4.5   (continued)

Illness Dimension	% Positive Association
3. Adults only	4
4. Adults mostly	89
5. Older people only	2
6. Older people mostly	9
Sex Relatedness	
1. Females only	2
2. Females mostly	49
3. Males only	2
4. Males mostly	7
5. Both males and females	31

Like Um Fahmy, ʿAmer Akhdar, a male household head who had gotten his first "role" (dor) of ʿuzr as a child, had a recurrence. As he explains,

Eighteen years ago . . . I fell into the deep part of the water and got frightened. They [members of his household] . . . took me to the hadra[14] and my body reacted to one of the turug.[15] [The assyad] talked and they said they wanted supper. They never come any more, they never came until today, I feel they are back. Now they came because they know I am sad, they know that my daughter wants to leave us alone and live with her husband in another house. Now I get the same pain all over my body. It starts in my head and then moves all over my body. The Sheika . . . talked to my daughter and tried to put some sense into her and she said she will make us a sulha.

While villagers, including healers, are in general agreement about assigning to supernatural creatures (awlad il ard or assyad) the role of efficient cause, they differ in their explanation of the manner in which these creatures relate to the human body. ʿUzr may be attributed to the invasion of the body or its "touch." Some villagers also make reference to the "winds" (aryah) of supernatural creatures as the specific means of their contact with the human body. Since the aryah or the jinn (assyad) are not stationary once they enter the body, the pain associated with ʿuzr is believed to move from one part of the body to another. This is a distinguishing diagnostic criterion which symptomatic persons themselves emphasize.

Non-localized pain is a diagnostic index which distinguishes the spiritual illness of ʿuzr (marad rawhani) from physical illness (marad gussmani). The spirits do not allow the pains of ʿuzr to subside until measures are taken to rectify the situation of distress. Yet even when measures are taken to address the afflicted person's source of distress, thereby pacifying the spirits, these supernatural creatures do not necessarily abandon their host/ess. They may remain dormant only to resurface once again under distress. This "telescoping" of illness explanations (Rubel 1964; Uzzell 1974) is illustrated by Bahiga's *ᶜuzr* as described by her mother-in-law:

> Bahiga was working, cleaning the wheat; she fell. But the *assyad* did not cause her any illness right then. Two years later she became ill. She complained that her whole body hurt and she kept sleeping all day long. We took her to two doctors but the more injections they gave her the worse she got. Finally her father took her to a Sheik . . . who made her a charm. . . . The death of her son caused all this; she used to cry a lot during the night.

The illness of *ᶜuzr* may also be a secondary effect of an untreated case of human gaze, i.e. the evil eye (*nazra insaniya*). It is therefore cautioned that if a person who is affected by the evil eye (*mahsud*) does not get immediate treatment through the recitation of Quranic verses (*ragwa*), the state of depression associated with the evil eye renders the *mahsud/ a* susceptible to *ᶜuzr*. This secondary precipitation of *ᶜuzr* may be detected by a diagnostician when he summons the *assyad*. When the *assyad* speak they indicate that they came under a wish, the wish associated with a covetous gaze (*taht nifss*). Similarly, the illness of sorcery (*ᶜamal bil marad*) predisposes people to *ᶜuzr*. Since sorcery causes sadness and passivity, the associated depression invites the *assyad* to act.

While the potential harm of *ᶜuzr* is feared by all adults, villagers recognize variable susceptibility to the effect of supernatural forces. It is said that

> there are bodies which are not touched by the children of the ground [*awlad il ard*]. But the good body gets noticed [*yitnizir*]. . . . It is only the beautiful which gets affected by the eye [*ᶜayn*] or the *assyad*.

Moreover, as one healer explained,

> The *assyad* go to those who have pure blood, they do not go to people who have polluted blood [*dam zifir*]. Polluted blood is inborn [*khilga*], people who have it are born this way; even the devil himself does not come to them.

To intrude upon an area where spirits are likely to roam is a necessary but not sufficient condition for precipitation of illness. A person's own constitution is considered an important intervening factor. Since women are considered emotionally weaker than men, villagers generally agree that women are more likely to be affected by *ᶜuzr* than men (see the Sex Relatedness section in Table 4.5). As one woman said,

> Men get *ᶜuzr* because they are more exposed to going out at night. But women get *ᶜuzr* by less frightening experiences than men. This is because women's nerves [*aᶜssab*] are limited. You know women have half the nerves of men.

According to a male healer, "men get *ᶜuzr* because they (go) . . . out at night, but women get it from the slightest fright or sadness . . . [because] women's emotions are limited." Consequently, although emotional distress is generally associated with the occurrence of the illness of *ᶜuzr*, when accounts of the illness among males are given there often is exaggeration of the emotional load which precipitated the illness. In the case of women, the affliction is usually attributed to crying in the dark or sadness.

Illness Explanations in Social Context

> Fatma's brother's wife's mother got leprosy only two weeks after she refused to give her sick relative some of the food she had cooked. Her relative pleaded to God that she may never be able to hold anything with her hands.

As in the case with other explanations of compromised health, the explanation of Fatma's leprosy is specific to its social context. Accordingly, "God's punishment" for wrongdoing (*zanb*) is given as an explanation of illness only in the case of other people, not in the case of one's self or in the case of one's loved relatives or friends. Thus when I tried to substantiate the above-noted account of illness with the afflicted person's daughter she denied that her mother suffers from leprosy. Not surprisingly, she did not attribute the illness to God's revenge. Instead, she said that, like any illness, her mother's came from God.

In another case several villagers explained a man's illness, and his hospitalization for surgery, as a revenge of God for his exploitation of a woman's poverty, innocence, and ignorance. It is alleged that under the man's pressure and intentional misguidance, the illiterate woman put her seal on a document which waived her former husband's obligation to support her and her infant son. Some villagers claim that the man was bribed by the woman's former husband, who is said to have paid him five pounds for this service. A few villagers, not one of whom is known to be a friend of the accused, noted that only three days after he had done this evil deed God's punishment came and the woman was avenged:

"He was [in the hospital] on the operating table in no time." Friends of the sick man, and his relatives, explain his affliction in terms of diametrically opposed causation, emphasizing his overexertion on behalf of community welfare.

Beyond generalized beliefs surrounding illness causation, interpretations of actual experiences of ill-health are contingent upon the duration of an affliction, its behavioral and physical manifestations, and associated social dynamics of interpersonal relations. Thus, if a child falls ill, a natural cause may be extended to explain his/her condition. Reference may be made to poor appetite, overexertion in work or play, or sunstroke. But a child may be labelled *mahsud* (affected by the evil eye) retrospectively, after he/she has been "seen" (*itnazar*) by someone who is disliked or feared.

The label "*mahsud*" may also be assigned to the child if the illness is considered to have occurred suddenly or if it lingers on beyond expected duration. In such cases, cause is also determined retrospectively. Thus, a child may feel tired and irritable, but if his/her condition persists, one or more members of the family may recall that earlier during the week, or even as long ago as a month or more, the child had been "seen" by a person whom the family perceives as possessing the evil eye.

Accusation of possession of the evil eye is dependent not on specific attributes of persons but on the nature of interpersonal relations. It is at once a reflection of and a justification for hostility. Thus, although some barren women are indeed believed to possess the evil eye (cf. Spooner 1970), barrenness is by no means a definitive criterion for such possession. The case of Zahia is instructive in this regard:

Zahia is a 45-year-old blind woman who is also barren. As is the case for other physically or mentally handicapped persons, she is considered *mabruka* (possessing *baraka*) by many of the village women. They bring their infants to her so that she can caress them and transfer some of her *baraka* to them. In contrast, her sister-in-law, with whom Zahia resides and who considers her a burden, says that she is a source of trouble and has the evil eye.[16]

In light of the account of tensions between extended family members elaborated in Chapter 1, it is not surprising to find that accusations of *hassad* are not uncommon among members of extended family households. By contrast, there is no indication of such accusations among members of a nuclear family (cf. Rubel 1966:204). It is only jokingly that villagers say, "No one envies wealth except its owners [*ma yihsid il mal ila sihabu*]."

The context-specific determination of illness causation is also manifest in relation to sorcery. For example, a wife may explain her husband's impotency by reference to sorcery because she might have taken him from another woman who is expected to take revenge. Similarly, a man enraged by refusal on the part of the father of a woman whose hand he has asked for in marriage may resort to sorcery. He may ask a sorcerer to "write" that the desired bride remain unmarried, fall ill, or even die. In short, the social conditions for implicating sorcery must exist in people's perception of interpersonal relations so that sorcery may be selected as an explanation of a case of illness. Even then, those making accusations are sensitive to the social consequences of implicating other members of the community. Hence the secrecy which guards the "discovery" of responsible parties. They are not confronted by their accusers.

Persons who are themselves the victims of supernaturally caused illness emphasize the action of supernatural beings as expression of concern:

> When my husband died he left me with three girls. They were all little. I took my share [of father's inheritance] and I brought my daughters up. I got them all married. Two are outside [her household]. My second daughter's husband is very poor so he lives with me. I became ill about five years ago when my daughter got married and I became sad because I have no son or husband, and my brother, God forgive him, would not help me. My sadness turned to illness. My sister took me to the doctor, but the more of the doctor's medicine I took, the worse off I became. So people said that I am *ma^czura* [afflicted by the illness of *^cuzr*]. The *Assyad* talked. They said that they are from Saudia, from the land of the Prophet. They told everybody that when I am not happy they make all my body blue. They knew that my brother was not saying the truth when he refused to help. The *assyad* from Saudia knew that I needed help. So in order to show my brother that I need help, they spoke to them all through me and made them know that I need their help.

When I questioned this *ma^czura*'s brother about his sister's *^cuzr*, he stressed the malevolent power of *ahl il ard* and even condoned their punitive actions, of which he regarded a "greedy woman" deserving.

The difference between medical beliefs as abstract cultural constructs and socially contextualized responses to illness is underscored by the case of a village government employee who consistently rejected the "nonsense" of supernatural explanations of illness by other villagers, whom he considered "ignorant," only to offer such an explanation himself when physicians failed to cure his own daughter.

Even hypothetical cases of illness presented to respondents in structured interviews reveal that there is no consensus among respondents about their associated illness dimensions (cf. Fabrega 1973). Table 4.4 provides numerical representations of the degree of consensus among a sample of 55 respondents. These males and females were asked to associate different illness indicators with the illnesses of *tarba, hassad,* and *ʿamal bil marad.* The absence of consensus illustrated in Table 4.4 is also evident when the sample population is differentiated into subgroups of practitioners and non-practitioners (see Chapter 5).

More pronounced than differences of cultural construction are those pertaining to the negotiation of claims to compromised health. This became clear even in the very early days of fieldwork. In the course of collecting census data I noticed a common discrepancy between mothers-in-laws' evaluations of their daughters-in-laws' health and the latter's descriptions of their own health condition. When I asked a mother-in-law about the health of one of her daughters-in-law, she asserted that it was normal by labelling her "as strong as a horse," or "like a *ʿafrita* [supernatural creature]." When daughters-in-law themselves were interviewed directly, they sometimes verbalized complaints which their older affines never even hinted at. When asked if they had fallen ill within the past year, many of these young women responded by saying, "of course," or "illness never leaves me." By contrast, a mother-in-law may justify her favorite daughter-in-law's or her own daughter's limited contribution to household labor by describing her as "weak" or "at her end in pregnancy" or "overworked."

While the illness role provides legitimacy for deviation from role expectations (Parsons 1972), the dispensation of such legitimacy is itself subject to social constraints related to power relations. Thus, a woman may claim illness only to be contradicted and overruled by her more powerful affines, parents, older sisters or brothers. Only under conditions of *socially* legitimated claims to illness is it considered permissible to subordinate the collective interest of the family to that of an individual member.

Aside from evidence of "the tendency to adopt the sick role" (Mechanic 1961), its legitimation is informed by the structural constraints of organizational power. In an extended family household, for example, legitimized claims to the sick role involve only a temporary mediation of the contradictions inherent in the social relations of production of extended families, and their attendant ideological elements. In fact the very process of legitimation of the symptomatic person's claim by more powerful affines or kin simultaneously reinforces relations of sub- or super-ordination within the household.

Since the explanation of a declared illness state may vary from the assertion of distress on the part of the afflicted person (and his/her supporters) to the outright dismissal of his/her behavior as "faking" (*dalaʿ*) by a non-sympathetic household member, an independent opinion is necessary. In such cases of contested claims a healer's evaluation is actively sought. Traditional medical practitioners willingly dispense

legitimacy to a symptomatic person's claim of distress. They even anticipate the types of problems which prompt people of different social positions to seek their help. Yet sometimes even their diagnoses are subject
to contestation among the parties concerned.

When diagnostic labels fail to match affected persons' (or their families') socially defined complaints, alternate diagnoses are sought. This is
precisely what happens in the village when a sick person or members of
his/her family reject a physician's diagnosis. Within the confines of their
biomedical logic physicians generally disregard the social dimensions of
compromised health which the villagers themselves consider central.
Depending on circumstances surrounding the illness at issue, this may
prompt relatives to seek explanations which are compatible with the
sick person's social reality and emotional state. However, if there is no
reason to assume supernatural etiology, they will continue to frequent
the physician and abide by his/her advice as long as they can afford to
pay the fees and purchase the prescribed medicines.

In sum, beyond multi-faceted cultural construction, illness experiences involve context-specific explanations. Interpretation of the state
of compromised health depends on the afflicted person and his/her
significant others' perceptions at any given point in the duration of the
illness. In general, villagers' selection of a specific cause to explain an
illness occurrence is a function of the duration of the affliction, its physical and behavioral manifestations, and its response to specific treatment. Additionally, and of particular importance, are the interpersonal
relations which surround the affected person and his/her significant
others.

As noted for other parts of the world, and in contrast to the biomedical explanatory model, ill-health in Fatiha is not a socially isolated
category of negative experiences (cf. Kleinman 1977). Broadly conceived, illness belongs to a general category of misfortunes which transcends a sharply delineated "medical" domain.[17] Compromised health
is understood not simply in terms of physical constitution but, more
importantly, in terms of social processes involving power relations.

Power Relations as Medical Discourse

The process of "making social" compromised health and the related
linkage between medical discourse and social power relations (Glick
1967; Frankenburg 1980; Young 1982) are well illustrated by the illness
of ʿuzr (Morsy 1978, 1991).[18] While the maʿzur/a[19] share with sufferers of
other afflictions a change in social behavior, including deviation from
gender role expectations (see Table 4.5), the social legitimation of
claims to the sick role is far from private. In the case of "tying" (rabt), for

example, whereas the state of illness involves a drastic deviation from expected male role behavior of sexual performance, the pronouncement of illness causation is private, shared only with trusted relatives and friends. For *ᶜuzr,* by contrast, the symptomatic persons themselves, or significant others, make a concerted effort to secure support of the claim to the sick role from as many members of the community as possible. The significance of "making social" *ᶜuzr* is evident in diagnosis and the associated healing process. These rituals are often performed in a public arena, in full view of an audience of relatives and other members of the community. Moreover, the very term *ᶜuzr,* which means "excuse," provides the illness with a social definition which insulates the "excused" (*maᶜzur/a*)[20] from otherwise enforced social canons. The significance of such social legitimation is understandable in light of the compromise of *pivotal* cultural norms, including gender role expectations.

Deviations from expected adult role behavior in cases of *ᶜuzr* are of a different order than minor infringements such as women's smoking or sniffing of *nishug* under the guise of "expel[ling] the moisture in the chest and the head." Compromised role behavior associated with possession illness involves what may be regarded as core cultural principles such as childlessness, threat to family livelihood, undermining of generational authority patterns, or incest. Illustrative of the last is the case of Fat'halla El Badri, who was surrounded by a large crowd in the field and restrained as he attempted to rape his son's wife. People rationalized his behavior by reference to his possession by non-Muslim *assyad.* Similar rationalization is extended for the behavior of a mother who refuses to nurse her child. Drawing on Islamic tradition to justify this mother's behavior, a literate villager noted, "There is no embarrassment for the afflicted" (*laysa ala al marid harag*).

Sickness and the Social Mediation of Powerlessness

In Fatiha the *maᶜzur/a* does not belong to an established institution of the type associated with traditional cults in other parts of Africa (I.M. Lewis et al. 1991). Nevertheless the "special position" of those whose claim to this sick role is legitimated involves privileged treatment. In addition to forcing attention to personal grievances and distress, the *ᶜmazour/a* experiences a temporary enhancement of social position. His/her sickness mediates asymmetrical power relations and allows dispensation from expected role behavior.

As noted earlier, women are believed to be more susceptible to *ᶜuzr* due to their weakness, which is considered natural (*tabᶜ*). As ideology, this belief legitimizes the power differentials between males and females, including those which prompt the illness of *ᶜuzr.* Villagers generally expect a higher rate of incidence of *ᶜuzr* among women:

> The *ᶜuzr* of women is heavier than that of the men because they are
> bossed [*mar'usin*]. If a man tells her to do something and she refuses, he
> will hit her and make her sad. . . . Women in the village have no opinion.
> A man forces his [will] on her because he is dominant, so she sleeps and
> says that she is *maᶜzura.*

In addition to the generalized belief about females' greater susceptibility to *ᶜuzr,* some villagers consider *ᶜuzr* to be indicative of powerlessness in general, whether women's or men's. A male villager clarified the meaning of the word *maᶜzur* as "someone who is ill and because originally he wanted certain things which could not be fulfilled, he sleeps and does not get up." It is also noted that beyond health status, the term "*maᶜzur*" is used to refer to someone who is short of money and, in a more general sense, to a person whose behavior is judged as legitimate in light of existing constraints.

Far from being shameful,[21] and once "made social," the culturally legitimated "excuse" allows the transgression of established power relations. Illustrative of this deviation is the experience of Nadia. The label *maᶜzura* permits this daughter to contradict the judgment of her father, an otherwise deplorable behavior. Nadia relates her experience of *ᶜuzr* as follows:

> I was engaged at the time. My father had hit me. I did not want to marry
> him [the groom]. My father hit me very hard. They tell me that I slept for
> three days. I did not eat. They found out that I have a *ᶜuzr* when they took
> my *atar* to the sheikh. I went to the *hadra* and they made me a *sulha.* The
> sheikh Abdel Salam el Asmar was the *sayid* who was wearing me. Be-
> cause of my father's hitting in the dark, the *sayid* came over me. He came
> to save me from my father's hitting. When my parents saw me in this bad
> state, they said that it was not necessary for me to marry the man who
> wanted to marry me. When I was cured, I married another person.

Possession sickness also provides Samra with "time out" from her responsibilities in an extended-family household. Neighbors who are sympathetic to Samra's tolerance of her "unbearable" mother-in-law explain that it is only because Samra is *maᶜzura* that she is allowed to leave the house (in order to go the *hadra* in the nearby village). They add that her weekly attendance at the *zar* is the only occasion on which she can "breathe."

In the case of Samra and others whose negotiated claim to *ᶜuzr* is legitimized, relatives become particularly sensitive to their needs. Care is taken to avoid the precipitation of another illness "attack," and by extension an emotional and economic crisis. Thus the reproduction of the household, including its central power relations, such as those which obtain between mother-in-law and her resident female affine, involves occasional mediation of power asymmetry through atypical accommodation of demands by those in positions of relative powerlessness.

The case of a young adult male, Gamal, also reflects the family's special treatment of the *ma^czur*. His brother described Gamal's condition as follows:

> Some years ago when he was playing in the street some kids hit him. When he came complaining to his mother, she hit him too. He fell in the doorway of the house. He kept crying and when we transferred him to the bed, he kept shaking. The following morning he had a fever. He became very hot. We took him to the doctor. He was cured. But every time after this, whenever anyone upsets him, he would get the "role" [*dur*] again. His head would shake. We took him to Sheikh . . . and he made him a *hijab* [charm] and he became better. But until now, whenever he becomes upset he starts shaking and so we have to be very careful with him. The sheikh had said that when he was hit over the doorway, because it is inhabited, [i.e., by supernatural beings], he became *malbuss* [worn or possessed].

Similar caution is exercised with Amira, a *ma^czura* who lives in a nuclear family household with her husband and children:

> About three or four years ago it started. I was very sad and then I started crying. Now I feel distressed and I know it must be the *^cuzr*. When my children upset me or if anybody tells me an unkind word I become sad immediately. I know it is a *^cuzr* because I lose consciousness. Four days ago I did not feel myself at all. I did not even know where I was sitting, it lasted for a while. It is mostly from the children that I get upset. My husband knows that I am *ma^czur* and so he doesn't like to upset me.[22]

In the cases of Nadia, Gamal, and Amira, the tolerance which they experience is clearly the result of willful abdication of authority by members of their household. This was also the case for Fadli, who is recognized as *ma^czur* by his acquaintances and affines. Yet, as his experience illustrates, certain actions on the part of the *ma^czur* may be considered intolerable even by sympathetic associates, prompting withdrawal of their legitimation of claim to sickness. According to Fadli,

> I was in the *tarhila* [migratory labor tour] and found a bunch of dates on the face of the water. I went into the water to pick the dates. After I

touched it, it disappeared from my hand. I screamed and so I got a *latah* [supernatural touch]. My body became worn [possessed]. [It is] the *safina* [ship, one of the forms taken by the supernatural *assyad*], if it is upset, it drowns a person in the mud, but if it is docile, it simply makes the person *maᶜzur* or takes him down with her for a few days. Sometimes it comes to people in the form of food, and sometimes in the form of jewelry. It came to me in the form of the dates. At the time I was only twelve years old. The *safina* [the ship, so named because it inhabits the waters of the river] is still with me until now. When I go to the *zikr*[23] she comes out and talks through my mouth. Whenever I am upset and if I get into an argument with anyone, she comes out and gives hell to everyone. After the argument when I come to [my senses], I apologize to everyone for what she did, they understand and forgive me. . . . [She came to me] . . . during the *mulid*, I was in the *zikr*. She said through my mouth that she wants to be happy, and she made me faint. That day I had been very upset with my wife. She had hit the child, although I had told her not to.

In the course of discussions with other villagers, including the *maᶜzur's* wife, another side of the story emerged. During the *mulid* Fadli had beaten his wife severely and her screams drew the neighbors. Some of her neighbors went over to her relatively affluent father's household and informed the family of what was happening to their daughter. The wife's brothers went over to Fadli's house and ordered their sister to collect her clothes and leave with them. Fadli pleaded with his brothers-in-law not to take their sister and said that it was not he who hit her. He said that he was lost (*tayih*, i.e., unconscious). He attributed his uncontrolled actions to the spirit possessing him. He kept crying and asking forgiveness but the men insisted on taking their sister along.

Fadli's friends support his claim of possession. Other villagers who support the action of the wife's brothers note that she belongs to a family which is "happy" (*mabsuta*, meaning wealthy). To the latter group, it is understandable that they would not allow their sister to be exposed to such degradation (*bahdala*). In this regard one villager pointed out that "she has mud [*di ᶜaliha teen*, i.e., she owns land] and [Fadli] has his eye on it."

Among other points, Fadli's case shows that "the tendency to adopt the sick role" is not independent of associated social power relations. Although the sick role legitimizes deviance as a strategy of indirect control, it is not without restrictions. While *ᶜuzr* denotes a position of relative powerlessness, the attendant social sanction which allows temporary transgression of such a position of powerlessness is itself subject to negotiation.

Contestation surrounding claims to the designation *maᶜzur/a* extends to children. As shown in Table 4.5 (under Age Relatedness), *ᶜuzr* is generally considered an affliction of adults. Whereas deviation from culturally prescribed role expectations demarcates *ᶜuzr* in adults, this is not the case for children. For children, whose social obligations are not as crucial to social reproduction as adults, no similar established indicators are operative. Thus, in association with children, the label *maᶜzur/a* is a significant "excuse" for the adult relatives of an allegedly afflicted child. It is this label rather than the physician's shameful diagnosis of "*marad ᶜasabi*" (illness of nerves, or mental illness), which a child's family prefers to use. For example, Baheera insists on describing her son's illness as *ᶜuzr* in spite of the physician's diagnosis of epilepsy. On his part, the son, a student who, like his literate peers, tries to distance himself from the "ignorance" of the *fallahin*, prefers the physician's diagnosis.

The identification "*ᶜuzr*" is also valued by adults who reject the labelling of mental illness and its shameful implications for themselves. This is the case for Nusa, a middle-aged barren woman. I learned from a number of villagers, including the village headman, that both Nusa and her brother had once been committed to a mental institution. Nusa herself believes that her committal was an error on the part of the physician, who could not recognize her *ᶜuzr*. Her friends support this explanation, but those who dislike her say that she is crazy (*magnuna*) and that is why she was sent to the mental institution. They say that "light mindedness" runs in her family.

ᶜUzr: Between Social Production and Biomedical Diagnosis

As noted in Chapter 1, as early as the nineteenth century Egyptian physicians tried to describe possession illness in terms of biomedical diagnostic categories. In the present century psychiatrists have continued to show interest in this affliction (Behman 1953; Okasha 1966; El-Islam 1967). Psychiatrically informed definitions of spirit possession yield the biomedical labels "hysterical," "anxious," "obsessional," and "schizoid" (Okasha 1966).

Undoubtedly influenced by my own earlier biomedical training, my research agenda for the community of Fatiha included the attempt to identify the biomedical diagnostic equivalents of possession illness. Informed by Devons and Gluckman's discussion of anthropologists' "limits of naivete" (Devons and Gluckman 1964), I relied on the collaboration of a physician and a psychologist to establish what I once regarded as an "independent scientific" measure of somatized distress (cf. El-Islam 1975) associated with an "emic" diagnostic category. The extended case studies of *ᶜuzr* in this section formed the focus of this attempt.

All the cases presented here involved afflicted persons whose illnesses were "active" during my residence in the village. Only those villagers who experienced "the role" (*el-dor*) during that time were subjected to a physical examination by the physician. To the same group of villagers I administered the Hakky Personality Test.[24] The psychologist-author of the test evaluated its results. She also evaluated the responses to the Cornell Medical Index (CMI), which I had administered to a group of *maᶜzourin* that included but was not restricted to those who manifested an active phase of the affliction.

As the following case studies show, *ᶜuzr* is an umbrella term which covers a variety of compromised states of health, defined primarily in terms of social causation and derivative emotional distress. As the villagers themselves recognize, these diagnostic criteria are very different from those utilized by the physician. In fact, the physician's inability to identify this socially defined illness is itself an important indicator in the diagnosis of possession illness. With regard to the psychologists' label, which is based on the Hakky Personality Test, this also represents a reduction of a wide and changing repertoire of expressions of distress associated with *ᶜuzr*. As for the CMI, its multiple and multi-faceted indicators, which include somatic and psychological elements, provide a measure of compromised health which represents greater approximation to villagers' own perceptions of sickness.

Ahmad's Illness Experience: The Case of a Dependent Husband

In Fatiha powerless men, like their female counterparts, are accorded temporary exemptions from positions of subordination through the social legitimization of claims to *ᶜuzr*. The case of Ahmad, a married man who resides in the household of his wife's family, illustrates the association of *ᶜuzr* with absence of control over culturally valued power bases.

I was informed of Ahmad's condition by a neighbor of his wife's family. On arriving at the house of the sick man, I was met by his wife and her mother and led into a room where the junior woman served us tea. In describing her husband's condition, Safeya emphasized how he had made their household "the show of the whole village" by his interchangeable crying and singing of a melancholy tune. According to Safeya, it was her mother who first suspected that Ahmad was *mᶜazur*. Concerned that his possessing spirits "would take advantage of his loneliness and harm him," Safeya spent the entire night sitting by his side as he slept. When he woke up in the morning Ahmad was surprised to see his wife sitting up and looking over him; he had no memory of the events of the previous night.

Upon my request, I was led to another room in the house where Ahmad was lying down in a corner, covered with a heavy blanket in spite of the heat. He apologized for not getting up to greet me and said that his legs were too weak to carry him. He said that he was feeling very cold and gets very dizzy when he tries to stand on his legs. When I asked him about the cause of his illness, he responded, "Only God knows" (*allah hua a‘lam*). In response to my inquiry about whether he planned to go out to work in the field, he replied in the negative and pointed to his reliance on his father-in-law ("*il baraka fi hamaya*"). The father-in-law assumed full responsibility for work on the land, which he owns.

During my first visit with Ahmad he agreed to see the physician, who gave him a physical examination and took urine and stool specimens. Aside from recording bilharziasis and noting Ahmad's blind eye, the physician pronounced this *ma‘zur*'s health as "normal." As for the result of the Hakky Personality Test (which I had administered to the *ma‘zur* about two weeks after his initial attack when he felt comfortable enough to sit up and engage in conversation), the psychologist's judgement yielded the diagnosis "hypochondriac neurotic."

According to Ahmad, compliance with the physician's directive of consumption of a vitamin tonic did not relieve him of his feeling of weakness. He did not go to the field and slept for most of the day. His wife and mother-in-law both reported that he would refuse to eat most of the time, and when he did, he would "only take a bite." The simultaneous laughing and crying, described for the first day, was not repeated, but he continued to complain of general weakness, headache, and shivering. Observing no noticeable improvement in his condition, Ahmad's father-in-law went to see a healer. Since the *ma‘zour* himself refused to accompany the senior man, the latter took his *atar*.

The healer's diagnosis confirmed the mother-in-law's suspicion of *‘uzr*. The Sheika specified that the *assyad* had come to Ahmad when he was in the field and "started quarreling with his brothers about the inheritance." Clarification of the reason for the quarrel by Ahmad's mother-in-law and wife disclosed tension between Ahmad and his sister, who allegedly owed him money that she refused to return. In this regard the mother noted that Ahmad had been advised to leave the money to his sister "because she has orphaned children" but added that "he also needs the money." In turn Safeya commented, "He wants to get it from her so that we can attend to our concerns. We cannot live here [in her father's household] forever."

Following the diagnosis of Ahmad's condition as *ma‘zur*, the sheikha performed a *sulha* for him. His sister contributed five pounds (a large sum of money by village standards) to buy the sacrificial poultry demanded by the *assyad*. When the *assyad* spoke through Ahmad's mouth during the *sulha,* they added to their earlier disclosure that they had come under fright (*taht tarba*). They had come when he became frightened as he turned around while speaking to his brothers about the inheritance and found the draft animal falling into a ditch.

During the two weeks following Ahmad's *dor,* he did not go out to the field with his father-in-law and still complained of weakness. Gradually he slept less and could get up and move around in the house. Occasionally he sat outside the house and chatted with friends and neighbors who constantly stopped by to inquire about his health. During our conversations he did acknowledge his condition of *ʿuzr* but referred to it only upon my inquiries about his health.

Reference to Ahmad's condition of *ʿuzr* and to the diagnostician's labelling of *maʿzur* seemed to be more crucial to his mother and father-in-law. His wife, by contrast, showed minimum interest in convincing others of his condition as *maʿzur,* encouraging him instead to continue to take the doctor's medicine. This literate young woman even suggested to me that the charm (*hijab*) which the sheikha had instructed her husband to wear was nonsense ("*kalam farigh*"). Her parents behaved differently.

To the parents-in-law the labelling "*maʿzur*" seems crucial to their attempt to lend legitimacy to Ahmad's financial dependence and related effort to bring his family's attention, particularly his sister's, to his unhappy condition. In support of this expectation, one of the neighbors anticipated that Ahmad's experience will expedite receipt of his share of the inheritance. As to why the parents had agreed to have their daughter marry a male who is incapable of supporting her, another neighbor responded, "Who else would have agreed to marry their ugly daughter? She must be at least ten years older than him." From Safeya's own reaction to her husband's sickness, it seems that she is conscious of her own culturally defined inadequacies. Consequently she tolerates her husband's inability to live up to male role expectations.

Zebeda's Illness: The Social Mediation of Affinal Authority

The significance of the labelling *maʿzura* as a culturally sanctioned form of deviance is also illustrated by the case of Zebeda. My initial acquaintance with her condition came during visits with two local healers. During my visit to sheikh Malek, he described Zebeda's condition as follows:

> There is a woman, she is about eighteen years old. She is married. . . . I went to see her. . . . They said her health is not well. Her thigh was swollen. They said they had taken her to two doctors but she got worse from

the injections. I threw the rosary and found that she is *ma᷐zura*, she has *rih* [wind] and when the *assyad* are on people they do not like injections and stuff like that. I gave the rosary to her mother-in-law and she whispered to the rosary to show the reason for the illness. I then spread the rosary and read its signs they [the *assyad*] had come to her under sadness [*taht za᷐la*]. The doctor had told them that the veins in her thigh were plugged up. I told them to take her to . . . [a nearby village]. Sheikh Muhammad made her a charm [*hijab*] although I told them that she needed the *dagga* [drumming of the *zar*]. If the pain had not been so irregular and so mobile, maybe the *hijab* would have worked. The *assyad* were still new and so they could have been pacified and they may have left her alone completely. It is when the *assyad* have been in her blood for a long time that they do not leave. . . . They do not settle in any of the important parts of the body except if the sick person is denied the status of *ma᷐zur* by his family or in cases where they iron on him [i.e. cauterize]. It all started because her mother-in-law had accused her of laxness in her work and spending too much time at her father's house after childbirth. She became sad and she probably went inside a dark room and cried. The woman who has given birth is like the bride, she is susceptible to the *assyad*.

Another healer who was also consulted by Zebeda's family gave the following account of her case:

She is about twenty years old. She has been married two years. She had a child and he died when he was two months. She was very sad. She became very weak; she could not eat, she could not walk. She went to her father's house because her mother-in-law could not stand her any more. They took her to many doctors. They gave her the injections but nothing happened. The pain had started in her arms first and moved to her head, and now it has moved to her legs. They came to me yesterday. The *sayid* on her talked last night. He said he had come because of her sadness when she screamed in the doorway when her son died. He has not made any demands yet. Tonight or tomorrow night they will drum for her. [Will you organize the *dagga* for her?] No, I will not go, they will call someone else. I do not do this type of thing any more. Women move around and expose themselves; it is below my dignity.

At night I went to Zebeda's father's house following a rather reluctant invitation by the father himself. During an earlier conversation, when I had recently arrived in the village, this literate government employee had firmly denied his belief in *᷐uzr*, dismissing it as "nonsense" which shows the peasants' ignorance. As he greeted me at the door, he promptly referred to that earlier conversation and shaking his head said, "This is God and this is his wisdom [*adi allah wi adi hikmitu*]; what can we do?"

In a room lighted with a butane gas lantern (symbolic of relative afflu-ence), Zebeda lay on the floor covered with a blanket and surrounded by her mother, sisters, and their children. The whole family's attention was clearly concentrated on her. Her sister's husband came in the room, sat near her head, and started feeding her an orange, which she ate reluc-tantly. A little while later, her mother-in-law came over to inquire about her health and referred to her presence as substituting for that of her son, Zebeda's husband, who was away from the village in the army.

Zebeda's sister explained to me that Zebeda had left her husband's ex-tended family household when her illness became incapacitating. She explained that it is customary for a woman to go to her father's house when she becomes ill for a long time and sometimes when she delivers her first child. Zebeda looked very pale and tired. She could hardly sit up and eat; members of her family took turns propping her up in a sitting position to feed her. Conversations with members of the family, includ-ing the mother-in-law, indicated that Zebeda's relatives had at that time dismissed the doctor's diagnosis. According to the relatives this attrib-uted her swollen thigh to a blood clot. When I spoke later with the physi-cian, he communicated to me his diagnosis of Zebeda's condition as "postpartum thrombophlebitis." He said that she had suffered from an occlusion and inflammation in the femoral vein and expected her re-covery from this condition to extend over a period of a few weeks.

Because the physician had failed to bring about the desired improve-ment in Zebeda's condition and had ignored her emotional distress as an important cause of her state of ill health, his diagnosis and con-sequent treatment were judged as inadequate. Everyone present at Zebeda's father's house during my first visit was convinced that the doctor had failed to recognize the *ᶜuzr*. Zebeda's mother said that they had taken her to two doctors who prescribed many medicines which brought no improvement over a period of two weeks. Her father turned to me and said:

> You never believe these things until they happen to someone you love. I would not have believed it myself if I had not heard the sheikh Muham-mad from the Sayida Zinab speak last night. . . . He was speaking through my daughter's mouth. He said that he had come to Zebeda be-cause she cried a lot in the dark after her son died. He said he wants a white dress, white shoes, and a gold ring.

As we sat surrounding the *maᶜzura*, she intermittently gave a few whimpers to which her family responded with comforting, loving words. A knock on the door was responded to by Zebeda's father, who ushered in the sheikh who had diagnosed her condition. Sheikh Saber was accompanied by another sheikh from a nearby village and by the latter's assistant. These men were received warmly by the family. They had been called over to the house because Zebeda herself could not be transported to the nearby village to attend the *hadra*. The sheikh and his party sat down to an elaborate meal. Then the drumming and music from a wind instrument (*salamiya*) started and the visiting sheikh started the chanting of the different *tarigas*.

Everyone's attention was concentrated on Zebeda, to see which *tariga* her body would react to. Finally there came the *tariga* of Sayid il Badawi, and her body started to sway from side to side. Two of her sisters pulled her up and she kept shaking her head from side to side and waving her arms. Her head kerchief became untied and her long hair came undone from its neat braids. She kept up this dancing for about five minutes and fell exhausted into her sisters' arms. They put her down on the reed mat and covered her with blankets. She said that she was very cold and started crying. She complained of her thigh, which she shamelessly exposed in front of the men in the room. It showed a large swollen red blotch. The local sheikh said that the pain was now very severe because the *assyad* were present (*hadrin*). He said that she could rest and later they would have a *sulha* when they prepared the items which the *assyad* had demanded. Zebeda fell asleep and all the visitors left her father's house.

The following day, Zebeda was in great pain; her mother said that she could hardly move her thigh. Relatives and friends advised her parents to bring another sheikh from a nearby village. One of Zebeda's father's friends recommended a sheikh who was described as a learned man who knows the Quran, "not just a drummer." In the afternoon this sheikh was summoned to Zebeda's father's household. Her father informed him of the progression of her illness, emphasizing the emotional distress to which she had been exposed as a result of the death of her son. He also emphasized the pain from her swollen thigh, her poor appetite, and her inability to do any housework. In elaborating the latter behavior, he noted, "This, as you know, is not tolerated by the family of the husband, they made her psychological condition worse." The sheikh listened attentively but did not touch Zebeda or examine her thigh. He said it was wrong to have her descend to the *hadra*. He said that this simply excites the *assyad* and gets them in the habit of wanting to hear the drumming.

When the sheikh did not make any visible sign of attempting to diagnose Zebeda's illness, I asked him if he would take her *atar* to make sure that she was *ma'zura*. He responded rather abruptly and said, "If the owner of the illness [*sahbit il marad*] says that she is *ma'zura* and her family have heard the *assyad*, so how can anyone say otherwise?" He then turned to Zebeda's anxious parents and told them that he would prepare a *hijab* for her to shield her from the pain inflicted by the *assyad*. He was ushered into another room, which he asked to have darkened. As Zebeda's father prepared to close the door, the sheikh asked him about her name and that of her mother. The sheikh emerged from the room about half an hour later carrying a *hijab* with a piece of white cloth enveloping it. He told Zebeda's father that the *assyad* who were with her included a child (reminiscent of Zebeda's own dead child whose loss caused her *ᶜuzr*). The sheikh was then ushered into Zebeda's room again. Her mother supported her in a propped-up position to listen to the sheikh's instructions. He told her to keep wearing the *hijab* and not to take it off for two weeks. He said that she could take it off after two weeks but she should wear it immediately whenever she started to feel depressed. He then turned to her mother and said, "I don't have to tell you, feed her well and let her bathe every day with rose water."

On the days following the sheikh's visit to Zebeda her condition started improving gradually. She had been following the sheikh's instructions and bathing every day and eating well. As a matter of fact, she was getting the choice food in her father's household, particularly poultry and baked rice. She said that she was starting to feel better, and she showed me how the swelling in her thigh had started to subside. Only two days after the sheikh's visit, she was attempting to walk without anyone's assistance. She apologized to me for not being too hospitable during the earlier days of her illness. She said, "I was lost [*tayha*], I did not even know what was going on around me."

During our conversations, it became clear that Zebeda was convinced that the sheikh's *hijab* had fulfilled its intended purpose and was the reason for her improved health. She said that as a precautionary measure she would still hold a *sulha* for the *assyad* when her father bought the gifts that they had requested.

Zebeda remained in her father's household for three months until her husband returned to the village. Prior to her return to her husband's extended-family household, whenever I asked Zebeda about when she would return to live with her mother-in-law, she would make such remarks as, "My condition now cannot bear it," or "You know how it is in the husband's home, the family of the husband has no pity," or "She [her mother-in-law] wants us all to work all the time. She seems to have forgotten what it was like when she was our age. She sure takes good care of her own health."

During the months that Zebeda remained in her father's household, she was up and around but was still the object of pampering by her parents and older sisters. She was still considered *maᶜzura* by her family and friends. When I visited Zebeda's mother she told me that her daughter would remain with her until she was completely cured of her illness. She remarked, "The house of the man [Zebeda's husband], [they] do not pity, . . . I would sell myself to make my daughter comfortable." Zebeda interrupted and said, "Once they see me up on my feet they will expect me to work. . . . The [child] *sayid* is still with me. The *hijab* is just to make him happy. The sheikh said that he may come once or twice a month but he won't make me uncomfortable like before. I could not sleep from him and he would try to talk to my parents all night long but they could not understand the talk of the child. Now I think he will come once or twice a month only."

Once in her husband's extended-family household, Zebeda started going to the *hadra* about once a month in spite of her mother-in-law's objections. Zebeda said that her mother-in-law takes her son's needs into account and is not too demanding of her in terms of housework as she used to be. This shift in the mother-in-law's treatment is obviously related to the presence of her son, a relatively educated villager, deserving of the respect of fellow villagers, including his own mother.

For Zebeda, her *ᶜuzr* provided temporary insulation from her affines' authority in the absence of her husband. When her husband was away from the village she was expected to go on living in his extended-family household. Under the labelling *maᶜzura* these cultural injunctions were temporarily suspended. Zebeda's neglect of her domestic duties, her disrespectful attitude towards her mother-in-law, her eventual abandonment of her husband's home, and her residence in her father's house were all considered legitimate forms of behavior. This shift from one category of socially sanctioned action to an opposite but equally approved form of behavior needed justification. In Zebeda's case, her vindication is not the physician's diagnosis, but her child's death. This shocking and emotionally devastating experience explained her affliction and, by extension, her deviant behavior.

Under ordinary conditions, Zebeda's departure from the role expectations of a daughter-in-law would have had some dire consequences, possibly her divorce. In this regard it is important to note that without the support of her father (whose power in the village rests on his status as a respected government employee and the owner of a few faddans of land), such legitimized deviance from role expectations might not have been so easily granted.

Sayeda's ᶜUzr: Restraining a Husband's Maltreatment

Sayeda, a woman of about forty years of age, lives in a fraternal joint family household. She attributes her *ᶜuzr* to a "gaze" (*nazra*). Her targeting by the "eye" coincided with distress resulting from her husband's maltreatment. This *ma'zoura* herself explained the actions of the spirit as mediating the power asymmetry between the couple. Her husband had hit her after she quarreled with his older brother's wife.

Because Sayeda was considered under the influence of a foreigner, a westerner (*khawaga*), her abandonment of religious duties was excused. His threat of killing the other members of her household, and providing her with alternate shelter if they upset her, was also emphasized by Sayeda. She blamed her possessing spirit for preventing her from doing "anything Islamic," causing her sleeplessness, weakness, loss of appetite, shortness of breath, and pain in the head, which then moved "all over the body." Yet Sayeda was quick to add that "he forced [her] husband to forgive [her]."

Physical examination by the physician disclosed that (aside from "normal" blood pressure of 130/70), Sayeda suffered from "umbilical hernia" and "chronic infectious bronchitis." Sayeda found this diagnosis "incorrect." Noting its similarity to that of other physicians who had examined her in the past, she considered the physician's evaluation still another proof of doctors' ignorance of *'uzr*. Although biomedical diagnosis lends credibility to Sayeda's complaint of shortness of breath, it does not provide an explanation for her sadness. Neither does it justify the action of the *khawaga*, who "caught [her] husband from the neck and told him, 'I will kill you if you lay a hand on her again.'" The psychologist's diagnosis of "severe hypochondria" is equally inadequate in this regard.

Fayza's Distress: A Case of Protracted Estrangement

Fayza, a young woman in her twenties, had returned to Fatiha with her infant son to live with her widowed mother after being expelled from the household of her husband's extended family in another village. As with other cases of possession illness, Fayza's experience partakes of the above-noted pattern of telescoping. Her first "role" (*dor*) came when a teacher screamed at her in school. At the time a *sayed*, Sheik Ibrahim, came to her. According to Fayza's mother,[25] after a *sulha* the *sayed* stayed with her daughter, making his presence known when she became sad, including at the time of her marriage. The *sayed* is also believed to have accompanied her to her husband's village, where he helped her with the inordinate amount of work that was imposed on her by her mother-in-law.

Sheik Ibrahim was soon to be joined by other *assyad* who came to Fayza as a result of the emotional distress she experienced after the death of her infant daughter. Unlike the sheik, the new *assyad* by whom Fayza had become possessed were Christians. Their presence was manifested in Fayza's extended periods of sleep, chills, rudeness to her mother, and refusal to care for or nurse her son. She is now divorced and relies on her mother and sister to support her through their work as wage laborers.

Fayza's neighbors and friends share her mother's diagnosis. They attribute Fayza's condition to her departure to another village, where she lived among people who are "without religion" (i.e., merciless). In contrast to the people in Fayza's immediate neighborhood, who stressed social causes and who also considered her harmless, a distant acquaintance of the family expressed her concern about Fayza's violence:

> You saw her joking around with me with that knife in her hand. I was scared to death. Her mother is afraid that she would kill her own son. She sometimes holds him very hard and has nearly smothered him to death on several occasions.

If this claim is true, then Fayza's mother's insistence that her daughter's condition is due to ᶜuzr takes on special significance. This is so particularly in light of the fact that it was a traditional healer who had suggested that Fayza be taken to a physician for electric shock treatment.

The mother's insistence on the *maᶜzura* label may well be a way of avoiding the shame of having a daughter who bears the physician's diagnosis of "sickness of the nervous system" (*marad ᶜasabi*). The physician's documented diagnosis reads, Chest: bronchitis; Heart: free; Liver: free; Spleen: free. Unlike the other *maᶜzourin* whom the physician has examined upon my request, Fayza was known to him, and his longtime familiarity with her case prompted the following commentary on what he described as the nervous system: "Psychic Depression, most probably due to accident or sorrow from husband's behavior." The psychologist's diagnosis declared the *maᶜzoura* "paranoid—persecutory."

Fat'heya's Affliction: Motherhood as Cure

Fat'heya, a married woman in her twenties, has been a regular visitor to the weekly *hadra* in the nearby village for a few years. Her illness was manifest two months after her father forced her to marry her mother's sister's widower, a man who is over thirty years her senior. Saddened by her misfortune, she became "worn" by two male *assyad* after being "eyed" by another woman from the village as she was bathing. Fat'heya's self-diagnosis is "subterranean gaze in house of child" (*nazra ardiya fi bit il weld*). In my presence this explanation of her barrenness has been offered by the village healers, as well as by other spiritualists whom I frequented in her company away from the village.

While Fat'heya's friends concur with the diagnosis of "subterranean gaze in the house of child," her rival sister-in-law, Sabha, dismisses this as "excuse," describing Fat'heya's barrenness as "inborn" (*khilga*). To counter this claim, Fat'heya asked Sabha to accompany us on one of the visits to the *hadra*. She reasoned that "maybe when she sees my condition in the *hadra* she will have pity on me and her tongue will stop playing [i.e., she will stop her gossip]. I want her to hear from [the] sheikh . . . when he sees my *atar*." Evidently, it is neither the projection of behavioral or physical symptomatology (both of which, as shown in Table 4.5, are quite fluid) nor the "tendency" of the symptomatic person to adopt the sick role which is important; social legitimation is indispensable.

About three months prior to my departure from the village, Fat'heya suspected that she might be pregnant. She was examined by the physician, whose diagnosis indicated "enlarged uterus of two months gestation." Following this announcement, she stopped going to the *hadra*. She even took Sabha with her to the doctor's office on the second visit "to make sure that she hears the doctor say that [she is] . . . pregnant."

Ghalia's Despondency: The Price of Urban Patronage

Upon hearing of the illness of 13-year-old Ghalia, I accompanied an acquaintance of the family to her house. We found the child sitting alone in front of the house. Her mother was not home and her siblings were all out in the fields. The child looked very unhappy. She looked pale and more undernourished than most of the village children her age. She responded to my question of her mother's whereabouts in a barely audible voice and showed a degree of deference unequalled by any of the village children of comparable age. She had her head leaning against the wall as she sat. Her hand covered the part of her face exposed to the sun. The next-door neighbor came out and told us that Ghalia's mother was out in the field and would be home shortly. As we sat waiting for the mother's arrival, I tried to talk to the child, but to no avail. She kept covering her face and turning towards the wall. The neighbor said, "Leave her alone, don't bother yourself with her, she has *assyad* with her and they are making her very unhappy, the poor thing." Shortly the mother arrived. In spite of her relatively old age she still works in the field to support her orphaned children after the death of her husband a number of years earlier.

When I asked the mother about what was wrong with her daughter, she said, "It seems that she has *assyad* with her. Her brother had taken her to work [as a servant] in Cairo. She worked for his superior who had promised him a promotion. The lady of the house used to frighten her and hit her at night." The mother then turned to her daughter and asked,

"What did she used to do to you? Tell them." The child, for the first time since our arrival in their house, raised her voice to an audible level and said, "She used to hit me with a long stick and a long hose." The mother then continued,

When her brother went to visit her over there to take her monthly wages, she held on to him and she kept crying and saying that she wants to go with him. Her brother took the lady's permission and told her that he would take her to visit us for a few days and would bring her back. When she came back [to the village], she kept crying and saying that she will never go back. Her brother kept imploring her [to go back to Cairo] because he said that he will get the promotion very soon. But she kept crying and did not want to eat or drink. On the third day of her arrival [from Cairo] she was sitting with us and suddenly we found her completely unconscious [*misurgah khalis*]. She remained this way for nearly an hour. We tried to revive her but she would not answer us. We put cold water on her face and rubbed her hands and legs, they were like ice. Finally she woke up and could not remember any of the things which happened to her. Our neighbor was here and she said that she had a brother who used to do just like that and he was *ma*c*zur*. So we knew that she has *assyad* with her but they may be mute. . . . No they have not spoken yet or asked for anything. They haven't talked yet, but we knew it. She's been like this for four days now. After [the *assyad*] come she does not eat and she insults us, and when we tell her to go to the fields with her siblings, she says no. Her brother said, well then, let her rest. Her ways have changed; she used to be very clever and used to be a very hard worker. [The *c*uzr] is probably from her crying when the lady hit her in Cairo.

Ghalia's condition remained unchanged over the following two weeks. She stayed home, refusing to join her brothers and sisters for work in the fields. As she sat outside the house alone, she faced the wall and spoke to no one. Her mother continued to report episodes of "complete loss of consciousness," but I observed none myself. As for the result of the physician's examination of Ghalia, his report reads as follows: Heart: free; chest: free; abdomen: no palpable organ; stool: o.k.; Nervous System: epilepsy, petit mal (absence of convulsion accompanying the state of loss of consciousness).

The physician's diagnosis of "*marad* c*assabi*" was rejected outright by Ghalia's mother. She said that the doctor does not specialize in illnesses like c*uzr* and therefore cannot recognize the illness. In trying to prove her own evaluation of her daughter's illness, she noted, "Now she complains of her hands and knees and head and she refuses to work. It is just as I told you, the pain is moving."

To legitimize her claim of her daughter's condition as c*uzr,* the mother

asked me to accompany her to a local diagnostician. Ghalia did not accompany us on this visit and the mother took along only her *atar*.
The sheika's diagnosis was indeed as the mother had predicted, *ᶜuzr*. The
sheika said that Ghalia had gotten a touch from the ground (*lamsa
ardiya*) since Ramadan (the fasting month which had passed about
three months earlier). She said that *assyad* came to Ghalia under sadness
(*taht zaᶜla*). The similarity of the sheika's diagnosis to that of Ghalia's
mother and her precision in defining Cairo as the place where the illness
was initially precipitated is understandable in light of the conversation
which transpired between us and the healer prior to her "seeing" the
atar. When we first arrived at the sheika's house she had turned to me
and asked, "How are your children?" I responded that they were fine.
The sheika then said, "The children and their father and his family are
what causes all the problems for us women." She then turned to Ghalia's
mother and said, "Isn't that right my sister." Ghalia's mother then
responded, "Yes of course, that is why we came to you, it's about my
daughter, she was in Cairo and the lady hit her and it seems that she has
assyad with her."

When I study Ghalia's case, it becomes clear that the labelling of
maᶜzura was constantly being reiterated by the mother. The power differential between the mother and Ghalia's oldest brother was evident.
He works in the city and has thus earned the prestige and authoritative
role concomitant with exposure to urban ways. The mother needed to
validate her little girl's resistance to carry out a command which was
clearly in the brother's self interest. The son expected Ghalia to go back
to work as a servant for his superior. As *maᶜzura*, the child's refusal to
obey her brother's wishes, mediated by her mother's and the healer's
judgement, served as a socially sanctioned way of resisting the relatively
powerful brother's demands. This was evident in other villagers' urgent
pleas to the brother not to take his *maᶜzura* sister back to Cairo. As one
neighbor of the family commented, "This would be sinful [*haram*], you
take her there and she will be alone. Then [the *assyad*] will have her all
to themselves [*ha yistafradu biha*]." Such rationalization represents a
much more significant line of argument on the child's behalf than the
physician's shameful diagnosis of epilepsy.

Gender, Power, and Distress

Whereas the experiences of possession illness detailed above are not
measurable in terms of biomedical indicators, they *do* represent a pattern of asymmetrical power relations and associated emotional distress
consistent with local-level organizational power as described in Part I.
This pattern is recognized by the villagers themselves, who also

interpret physicians' failed diagnoses as further proof of their own identification of *ᶜuzr.*

As illustrated in Table 4.6, it is not gender status only which predisposes villagers to the illness. Contrary to the assertion of a culturally mediated biological predisposition of women to spirit illness (Kehoe and
Gilleti 1981; cf. Lewis 1983; Natvig 1991:187), the affliction is correlated
with power differentials in general, and not only those pertaining to
gender. Subgroups of women, and men, may be subjected to the authority of males or females in superordinate power positions during specific
phases of the developmental cycle of the family (e.g., daughters-in-law
and the brother of the household head in fraternal joint families). Wom-
en's and men's relative powerlessness may also be related to their failure
to live up to culturally defined role expectations (e.g., sterile men, barren women, men who do not approximate the ideal of "breadwinner").
Differences in power among women, as among men, may also be correlated with variation in access to culturally valued power bases (e.g.,
mother/father of sons as opposed to mother/father of daughters only;
landownership; literacy). Moreover, as in the case of the child Ghalia, the
distress which predisposes people to possession illness may be associated with power differentials involving males and females well beyond
the boundaries of the village community. In short, given the association
between spirit illness and power relations, the epidemiology of *ᶜuzr*

TABLE 4.6   Distribution of *ᶜUzr* in the Sample Population

Population	N	Total # of ᶜUzr Cases	Percentage of Affected Persons
Sex			
Males	166	13	7.8
Females	202	21	10.4
Relation to HH head			
HH him/herself	94	5	5.3
Wife	74	6	8.1
Daughter	42	3	7.1
Son	61	1	1.6
Brother	16	4	25.0
Sister	9	1	11.1
Brother's wife	8	1	12.4
Brother's daughter	10	1	10.0
Mother (married sons)	32	1	3.1
Daughter's husband	2	1	50.0
Son's wife	30	10	33.1

(cf. Rubel 1964), as expected, shows a higher frequency of illness among villagers who are identified as less powerful than their cohorts, whether women or men.

A survey of the incidence of *ᶜuzr* and the social characteristics of *maᶜzourin* in the sample population yielded 34 cases of this possession illness among 166 males and 202 females. Table 4.6 shows the distribution of *ᶜuzr*. Although a somewhat higher frequency is registered when females are compared to males, the significance of intervening variables in mediating gender status is illuminated by further differentiation of the sample population. Once distinguished according to culturally meaningful social relations of consanguinity and affinity, and attendant status changes pertaining to the developmental cycle of the family, the incidence of *ᶜuzr* takes on a different significance. With a focus on dimensions of identity other than gender, Table 4.6 shows the higher frequency of *ᶜuzr* among members of the male category "brother of hh head," which contrasts with the low frequency of the illness among relatively powerful females, notably "mothers [of married sons]." Additional differences of particular significance are those which are manifest when gender identity is a constant. For example, among women, such differences exist between the category "mother [married sons]" and "son's wife."

Among the five household heads recorded as *maᶜzourin* in Table 4.6, two had experienced the first *dor* as children, two are sterile males, and one has been diagnosed epileptic by the physician. Of the six wives of household heads, four are barren women. Among daughters of household heads, the three recorded cases of *ᶜuzr* are those of young women subjected to forced marriage. As for the four cases reported for the brothers of household heads, these involve younger brothers who are economically dependent on their older male siblings. The only case of a *maᶜzoura* mother-in-law applies to an elderly and physically debilitated woman experiencing maltreatment at the hands of her son's wife after the breakup of her extended family. A similarly limited single case of possession illness in the sample population involves a daughter's husband who resides in his affine's household; he does not have the support of his own kinsmen and remains without access to independent means of livelihood. Finally, the largest percentage of *ᶜuzr* cases is, predictably, recorded for sons' wives in extended-family households. The subservience of this group of women to the authority of senior household members, whether male or female, is legendary.

Villagers are concerned with emotional distress and its somatization, but the physician's biomedical diagnosis of the health status of *maᶜzourin* is not generally informed by these priorities. Among villagers, explanations of a symptomatic person's illness may vary from the assertion of stressful experience by the symptomatic person to dismissal

TABLE 4.7   Percentage Frequency Distributions of CMI
            Psychiatric Ratings According to Sex and
            Relation to HH Head

	1	2	3	4
Rating		*Percentages*		
Sex				
Males	33.7	34.9	22.9	8.4
Females	27.7	34.7	23.8	13.4
Relation to HH head				
HH him/herself	28.7	30.9	25.5	14.9
Wife	27.0	41.9	23.0	8.1
Husband	0	50.0	0	50.0
Daughter	28.6	38.1	9.5	23.8
Son	34.4	32.8	26.2	6.6
Brother	37.5	56.3	6.3	0
Sister	22.2	55.6	22.2	0
Brother's wife	50.0	0	12.5	37.5
Brother's son	100.0	0	0	0
Brother's daughter	66.7	33.3	0	0
Son's wife	16.7	36.7	46.7	0
Mother (married sons)	46.9	31.3	15.6	6.3

of his/her claim as faking by a non-sympathetic household member. To
get a crude measure of individual villagers' *own perceived* health status,
defined both physically and psychologically, I utilized the Cornell Medical Index (CMI).

After its modification with the assistance of the physician, the CMI
consists of some 186 questions that collect extensive medical and psychiatric data corresponding to those elicited in a general medical history
(Scotch and Geiger 1963:305). In other parts of the world, the CMI has
been shown to yield accurate general medical and psychiatric diagnostic evaluations of patients (Broadman et al. 1951; Chance 1962; Finkler
1985a; Scotch and Geiger 1963). For its use in Fatiha I translated it into
Arabic, relying on the physician, who is familiar with local medical terminology and who has resided in the region of the village for some
twelve years. Upon his advice I also modified some questions and elimi-
nated others on the basis of their conceptual disjunction with local
medical culture.

Administration of the CMI was restricted to adult males and females
above fifteen years of age; they were actively involved in defining themselves as ill. In the case of younger persons, it is their older relatives who
help define their health status and label their afflictions. The CMI scores

(i.e., the number of symptoms reported by respondents) were rated on a scale of 1 to 4 by the psychologist. These CMI psychiatric ratings of sub-groups of the sample population, differentiated on the basis of the same social criteria used for the distribution of *ᶜuzr* in Table 4.6, are summarized as percent frequency distributions in Table 4.7. As shown for the incidence of *ᶜuzr,* which is associated with emotional distress, higher psychiatric ratings (indicative of respondents' perceived distress) correlate positively with positions of relative subordination.

As shown in Table 4.7, and similar to the pattern of the incidence of possession illness, higher psychiatric ratings (3 and 4) occur somewhat more frequently among women than among men. Yet, once again, as noted for *ᶜuzr,* perceived distress and associated social status are not simply a function of gender. Higher ratings among relatively larger proportions of husbands of female household heads, brothers' wives in fraternal joint households, and sons' wives suggest that intervening variables relating to the developmental cycle of the family and role expectations are operative. Hence, as shown in Table 4.8, there are relatively low psychiatric ratings among higher proportions of mothers of married sons and higher ratings among males and females who deviate from culturally stipulated role prescriptions, notably economically dependent males and childless males and females.

In sum, the distribution of *ᶜuzr* cases and psychiatric ratings presented in this section takes us beyond the cultural construction of

TABLE 4.8   Percentage Frequency Distributions of CMI Psychiatric Ratings According to Role Expectations

Rating	1	2	3	4
	Percentages			
Economic role				
Male breadwinner	35.0	36.3	21.7	7.0
Dependent male	0	0	40.0	60.0
Dependent female	28.3	35.3	24.9	11.0
Contributing female	36.8	42.1	15.8	5.3
Sexual/reproductive role				
Father	36.1	34.8	21.3	7.7
Sterile male	0	30.0	50.0	20.0
Father, daughters only	18.8	37.5	37.5	6.3
Father with sons	35.6	33.3	21.8	9.2
Mother	31.4	36.6	22.3	9.1
Barren female	3.7	22.7	33.3	40.7
Mother, daughters only	17.4	30.4	26.1	26.1
Mother with sons	30.9	31.8	28.2	8.2

male-female power differentials to illuminate the social mediation of gender identity, whether in relation to women or men. Both women *and* men in positions of relative powerlessness, when granted the social sanction of the sick role, are allowed temporary deviance from culturally prescribed role expectations and/or transgression of their positions of relative powerlessness. Yet, the low incidence of 34 cases of *ᶜuzr* in a combined group of 368 adult men and women suggests that the "making social" of claims to this culturally sanctioned strategy of indirect control is subject to structural constraints. When I expressed surprise upon hearing from a local healer that he only diagnoses "not more than four or five" new cases of possession illness per year, he responded: "What more do you want, otherwise the whole village would come to a standstill."

Notes

1. A taxonomy is "a culturally specific way of ordering and specifying a particular domain" and "also reflects (and may be taken to embody) a *theory* about how that domain is structured and works" (Fabrega 1976:195, original emphasis).

2. In utilizing the idea of levels of causation, Glick traces it to the work of W. H. R. Rivers (Medicine, Magic, and Religion), who distinguished agents of disease from the means employed and from their reasons for acting (Glick 1963:111). The concept was accorded further attention in the work of Hallowel, who differentiated three aspects of causation (proximate cause, technique, and agent), emphasizing that these cannot be considered as distinct causes but must be "related to some explicit and comprehensive scheme" (Hallowell 1935:366 as cited in Glick 1963:111; cf. Caudill 1953:722; Willin 1977).

3. Villagers are generally familiar with a variety of illness labels used by physicians, ranging from influenza to rheumatism, to illnesses of the spleen, jaundice, liver, and heart. This familiarity is in many ways attributable to the numerous post-1952 Revolution health education programs on radio, and later TV, as well as School Health programs which targeted rural populations.

4. *Tarba* is caused by supernatural beings said to appear in the shape of animals, including wild dogs and cows. Spirits may also appear to people in visions and frighten them during their sleep.

5. The list of illness dimensions found in this and other tables derives from unstructured interviews, including those associated with the pretesting of this and other questionnaires. The idea of evaluating the degree of consensus about illness correlates derives from Fabrega's work in Mexico (Fabrega 1970, 1974)

6. Other villagers express no knowledge of such differentiation and readily defer to this "carrier of the Quran."

7. Death from fire among crawling young children who are left unattended is also attributed to their supernatural siblings, who punish the mothers for leaving the child unsupervised. Two such cases took place during the study period.

8. Since husbands are also known to value children, such punishment may also be interpreted as targeting them for having caused their wives' sadness.

9. There is no general agreement among villagers, including healers, as to the actual mechanism through which supernatural beings inflict illness. Illness is attributed to their presence or to their supernatural "touch," but not to physiological or anatomical alterations.

10. Emotional disturbances resulting from interpersonal conflict are incriminated in the incidence of a variety of other misfortunes, sometimes extending to injuries of the external body. Khalil, who is a horse carriage driver, had a fight with his wife. He then left the house very upset and set out to the train station in the nearby town, where he was loading flour. His father said that because Khalil was not paying proper attention to his work, since he was thinking about his wife and her rudeness, he did not tie the horses securely and they moved, causing him to slip and injure himself.

11. The people of Fatiha have two labelled illness states which clearly illustrate Evans-Prichards' classic distinction between witchcraft and sorcery. He associates the former with persons possessing inherent power to harm and the latter with those who harm by tapping outside power. *Hassad* exemplifies the first type of power, and *ᶜamal bil marad*, the second.

12. In the case of the illness of *ᶜuzr*, a gaze may be isolated as an indirect cause of illness. A person affected by the evil eye becomes sad and depressed, thus predisposing him/herself to a "touch" (*lamsa*) by supernatural beings.

13. Villagers distinguish between different types of *ᶜamal* (deed). They refer to *ᶜamal bil marad* (deed for illness), *ᶜamal bil kurh* (deed for hatred), *ᶜamal bil nazif* (deed for hemorrhage), *ᶜamal bil mahaba* (deed for love). Furthermore, a sorcerer may write Quranic verses for loss of hair, back pain, impotency, hatred (e.g., between a woman and her husband), or loss of control which prompts a person to suddenly go berserk, hitting people within reach.

14. The terms *hadra* and *zar* are usually used interchangeably to refer to a ceremonial form of diagnosis/treatment where possessing spirits are enticed to speak through the possessed person. This is an important ritual in the protracted healing process which leads up to a *sulha* (reconciliation ceremony) where the demands of the possessing spirits are granted.

15. During the *zar* a variety of musical melodies are performed; each of these melodies is said to represent a specific supernatural personage When a *tariga* is drummed, it is believed that the corresponding spirit, couched in the body of the *maᶜzur/a*, induces its host/ess to react by dancing, often to the point of complete exhaustion and collapse.

16. Zahia's case is also instructive as illustration of how sickness legitimizes deviance from role expectations. When a friend tried to convince Zahia to see a physician, who might have found a remedy for her condition, the blind woman responded, "I would be ashamed to look people in the eye and to be able to see them. Then everybody would expect me to work and be like I used to [before becoming blind]." Some of Zahia's acquaintances believe that she is actually content with her state of blindness. They suggest that in this condition she obligates many people to look after her.

17. In explaining illness villagers may simultaneously refer to the diagnosis of a physician and that of a traditional diagnostician.

18. From the 1978 article, published in *American Ethnologist* 5(1), numer-
·ical data on *ᶜuzr* is reproduced here by permission of the American Anthropological Association. For a discussion of scholarship pertaining to the origins of
spirit possession in Egypt and a comparison between *ᶜuzr* in Fatiha and another Nile Delta village, see Morsy 1991.

19. These are the male and female terms for persons affected by *ᶜuzr*.

20. The alternative term *malbus* (worn or possessed) is seldom used by the
majority of villagers.

21. When confronted with a hypothetical case of the illness, and the possi-
bility that the *maᶜzur/a* may actually be faking and tricking other people, it is
explained that "the *ᶜuzr* comes only to the pure, it does not come to people
who trick others." In light of the negotiation of meaning in the course of
making social of illness, one cannot realistically anticipate such a response to
all claims of *ᶜuzr*.

22. An acquaintance of the *maᶜzura's* privately said to me, "It is because
she is jealous for her husband, she is afraid that he will marry another. He is
like a bull and she is yellow [pale] and ugly."

23. Persons joining such processions sway in a rhythmic fashion to the
loud singing of praises to God and the Prophet.

24. This personality test, developed by the collaborating psychologist
(Hakky 1974), is a projective instrument consisting of twenty photographs. Respondents are provided with a choice of four different responses, including a
non-restrictive one in which he/she may provide his/her own evaluation of
the situation depicted in the picture. Each of the four responses is given a
numerical score which estimates the degree of personality maladjustment.

25. It was the mother who always talked to me on her daughter's behalf,
even when the latter was present.

5

HEALTH CARE: PREVENTION, RESPONSE TO ILLNESS, AND THE SOCIAL CONTEXT OF HEALING

On a daily basis the people of Fatiha operationalize the popular proverb "prevention is better than cure" but admit to the inevitability of misfortune, including ill-health. In response to the latter, villagers rely on a variety of health resources, either serially or simultaneously. As with negotiations of claims to the sick role, the selective allocation of valued resources for the protracted process of healing is determined by the rank (*magam*) of the symptomatic person and by associated power relations. Although gender differentiation is a notable element of the organizational power which determines healing, this cultural construction is not without its social mediation. Choice of treatment is also determined by the progression of illness and its response to initial diagnosis and derivative treatment, as well as by the material requirements of different therapeutic interventions.

Concerned with healing and its constituent elements (Csordas and Kleinman 1990), this chapter maintains the focus on the underlying logic and social implications of the component traditions of medical pluralism in the village. This methodological emphasis takes into account the role of the state and the related implication of peasant status in health care.

Prevention

Among villagers, preventive health care occupies a prominent place. The written "words of God" are generally regarded as the most effective protection (*hirz*) against ill fortune, including all types of illness. Utterances of Quranic phrases are also repeated throughout the day to prevent misfortune. Traditional healers who are frequented for the diagnosis and treatment of illness are also visited for the explicit purpose of its prevention.

Concern over the potential threat of loss of health is reflected in daily conversations, idiomatic expressions, and the constant sharing of the advice "Health, protect it; it will protect you" (*Il siha, sunha, tisunak*). Other frequently pronounced idiomatic expressions include "May you be spared the bad fortune of illness" (*Yikfik shar il ᶜaya*); "Do not be sinful, spare yourself," i.e., rest yourself either physically or emotionally (*Haram ᶜalik, irham nafsak*); "May good health protect you," verbalized in response to a standard salutation (*Sa'alit ᶜalik il ᶜafiya*); "strength or good health," a standard form of greeting (*ᶜawafi*); "May God give you strength or good health," used in response to the greeting *ᶜawafi* (*Allah yiᶜafik*)."

The constant reference to health is matched by a variety of preventive measures against the onset of illness. In Chapter 3 reference was made to villagers' belief in proper nutrition, rest, avoidance of overindulgence in food, drink, and sexual activity for the preservation of the proper functioning of the body. In addition, they rely on the periodic ingestion of medicinal plants and pharmaceuticals for the maintenance of good health. Infusions of boiled herbs or inorganic salts (which are purchased from the pharmacy) are taken occasionally to "flush out" the body and get rid of undesirable elements, including worms and salts, which are believed to accumulate and form kidney stones. Prevention of the latter condition also involves occasional drinking of herbal teas, which are believed to "purify the blood" and remove any "crowding" which causes the precipitation of salts.

Prevention also includes immunization. Acting upon the directives of the Ministry of Health, the *ᶜumda* sends one of his men from house to house informing villagers of the day and time of vaccination. On the appointed day a clinic is held in the village headman's courtyard, attended by a physician from the Ministry of Health and an assistant. On this occasion children are vaccinated against the common childhood diseases. Although immunological mechanisms are not part of the repertoire of medical knowledge of the adults who bring or send infants to this makeshift clinic, this preventive measure is nevertheless much appreciated. Far from having any concern over "cognitive dissonance," a mother standing in line with her infant on her shoulder responded to my inquiry about her reason for bringing her infant with the remark, "It is useful, isn't it? That's all I have to know." Indeed, within the framework of medical pluralism, with its multiplicity of underlying explanatory models, biomedicine is but one additional alternative. Its conceptual inconsistency with other forms of diagnosis and treatment in no way undermines its valorization (cf. Kunstadter 1975). Like other biomedical procedures, vaccination is appreciated as a symbol of peasants' "enlightment" (*tanwir*) associated with the Nasser era.

Another complex of preventive measures is that employed to deter illness attributed to supernatural etiology such as the evil eye and sorcery. When the covetous gaze typical of the evil eye is noticed, the victim (or his/her adult relatives in the case of children) immediately murmurs to him/herself a specific Quranic verse which seeks the protection of God against the evil eye. People also verbalize such phrases as "in the name of God the merciful and the compassionate" (*bism e'llah il rahman il rahim*) on numerous occasions throughout the day. They pronounce such words on entering a house, on entering a dark room, on looking at a child or an admirable object, or even on looking at their own or other people's animals or farm products. People who fail to recall the name of God before stepping in a body of water predispose themselves to the attack of the supernatural subterranean creatures which inhabit rivers and ponds.

The written form of the Quran is believed to be even more powerful than verbal recitations. Physicians' clinics in the region of the village, as in Egypt's major cities, often have wall hangings with Quranic verses or narratives attributed to the Prophet (*hadith*). Literate healers in the village and elsewhere are frequented for the writing of charms (*hijab*) which are made of folded paper inscribed with Quranic verses. These are worn by children as well as adults. The wearing of a *hijab* is also associated with culturally marked life cycle events, including birth, the circumcision of boys, the graduation of a son or daughter from elementary or secondary school, and marriage ceremonies. In spite of some villagers' description of girls' circumcision as "Islamic," this ritual does not involve use of a *hijab*. Like other Quranic inscriptions, this is also distanced from menstruating women, who also do not pray or fast for the duration of their periods.

Bridegrooms often obtain a Quranic "shield" (*tahwita*) inscribed by a local healer before their wedding night. This form of protection is intended to prevent sorcery-induced "tying," expressed as sexual impotence. In addition, they often invite a village traditional healer who is rumored to be a sorcerer. This man is well fed and entertained by the family of the groom in an effort to neutralize his potential harm and to undermine the efforts of others who might commission his services.

In view of the pervasive danger of the evil eye, several prophylactic measures are employed as deterrents to its harmful influence. In their almost unceasing efforts to avoid the harmful effects of the *ᶜayn*, parents, particularly mothers, constantly understate their offsprings' positive assets. They complain about their children's ill health, their loss of appetite, and every other conceivable negative quality that may be associated with a child. This is particularly true for boys; mothers exercise greater care in performing regular preventive rituals for protecting male children than they do for their female siblings. Since male children are more desirable than females, boys may be dressed like girls, have their hair left to grow long, be called beggar (shahat), or even be called by girls' names.

Charms are also used to ward off the effect of the evil eye. Such charms include the verbal religious recitations noted above as well as object charms or amulets. The blue bead and the five-fingered hand[1] are used to protect children from the evil eye.[2] Protection from ills also involves the fumigation of a child with smoke from burning alum and tar combined with the *atar* from the suspected giver of the evil glance. The bursting crystals of alum and the melting tar symbolize the destruction of the evil eye.

Protection against the evil eye extends to adults and also involves undermining positive assets, including good health. Contrary behavior threatens health:

> Ali had lots of strength but he showed it off in front of everybody. He even placed bets with men to eat a glass jar and since that day he had been in great pain. He went to many doctors until he got to the army and they operated on him.

In prevention, as in treatment, women play a primary role as domestic health care providers (cf. Browner 1989; Ferguson 1986; McClain 1989). In the preparation of food, older women in particular are informed by preventive rituals for the avoidance of "pollution" (*nagasa*). In addition to uttering Quranic passages at the beginning of food preparation, some women take great care to wash their hands, particularly after handling urine or feces, whether their own or their children's. Some make a point of using their left hands to touch these bodily substances, reserving their right hands for the handling of food.

Through the discriminatory allocation of food noted earlier, senior women consciously exercise preferential protection of health. They are also instrumental in instructing children in preventive health care and in directing younger women towards a variety of preventive practices. Senior women's health management ranges from insistence on periodic cleansing of the water storage containers by junior women, including the use of alum, to the removal of waste from the vicinity of food and the preparation of charms for children. Whether as members of the same household or as neighbors, older women in particular give unsolicited advice about child health, whether in relation to nursing, ear piercing, or weaning.

Health Care Resources

In response to perceived compromised health the villagers avail them-selves of a multitude of health resources. These are summarized in Table 5.1 and include two major categories: household care and specialist care. Practices of the first category are associated with family members, particularly women, as well as neighbors and relatives. More serious cases of illness are brought to the attention of specialists. Within this category, villagers distinguish between traditional forms of diagnosis and treatment (*ᶜilag baladi*) and professional biomedical health care, which they refer to as the treatment of the physician (*ᶜilag il hakim* or *il doctor*).

Traditional healers are available within the village itself. If they fail to bring about the desired relief, the sick person and/or support group of family and friends (that Janzen terms "therapy management group" [1978]) may turn to a similar form of treatment available in nearby vil-lages or provincial towns. If necessary, still other traditional healers may be visited in major urban centers. Some of the more famous of these practitioners of spiritual medicine (*tib rawhani*) are located in the ma-jor cities of Cairo, Alexandria, and Tanta.[3]

The same pattern of gradual movement away from the village obtains for the utilization of cosmopolitan forms of medical care. When cure does not result from the medicine of the village paramedic, known as *halag il siha,* or the physicians of nearby towns, villagers seek this form of treatment in larger urban centers.

Household Health Care

The significance of the familial household labor process in produc-tion extends to reproductive activities of health care. In their initial response to illness, villagers rely on domestic care, which is often the only form of care administered to a symptomatic person. Although male and female members of households share knowledge of self-healing, including home remedies, it is women's duty to prepare and administer remedies. This is but part of their broader responsibility for the general well-being of all members of the family. As with prevention, it is women, and particularly older women, whether household residents, neighbors, or relatives, who play a major role in household care. Their authority in domestic health care is accorded cultural legitimation. The very pres-ence of older women (and men) in the household is rationalized as a blessing (*baraka*).

Women initiate diagnosis of illness and the acquisition of herbal medications and pharmaceuticals. Whereas men play a more promi-nent role in dealings with medical professionals (including those who

TABLE 5.1   Health Care Resources

I. Household health care
   Herbal remedies; prayers; purchase of pharmaceuticals; visits to religious shrines; midwifery[4]

II. Health care specialists
   A. Traditional healers (*ilag baladi*)
      1. *Tib Tabi^ci* (natural medicine)
         a. Arabic medicine (*tib ^carabi*): treatment of headaches, rheumatism, barrenness, poor eyesight, hernia, and fright (*Tarba*).
         b. Bone setter (*mijabarati*): setting of broken bones; massage and realignment of back, ankle, or shoulder.
         c. Herbalists: sale of herbs; advice on home remedies.

      2. *Tib Rawhani* (spiritual medicine): diagnosis and treatment of *^camal bil marad, hassad, ^cuzr*
         a. Diagnosticians: diagnosis of illness through practitioner's own possessing spirit. Diagnosis includes use of rosary, "opening of cards," and/or visions of precipitating causes of illness. Relatively limited power in dissolution of sorcery (*fak*).
         b. *Zar* organizers: performers of *dagga* (drumming) and *sulha* (reconciliation).
         c. Quranic diagnosticians/healers: usually literate males who diagnose and treat illness of supernatural etiology through knowledge of the Quran and control over supernatural servants (*khudam*). They also practice sorcery and utilize their *khudam* for the dissolution of sorcery.

   B. Cosmopolitan Medical Care
      1. Paramedics
         a. Sanitary barber (*halag el siha*): diagnosis, prescription of pharmaceuticals, administration of injections; male circumcision; tooth extractions.
         b. Nurse/midwife [*hakima*]: pre/post natal care; childbirth.

      2. Professional Medical Personnel (*^cilag il hakim/doctor*)
         a. Public health unit/hospital physicians: immunization; diagnosis and treatment of disease; prescription and dispensation of medication; surgery; obstetrics and gynecology; school health care program [*al-siha al madrasiya*]; dressing of wounds.
         b. Private physicians: diagnosis and treatment of disease; prescription of medication; house calls.
         c. Pharmacy: sale of pharmaceuticals, including contraceptives; sale of some packaged herbs; administration of injections; medical advice; dressing of wounds.
         d. Dentist: primarily tooth extractions.

evaluate their health status in the state's public productive sector), it is women who accompany other members of the household to traditional healers or shrines. They also bear primary responsibility for caring for the sick, including regulation of their diet. When pharmaceuticals prescribed by physicians are involved, men or literate male or female members of the household take a more active role in regulating the administration of medication.

Among themselves women share knowledge related to contraception, barrenness, male sexual potency, abortion, childbirth, and post-partum care. Older women help deliver infants in their own households, in neighboring households, or anywhere else in the village. Whereas women are far from reluctant consumers of cosmopolitan medical care, the majority of women continue to deliver at home. Under legal duress they have come to rely on medical and paramedical professionals, but only for what are perceived to be complicated births, and generally *after* attempts to deliver with the assistance of other village women fail. Even the women of the Turkish descendants prefer delivering at home with the assistance of a local midwife.

Local women have resisted the state's attempt to appropriate the traditionally female domain of midwifery by delegalizing the activities of local *dayas* (Nelson 1983:18–19) and defining pregnancy and birth as within the realm of responsibility of (primarily male) medical professionals or the Ministry of Health's female trained/licensed *dayas* and *hakimat* of public health care facilities. Even male literate villagers who advocate "modern medicine" consider older women the primary authority on matters related to childbirth. Remarking on his mother's role in managing his wife's delivery of their baby, a son acknowledges that "after all, she is more experienced in these matters, she has had fourteen children herself, she should know."

As with matters concerning childbirth, other health-related knowledge is not confined to a specific group in the village. Some information about the healing power of herbal infusions and popular pharmaceuticals even extends to some children. Knowledge of home remedies is freely exchanged among neighbors and relatives and shared by the herbalists of the weekly markets and the nearby towns with their clients from the village. Similarly, some people who are literate in Quranic knowledge provide villagers with charms free of charge. To some villagers the commoditization of this form of mutual aid undermines the healing power of the charms. As a patriarch explained:

A person who has *baraka* [blessing] is an intermediary between God and the sick person; he should not profit from this. My wife and I had lost nine children. We went to a sheik, he made us a *hijab* that we paid him for. But we still lost our children as soon as they were born. So I was sad and went to another sheik. He made me a *hijab* and my wife wore it. He would not charge me [money]. He said "I do this for my love of God. If I charged any money it would not be right." His *hijab* worked and now we have many children. His *baraka* is from his worship of God and from his generosity to people.

Home remedies used directly by the sick person or his/her family without the intervention of specialists include massaging with oil. For example, camphor oil or castor oil is used for pains in joints, including those described as rheumatism. Care is also exercised in the form of a special diet. "Light eating" is recommended for fever, and the ingestion of mint and watercress is advocated for heartburn. The afflicted person may be given boiled cumin for intestinal disorders; honey and milk are fed to those who are considered weak. Lemonade, guava leaves brew, and extracts of gum arabic are used to suppress coughs; crystalline sugar (*sukar nabat*) and sulphur (*kabrit*) are administered to those suffering from jaundice, and Coca-Cola is served to relieve indigestion.

Additional home remedies include the consumption of water in which fava beans have been soaked in the "pan of fright" (*tasit il tarba*) to overcome fright (*tarba*). In addition people make use of a variety of ointments and natural products for surface injuries (e.g., oil on burns; ground coffee or mud to stop the bleeding of a wound) and Quranic prayers (*ragwa*) against the evil eye.

Household-centered self-healing also involves the use of drugs purchased from the two pharmacies in the nearby town and aspirin from the local grocery store. The pharmacies are frequented by villagers who seek diagnosis of their own ailments or those of their family by describing symptoms to the pharmacist, who then recommends an appropriate medication. The pharmacist is also frequented by villagers who, having diagnosed illness either on their own or with the aid of relatives or neighbors, come to purchase the required medication. A variety of state-subsidized antibiotics and medications are available to villagers at low prices, and without prescription. Consequently, when a man feels out of sorts he may well "just go down and buy a couple of penicillin injections and have *halag il siha* give them to [him]."

Treatment of a sick person by members of his/her own or other village households may also involve visits to the shrines of holy men/women (*awliya*). It is believed that the mere presence of a person near the burial place of a holy person is enough to transfer blessing (*baraka*) to his/her ailing body (cf. Von Denffer 1976). This type of grace is available to villagers within the boundaries of their own community at the shrine of Sayeda Amna.

The shrine was built by a descendant of Tusun Bey in 1912 to com-
memorate the life of his third wife, a descendant of the pious Sidi
Ibrahim of Desuk, who is himself genealogically linked to the Prophet.
Like her ancestral Muslim "pious ones" (*wali*s or saints), Sayeda
Amna is believed to partake of God's *baraka*, passing it on to her
devotees to ward off misfortunes, including illness (cf. Eickelman
1989:289–301). Amna's miracles (*karamat*) are said to have been manifest when she was in her twenties. The first expression of her holiness
came during a quarrel with her husband. When he slapped her "his
arm stood still and the nerve would not move. His arm was not cured
until he begged her forgiveness and she finally massaged it for him while
reading verses from the Quran." After this "sign" Amna lived a life of
austerity, refraining from sexual intercourse and devoting her life to
reading the Quran. Her healing power was renowned during her lifetime
and still draws those seeking health from the village, and beyond, to her
shrine

In case the sick person is unable to visit shrines, a member of his/her
family makes a vow (*nadr*) on his/her behalf. When the plea for cure is
"answered" through the holy person's intercession with God on behalf
of the afflicted, the person who made the vow must fulfill it under threat
of continued misfortune, including illness to him/herself, the afflicted
person, or significant others.

Beyond the boundaries of the village, those seeking cures for illnesses
and a variety of other misfortunes, including spinsterhood, sterility, and
infant deaths, visit the nearby religious center of Disuk, the burial place
of a highly revered wali, Sidi Ibrahim, the namesake of the Burhamiya
Sufi spiritualist path (*tariqa*). The annual *mulid* held in Disuk, his place
of birth, commemorates his life and miracles. Some of the learned devotees of the *wali*, including a descendant, Sheika Faheema,[5] associate
some of his miracles with the Muslim victory over the Crusaders and
with the defeat of the Mongols at the hands of Baybars, the famous
thirteenth century Mameluke sultan. Like other *walis' barakas*, Sidi
Ibrahim's remains effective even hundreds of years after his death. His
power, and that of his current successor (*khalifa*), brings thousands of
people from different parts of Egypt to his annual *mulid* for a variety
of purposes ranging from commerce to healing.

To partake of Sidi Ibrahim's *baraka*, some villagers from Fatiha go to
serve in his shrine during the celebration of his *mulid*. A barren woman
explained that she would go to serve in Desuk so that the *baraka* of Sidi
Ibrahim might come on her and she would get pregnant. Of this holy
man other villagers say that "if a sick person goes to visit him, he need
only touch his tomb [*darih*] with his hand and he would be cured."

Traditional Health Care Specialists

Two major types of traditional health care specialists are accessible to the people of Fatiha: the practitioners of natural medicine (*tib tabi⁽i*), which bears resemblance to the ancient humoral traditions of the Mediterranean and Islamic worlds; and practitioners of supernatural medicine (*tib rawhani*) who partake of Sufi healing traditions.

Tib Tabiᶜi. Within the boundaries of the village itself, *(tib tabiᶜi)* is practiced by a woman of bedouin origin. The parents of this healer, whom some villagers refer to as Sheikit il ᶜ*Arab*,[6] originally came from Libya. She relies on the knowledge acquired through her mother, who was a healer herself, to treat health problems which she attributes to natural causes. People who frequent this healer may come complaining of any of a variety of illnesses which include headaches, rheumatism, barrenness, poor eyesight, hernia, and fright (*tarba*). Secondary to visiting more renowned bonesetters in adjacent towns, villagers also visit her for treatment of broken bones and other bodily dis-alignments. The sheika is also known for her practice of midwifery.

Unlike some other types of healers in the village, this practitioner of *tib tabiᶜi* does not claim any communication with the supernatural world and neither does she attribute her healing abilities to supernatural power (*baraka*). Nevertheless, villagers themselves attribute *baraka* to this healer, and they explain this not in terms of inherited supernatural healing power or reliance on supernatural servants but by reference to the fact that she is a good Muslim.

On her part, Sheikat il ᶜArab emphasizes her specialized knowledge about the care of the human body:

> I treat people who are sick and I also help deliver babies. I cut the umbilical cord and use some of the blood to push up the roof of the child's mouth so that he can eat properly; this is repeated after the fortieth day. . . . I inherited my mother's profession. My mother originally came from Libya. I used to watch my mother and I learned. For the person whose head hurts and who has tears coming down from his eyes, I use a nail, a hot nail in the middle of his head, then I put a piece of castor leaf on the burn. This stops the headaches and the tears. This headache could be from sadness or depression [*zahag*] and this brings about the boiling [*fawaran*] of the blood. The blood expands and rises to the head and it plugs up the eyes. When I iron on [cauterize] the head, the water secretion [*nashᶜ*] from the burn brings out the excess pressure and the person is relieved. . . . These days everybody goes to the doctor, but they come to me after the doctor cannot cure them. I never charge them anything but when they are cured they bring me a gift [*halawa*].

Although this healer defines herself as a specialist in illness of natural cause, it is worth noting that, like other villagers, her perception of illness causation is far from unidimensional:

All illness is from God. A person may get moisture when he is young and when he gets older the chill shows up as rheumatism and weakness. Dirt can also cause illness and people who eat or drink after a sick person also get sick. But illness is usually caused by sadness or depression. When people get upset all sorts of illness can come to them in many parts of their bodies. First they may go to the doctor or sometimes, if they have had experience with me, they come to me first. If the person's eye hurts, it is because the main vein in the head has excess blood and so I lift the vein and tie a thread around a person's ear. If the person has clouding over the eyes and cannot see well, I pass a thread in the back of the ear and this relieves pressure from one part of the body; pressure then has to be relieved from another part of the body. So if a tiny boy comes with an enlarged testicle because of trapped air from neglect and being left alone uncovered and crying, I do the same thing. The pressure on his lower body part is relieved by the thread in the back of the ear. When the doctor tries to relieve the pressure from an enlarged testicle he cuts the boy open and when he does this he may cut the vein of birth. On my part, if the two testicles are affected, I treat the two ears to relieve the pressure. For grown men of course I cannot examine them, so I ask. If it is the left testicle I take the left ear and if it is the right testicle I take the right ear. The men get this pressure from carrying heavy loads.

Regarding the treatment of broken bones, she explains,

I heat water. I feel the bone and I use hot pads to push the bones together. I use an egg and flour dough and I put a layer of this between a layer of rags. When this mixture dries it becomes just like the *gibss* [cast] of the doctor. But the doctor's treatment can harm the veins. On the third day I go to see the broken person. I use a spoon with oil to soften the dough, this moistens the veins and it allows the blood to run freely in the veins.

Sheikat il ᶜArab also treats *tarba*:

If a person gets frightened [*matrub*] I can know by looking at the lower lip, if it is yellowish I know that he is frightened [*marhug*]. The blood disappears from this area because of the shock and he may even be unable to father children. The blood dries up and he weakens very much. If he passes semen it is just like water. There is a cure for this. I iron on the bone of planting [ᶜ*admit il zar*ᶜ, i.e., the lower vertebra of the back]. The man should not have intercourse for forty days so that he should not bathe because if he bathes the water will prevent the healing of the wound. We want the wound to stay for a long time so that it will bring [out the] pus and pull out the yellow water from his body.

Unlike Sheikat il ᶜArab, who makes explicit her expertise in "natural" medicine, another female healer, also a descendant of bedouins who followed in the footsteps of her healer mother, claims knowledge of both natural and supernatural etiology. As a woman her practice of the former is limited to the touching of women's and children's bodies.

When someone is ill they come to me. I separate the egg white and yolk. I put the yolk on the body of a child and it spreads at the location of the pain. . . . The yolk spreads from the heat because this area is inflamed. . . . My mother was also a healer and taught me. I have visions of my patients before they come. My mother had learned the trade from her family; they were Arabs who used to iron and cure. . . . My clients are mostly children and women. I am a widow and so if men come to me other people will talk. But if a woman's husband is not well she tells me his symptoms and I tell her what to do for him after the vision.

Traditional healers who deal with illness from "natural" causes are also sought out by the villagers of Fatiha at the *mulid*s of nearby villages, and more importantly at the adjacent religious center of Disuk. There, during the celebration of the *mulid* of Sidi Ibrahim il Disuki, a variety of healers set up stalls in the large square surrounding the mosque, the site of the holy man's shrine. As in the case of Sheikat il ᶜArab, some of these healers who regard themselves as practitioners of "natural" medicine in fact rely on supernatural power in healing.[7]

For villagers who cannot travel outside the village, the services of itinerant practitioners of traditional healing represent an addition to their local pluralistic health care resources. Barren women, who "try everything," eagerly await the visits of such healers. In this regard, a well-known story among villagers relates to Sheik Badrawi, who "used to come and live [in the village] for months at a time and people would serve him their best food." The Sheik eventually lost "everybody's respect" when his efforts to deal with the desperation of childless women combined supernatural and natural treatment in a manner which villagers deem unacceptable. As Hanem, a childless woman explained,

People said that he knows about procreation [*khalaf*] so I went to see him at [a friend's house]. He told me to bring the leg of a camel which has [bone] marrow and to smear the marrow on two [pieces of] wool [*sufa*] to wear after my period and remove them when I unite with my husband then put them back in after [ritual] bathing. He said if this does not work I will tell you about another method [*wasfa*]. When I went back, he said, [on the basis of a supernatural vision], "your husband has nothing for women, I will put it in for you," which means that he wants to unite with me. He pushed me on the floor and lay over me but I screamed and yelled and pushed him and ran out. I ran and told the *ᶜumda* and the whole village found out. The scandal caused him shortness of breath and so he died.

Tib Rawhani. The second major type of traditional healing specialists, the practitioners of spiritual medicine (*tib rawhani*), are represented in the village by six persons. Diagnosis of illness by members of this group includes the "opening of the book" (the Quran) or cards and the "throwing" of the rosary.

In contrast to the direct treatment of the body associated with the practitioners of *tib tabiᶜi*, spiritualists (*rawhaniya*) diagnose illness and induce symptomatic relief through the manipulation of supernatural forces. Their concern with the mechanisms of bodily functions is minimal and they specialize in illness of supernatural etiologies, e.g., *ᶜuzr*, *ᶜamal*, and *hassad*.

During visits to *rawhaniya*, short of reliance on the *atar*, the interaction between the healer and the sick person may be minimal. Communication often involves the healer and the older person, male or female, who accompanies the sick person. The *rawhani* makes no attempt to examine the body of the sick person. Instead, his efforts focus on what Irvin Zola (1978) has described as "divulg[ing] the symptoms of daily living . . . habits and worries," for which the presence of the symptomatic person is not necessary.

As in the case of Sheikat il ᶜArab, whose very use of certain terminology (e.g., "yellow water") and knowledge of maintaining bodily equilibrium (e.g., by releasing excess pressure or excess blood) is reminiscent of historically antecedent naturalistic humoral medical traditions, the orientation of the *rawhaniya*, including registered Sufis who are frequented by the villagers, resembles that of the eighteenth and nineteenth century orders discussed in Chapter 1. Like their predecessors, and in addition to representing a contrast to desocialized biomedicine with its focus on organismic performance, the present-day spiritualists uphold the concern with emotional catharsis (Bates and Rassam 1983:69). Yet it is important to bear in mind that although this cultural continuity exists, the macro-social context in which traditional healers operate in 1974–1975 differs profoundly from that surrounding practices informed by the above-noted Arabic/Islamic traditions in earlier historical periods (cf. Gran 1979b).

Beyond the abstract contrast between the Islamic *shariᶜa* (literally, "the way") and attendant concern with "the well-being of the Islamic body politic" on the one hand and Sufi attendance to "the social and spiritual life of the individual . . . and . . . social groups" on the other (Eickelman 1989:289; see also Tibi 1990:23–24), the post-1952 years found the Sufi *tariqas* on a collision course with the state's program of Arab Socialism. Popular Sufism was disdained as the epitome of ignorance and backwardness; the state portrayed this form of spiritualism as an impediment to the country's progressive path (Gilsenan 1973, 1982).

While the political power of Sufi orders and their role in national political discourse has been effectively held in check, the importance of the popular form of their spiritualism in the everyday lives of rural people has not been terminated by any means. Although generally not recognized as Sufi per se, spiritual (*rawhani*) healing traditions continue to be significant to peasants as they cope with the health problems of their daily lives, which are not dealt with by the state's professional biomedical health care. To educated villagers who are propelled towards "progress," the Sufi *rawhaniya's* multiple paths (*tariqas*) to God in pursuit of health is not only an illegal act of practicing medicine (read hegemonic professional biomedicine) without a license but a sign of peasants' legendary "ignorance" and "backwardness."

Although clearly curtailed, during the post-1952 years, spiritualist activities were not terminated. Indications of selective tolerance on the part of authorities are in evidence. These coexist with regulation by agencies of the state. This is evident at major religious centers, and particularly on special occasions of celebrations of the *mulid* of one or another of Egypt's famous *walis*. This is the case at the Sidi Ibrahim il Desuki's *mulid*, to which villagers from Fatiha travel in pursuit of health resources. Here they obtain diagnosis and/or treatment at the hands of the many *rawhaniya* who gather during the week of celebrations.

In addition to the fact that the state has a permanent representative in the person of the *khalifa* (successor of Sidi Ibrahim) himself, who is a government employee receiving a token monthly stipend of 6 L.E., public funds are contributed to the purchase of sacrificial animals. A tent is also set up as a forum for speeches by officials. A police force of some 500 soldiers is sent to Desuk to maintain order among the thousands of people who come to the *wali's* burial place to partake of his *baraka*.[8] Moreover, the *nadr* of money and jewelry left in a collection box in the shrine, considered the property of the *khalifa's* household in the past, is now appropriated by the state treasury, which also allocates funds for the maintenance of the shrine and its grounds.

Whereas the *mulid* of Fatiha seems dwarfed in comparison to that of Sidi Ibrahim, whose miracles and renown surpass his local descendant/saint's power by far, the grand *mulid* in Desuk legitimizes the tradition of *mulid* celebration locally. Moreover, the renown enjoyed by the *rawhaniya* who attend the *mulid* reinforces the legitimacy of the local diagnosticians, *zar* organizers, and Quranic healers.

Diagnosticians

Among the practitioners of *tib rawhani*, there is a distinguishable sub-group of men and women whose talents are restricted to diagnosis. As a female member of this group explains: "If someone is *ma˓zur* or has *nazra*, I can tell from the cards. I only know how to identify the ˓*uzr* [then] I . . . send people to the specialists [for treatment]."[9] Those who have limited or no knowledge of the Quran base their diagnosis on communication with possessing spirits, the use of a rosary, and the "opening" of cards. To the healers whom I frequented, the details of the last two forms of diagnosis are considered "secrets of the trade," which they refuse to divulge. This is similar to the secrecy surrounding the specific Quranic passages used by sorcerers to summon the *khudam*. Such limitations aside, and in spite of the fact that, strictly speaking, their practices are considered illegal and described in the national press as charlatan (*dagal*), traditional healers are generally uninhibited in boasting of their ability to "see" that which is "hidden."

Among healers who themselves are *ma˓zurin*, the possessing spirit, now pacified, is enlisted in the diagnosis of the illness of others. As a possessed healer remarked, "The ˓*uzr* knows another ˓*uzr*." Thus, while the healing power of practitioners who are literate and who have memorized the Quran is generally acknowledged as greater than that of other healers, some diagnosticians claim that in the diagnosis of ˓*uzr* in particular "it is the ˓*uzr* which can recognize another ˓*uzr*." In other words, direct experience with affliction is itself a qualification for adoption of the role of diagnostician. As one *rawhani* reasoned, "This is why the doctor cannot identify the ˓*uzr*, because he himself is not *ma˓zur*." Indeed, to *rawhani* healers the outcome of medical treatment by a physician represents an important element in their judgement of the nature of the afflictions brought to their attention:

> The person goes to the doctor first. If the doctor's medicine does not bring about the desired cure he turns to the spiritual method [*tariqa al rawhaniya*]. . . . His family takes him to a ˓*araf*.[10]

Exemplary of healers' reliance on visions is the case of a local Sufi, a member of the Burhamiya order:

> When the sick person comes, I ask him where the pain is. I also ask if the pain moves around from one place to another. If it does, then I know

that it is *ᶜuzr*. I ask, "did you go to the doctor?" Then the patient says yes.
So I take her handkerchief and I keep it under my head for a night only
on Mondays and Fridays because these are nights which are blessed
[*mabruka*]. These are nights when the *awliya*[11] roam the world. When I
have the *atar*, I get a vision after my prayer. The vision is like a television
screen. I can see exactly what caused the patient's illness. It could be
that she could have had a disagreement with her husband. If he hits her
in a dark area, she may scream and become . . . possessed. Inhabitants
of the underground [*sukan il ard*] then enter her body. They do not remain in one place. This spiritual wind [*rih rawhani*] enters all her blood
system.

Zar *Organizers*

Once a person's illness has been diagnosed as spiritual (*rawhani*),
healers may recommend differing forms of treatment by other specialists, and some may administer the treatment themselves. Some
healers recommend that their patients go to the *hadra* (*zar*). Sometimes
a diagnostician may even accompany an afflicted person to the *hadra*.
When the suffering person's body responds (*yihim*) to one of the musical
tunes (representing the familiar *wali*s, their associates, or according to
some villagers, malevolent spirits of unknown origins), he/she gets up
to dance. This continues up to a point when the dancer reaches what is
regarded as an altered state of consciousness. At this point the sheikh
proceeds to ask the possessing spirit where he/she comes from and
what his/her demands are. The spirit responds by saying that he/she
comes from one of the shrines of the famous *wali*s which are found
throughout Egypt or beyond. Speaking through the mouth of the afflicted person, he/she/they describe(s) the circumstances under which
he/she/they came to the sick person. The possessing spirit(s) also set(s)
the conditions for reconciliation (*sulha*) and attendant relief of the
afflicted from the ravishes of illness. The demands made by the spirit(s)
are generally to the personal advantage of the *maᶜzour/a*.

At the *sulha* the demands of the *assyad* are met. In addition to dress-
ing up the sick person in the expensive items of clothing and/or jewelry
demanded by the *assyad*, his/her family may be required to make sacrificial offerings of poultry or cattle. During this ceremony the *maᶜzour/a*
is also reminded to honor his/her promise (*ᶜahd*) to the *assyad*. He/she
is asked to reiterate a commitment to paying regular visits to the *hadra*
and joining the *tariga* of the possessing spirit in the dance arena. It is
expected that the *assyad* no longer cause physical discomforts to their
host/ess after the *sulha*. But their action may be triggered again under
distress (*taht zaᶜla*).

In association with the *zar* there is a distinguishable subgroup of *rawhaniya* who organize *zar* ceremonies.[12] Such groups also arrange private drumming sessions (*daga*) if the sick person is unable to go to the *hadra*. Usually the *zar* ceremony is recommended by a healer, but in some cases members of this second group may be diagnosticians themselves. Relying on the power of spirits which possess them, they may also be the ones who perform the *sulha*.

Quranic Diagnosticians/Healers

A third subgroup of practitioners of *tib rawhani* are those who are not necessarily *ma'zurin* themselves but command supernatural servants (*khudam*) through their knowledge of the Quran. Members of this group have the power to diagnose illness, cause it, and also "dissolve" it, as in cases of sorcery.[13] Their powers also include the capability of alleviating pain attributed to spirits.

A literate healer describes his method thus:

> The knowledgeable one [*'araf*] takes the *atar* in which is wrapped some money. The *'araf* measures the handkerchief after reading a passage. . . . This involves resolve [*'azima*] on the part of the reader of the Quran, any *sura* of the Quran . . . [which] is all *baraka*. The change in the length of the handkerchief determines the type of illness. If it becomes short it means that the illness is from the *jinn*, it is from *lamsa ardiya*. If it becomes long, the cause is from a human [*inss*]. This means a human gaze [*nazra insaniya*, i.e., the evil eye]. If it remains the same then the illness is from Allah; it means that the illness is due to bodily dysfunctions which are natural. If it is *nazra ardiya*, the pain is mobile. In this case a *zar* ceremony is performed and the person descends the *hadra* [literally "presence," i.e., presence of the possessing spirits] on a specific *tariga* or on any *tariga*. After two or three *hadra*[s] the *assyad* start to talk through the mouth of the affected person. At this time the pain becomes more severe and the *assyad* start to make their demands known. If the cause of the illness is *nazra insaniya*, the pain is localized, not necessarily in any specific part of the body.

Members of the literate group of practitioners who have studied and memorized the Quran consider themselves the only true practitioners of *tib rawhani* and refer to some other practitioners as "nothing but musicians." As a learned carrier of the Quran (*hamil il Quran*) remarked, "It is true that *'uzr* is recognized by another *'uzr* but the power [*baraka*] of the Quran is above everything else." Indeed, the power of this healer and of other healers of his caliber is the object of cultural sanction, given the "authority of learning" in Muslim society (Eickelman 1989:304–315). Whereas the political authority of the religious establishment was held in check under Nasser (Tibi 1990:140), this in no way undermined the authority of Islamic texts, and more generally, for peasants, the power of the written word.

Although the treatment of illness of sorcery (ʿamal bil marad) is sometimes undertaken by practitioners who are maʿzurin and who command their possessing spirits to diagnose the illness, it is generally assumed that rawhaniya with knowledge of the Quran are better able to dissolve sorcery (yifuk ʿamal). One such practitioner recalled his latest case of dissolution:

> She had a hemorrhage. She went to Dr. Badr and stayed in his clinic for ten days, but to no avail. She came back here [to the village] and got worse. They sent for me. I knew right away that it must be sorcery [because of the continued bleeding after injections]. I wrote her three papers [i.e., Quranic charms]. She wore one in the hem of her dress, another in the back, and a third under her navel. Within less than an hour the bleeding stopped. . . . I cannot know who did [the sorcery]. Only with fat'h il mandal one can find out. . . . This means that I bring a cup with a drop of olive oil and a child, a male, who has not reached puberty. The child looks in the cup and the rawhani reads a ʿazima and the child sees the khadam and they show him a view of who did it. . . . I don't want to do this [procedure] because it brings hatred between people.

When I checked the sheikh's account with the woman who had suffered from the severe case of bleeding, she confirmed his narrative, corroborating his claim that her bleeding stopped less than an hour after the sheikh's charms (hijiba) touched her body. Unlike the sheik, she showed no reluctance in charging her future mother-in-law with sorcery. She did not blame the rawhani for not attempting to reveal the identity of those who commissioned the sorcery against her.

Villagers generally agree with healers' wisdom of concealing the identity of persons who initiate sorcery against adversaries. As one woman reasoned, "[The rawhani] never tells people [about] who made the ʿamal for them. Otherwise people will all start killing each other, and he will be blamed. People of course can guess who is the one who went to a sheik for ʿamal against them."

Whereas villagers generally agree that the diagnosis of spiritual illness (marad rawhani) can be undertaken by anyone who has been himself/herself maʿzur/a and who maintains control over possessing spirits, this expectation does not extend to treatment. It is believed that treatment of spiritual illness, particularly sorcery, is more effective at the hands of those who have good knowledge of the Quran. All things being equal, including the "comfort" experienced by the sick person or members of his family with one or another healer, this implies differential valorization of the healing power of literate healers, who are more likely to be men.

Given the higher rates of illiteracy among rural women in general, female practitioners seldom enjoy the prestige of literate males. The basis of their relative devaluation is not their gender per se, as suggested by the villagers' reverence toward the village's female saint, but blocked access to a culturally valued power base, literacy. Nevertheless, there are exceptions to the association of literacy and its attendant prestige with men. This is so in the case of some learned women who practice in the vicinity of the shrine of Desuk. It is of their knowledge of the Quran that villagers boast when recommending them to relatives and friends in distress.

In terms of actual experiences with specific healers, villagers' rationalizations of their preference for one healer or another draw upon culturally meaningful constructs pertaining to age and gender identity. Accordingly, it is said that "the longer a spirit possesses a person, the stronger it becomes. It matures in the body of the person. The strength of the healer depends on the strength of the *assyad* that are possessing him." Such preference for seasoned spirits also applies to the length of association that other types of healers have with the *khudam* at their command. Similar cultural preference pertains to gender. As one man remarked, "[T]he sheika was the only one who can cure me. She is the sibling of [*mikhawiya*, i.e., possessed by] Sheik Mussa, not like [the healer] Sheik Hassan, who has [i.e., is possessed by] a woman."

Aside from their claim of supernatural powers, practitioners have no distinguishing social characteristics. With the exception of literate practitioners, the *rawhaniya* resemble other older peasants in terms of social attributes. None of the village medical practitioners are full-time specialists. With the exception of one, who is the master of the *kutab*, they are all peasants who till the land. This includes one *rawhani* who is also a carpenter. The amount of land they own is typical of the majority of peasants in the village. The male practitioners are married and have children.

Female *rawhaniya* in the village are all widowed. One of them suggests that their status as widowed women is probably coincidental. However, she remarks that "when a woman is younger she is more occupied with her young children and if men come to her house [for diagnosis], people may talk." Another female practitioner explains that when a woman gets older she becomes more mature (*rasya*, i.e., settled or more reflective), "like a man." Still another *rawhaniya* says she resorted to healing as a way of making a living:

[My husband] died during the [early] days of the Revolution, during the days of Muhammad Naguib. I did not get a pension or anything. I had only one daughter. I did not remarry The assyad came to me right after he died . . . then God blessed me and I started working the *atar*s.

Female practitioners' reasons for their practice of healing extends to males. For both sexes there is no fixed pattern of recruitment to the healing role. Conditions under which the role of healer was adopted by village practitioners include possession illness, a call through vision, and adoption of an older relative's specialty. As for the *rawhaniya*'s knowledge of compromised health, there is evidence to suggest that they do not share a body of specialized knowledge which distinguishes them from other members of the community. Following Fabrega and Silvers' example of determining the extent of shared medical knowledge about illness manifestations among *h'iloletik* and laypersons in Zinacantan (Fabrega and Silvers 1973), I administered a questionnaire to the six practitioners of *tib rawhani* in the village, and to a control group consisting of an equal number of non-practitioners matched for age and socio-economic status. The percentages of each group of respondents who provided positive associations between illness dimensions (related to causation and physical manifestations) and three states of illness (*hassad*, *ᶜuzr*, and *amal bil marad*) are summarized in Table 5.2.

TABLE 5.2   Comparison of *Rawhaniyas'* (R) and Non-Practitioners' (N.P.) Consensus on Illness Dimensions Associations

Illness Dimensions	% Positive Association Hassad		% Positive Association ᶜuzr		% Positive Association ᶜamal	
	R	N.P.	R	N.P.	R	N.P.
Cause						
Instrumental						
1. Nat. envir. & subs.	0	0	0	5	0	5
2. Phys. constitution	0	0	17	9	0	0
3. Spirit intrusion	0	5	100	100	0	0
4. *Hassad* [gaze]	100	95	17	19	0	0
5. *ᶜAmal* [sorcery]	0	0	0	0	100	100
Efficient						
1. God	0	5	0	14	0	5
2. *Hassid* [witch]	100	100	17	23	0	0
3. *Assyad* [spirits]	0	0	100	90	0	0
4. *Sahir* [sorcerer]	0	0	0	5	100	100
Ultimate						
1. Sadness	0	0	100	100	0	0
2. Anger	0	10	83	90	67	57
3. Jealousy	100	100	17	10	100	95

(continues)

TABLE 5.2   (continued)

Illness Dimensions	% Positive Association Hassad		% Positive Association ᶜuzr		% Positive Association ᶜamal	
	R	N.P.	R	N.P.	R	N.P.
4. Hatred	100	100	0	10	100	100
5. Punishment by God	0	0	0	0	0	0
6. Fear	0	0	84	86	0	0
Physical symptoms						
1. Weakness	100	100	100	100	100	100
2. Headache	100	100	100	100	100	100
3. Aches all over	100	100	100	100	100	100
4. Trembles	67	43	50	52	33	57
5. Hot-cold spells	55	19	33	19	33	29
6. Cough	17	5	50	14	17	5
7. Chills	17	5	50	29	17	15
8. Nausea	33	10	50	33	50	24
9. Weight loss	67	29	100	76	100	95
10. Vomiting	33	14	50	24	17	19
11. Swelling	0	5	50	33	17	29
12. Loss of balance	33	29	50	71	50	71
13. Difficulty in breathing	67	43	67	71	17	48
14. Lump in throat	50	19	67	57	0	24
15. Diarrhea	0	0	0	5	0	29
16. Fever	67	38	33	43	17	38
17. Pain in joints		62		90		67
18. Earache	33	19	67	67	50	48
19. Watery eyes	67	43	50	71	50	52
20. Rash	0	5	17	14	0	14
21. Back pain	50	48	67	86	100	76
22. Dizziness	67	76	83	95	83	86
23. Chest pains	17	14	67	57	17	38
24. Stomachache	17	10	67	57	17	33
25. Excess blood in body	0	0	0	10	0	10
26. Excess water in body	0	0	0	5	0	0
27. Drying of blood in body parts	67	57	83	67	100	76

As in the case of the indigenous Indian *h'iloletik* of Zinacantan, the *rawhaniya* of Fatiha do not appear to rely on specialized, exclusive knowledge. Among the *rawhaniya,* as among non-practitioners, a high degree of consensus obtains with regard to illness causation relative to consensus on the association of physical symptomatology. Healers tend to associate some of the latter with illness states more frequently than do non-practitioners. On the basis of unstructured interviews, this difference may be attributed to healers' assertions that the harmful effects of supernatural forces on humans is infinite. In diagnosis, as in treatment, specific physical symptoms are far from central.

As with symptomatology, the specific mechanism by which supernaturally caused illness is precipitated is by no means a subject of complete agreement among the *rawhaniya* themselves. Thus with regard to *ᶜuzr*, although Table 5.2 displays complete agreement with regard to implicating spirit intrusion, as is the case among non-practitioners, there is no agreement about the precise operation of the supernatural creatures on the human body. While one diagnostician may assert that the spirit itself does not actually reside in the *maᶜzurla's* body ("or else it would burn it completely"), and that it is simply the "wind" (*aryah*) which actually enters the human body, another practitioner provides a diametrically opposed description. When I asked about the process by which the *assyad* inflict physical pain on the *maᶜzurla* and whether it is only the wind of these spirits which is responsible for the pain, a female diagnostician responded,

> Of course it's not only the wind, they themselves come inside the person and control the person and put him in a daze. People cannot feel themselves. The *assyad* move from one place of the body to another. They go from the head to the heart, to every part of the body. The doctor doesn't know them. No doctor will ever know them. People become well only in happiness.

The *rawhaniya* themselves do not claim any specific knowledge about the functioning of the body. In response to my inquiry of this matter, one of them answered,

> I do not know anything about these things, I only know about spiritual illness [*marad rawhani*]. This [knowledge of the functions of the human body] is the work of the doctor. The doctor does not know the symbols of the rosary [a form of diagnosis followed by this spiritualist]. . . . The doctor recognizes the physical illnesses which come on suddenly. Spiritual illness comes on gradually. The person with *marad rawhani* does not necessarily become ill right after the *assyad* come to him, that is why people do not remember.

Villagers who are not healers also believe that the *rawhaniya* are not distinguished by specialized knowledge. While recognizing the special association of *rawhaniya* with supernatural powers, on which they depend in diagnosing and treating illness, villagers generally believe that the diagnosis of such illness on the basis of symptomatology can also be undertaken by non-healers. For example, when a villager told me that her neighbors had advised her to go to the *hadra* and when I inquired about how her neighbors were able to diagnose her illness, she responded, "Because the same cases have happened to many other people before me and everybody knows these symptoms and what they mean."

In light of such reasoning, frequenting the *rawhaniya* may represent an attempt on the part of the symptomatic person and his/her family to legitimize the sick role through reaffirmation of their own evaluation of the illness state. In fact, it is possible to actually start the process of pacification of the spirits through attending the *hadra* without the assistance of a *rawhani*.

Deprived of the legitimacy endowed by formal specialized diagnosis, or legitimation of claim to the sick role by significant household members, a *ma^czour/a* attempts to dispel charges of faking illness. In the *hadra* she may sing a song entitled "They Blamed Me" (*Lamuni*). The song goes, "Why do you blame me? Oh free one, oh free one, what is your concern with me? Tomorrow [i.e., in the future] you will see what will befall you and what happened to me will happen to you." While some adversaries' hearts may be softened by such moaning, for others, nothing less than a reputable spiritualists' judgement may be necessary

Far from being a monopoly of specialized knowledge of illness causation and symptomatology, spiritualists' cultural capital entails the reputation of access to the supernatural realm and religious literacy. It is on these bases that they extend legitimacy to the sickness role and attendant deviations from role expectations.[14] Moreover, the *rawhaniya* accumulate a tremendous amount of information about the members of their community; they make very good listeners. Their familiarity with local culture, along with their eagerness to inquire about "the well-being" of others, allows them to anticipate the types of problems which people of different social identities in the village are likely to bring to their attention as the basis of their distress and subsequent illness.

It is also important to point out that the *rawhaniya* are not reluctant to modify their diagnosis of illness as the need arises. They change their assessment as new information about the sick person comes to their attention. Thus while Sheika Aziza had attributed Fat'heya's barrenness to *^cuzr* on the occasion of my first visit to her in the company of Fat'heya, a few months later when rumors of the *ma^czoura*'s pregnancy spread through the village, the sheika changed her diagnosis. Taking credit, she assured Fat'heya that the *assyad* had been barred (*inhagazu*) from her and that she would have a child within the year. Far from pointing to the sheika's contradictory prognosis (possibly to avoid the harm that the healer might have inflicted on the unborn child), Fat'heya eagerly accepted the healer's vision.

In sum, the power of the *rawhaniya* does not rest on their specialized knowledge of illness causation or symptomatology of illness, nor even on a shared view of the mechanisms of illness precipitation. It is derived from their culturally valued control over elements of the supernatural realm. This lends their diagnosis of illness its authoritative, legitimizing character. The reproduction of spiritualists' culturally legitimated claim to supernaturally derived power involves a marked level of knowledge of their social surroundings. They are well-tuned to local culture, the distress associated with asymmetrical power relations, and the role of these societal elements in the precipitation of illness.

Villagers do not anticipate complete cure at the hands of spiritual healers. This is understandable in light of the structural embeddedness of afflictions brought to the attention of the *rawhaniya*. What people do expect is disclosure or confirmation of culturally meaningful events which precipitate ill-health. They also expect a *rawhani* to negotiate cessation of pain inflicted by the spirits. Although the healer's pronouncement of precipitating events legitimizes temporary transgression by symptomatic individuals, it simultaneously reinforces the structural relations which generate illness and its attendant deviance.

Far from having specialized medical knowledge, healers have the ability to weave coherent scenarios of culturally meaningful processes of illness production from the disparate elements of events, social profiles, and experiences. These are not necessarily provided by symptomatic persons themselves but may be presented even in their absence by kin, other companions, or neighbors.

The *rawhaniya*'s ability to provide coherent interpretations of their social environment is manifest beyond the context of diagnosis/ treatment. In an attempt to assess the *rawhaniya*'s capacity to impose coherence on equivocal representations, I administered a modified form of Shweder's cognitive capacity test to all the *rawhaniya* in the village, and to a control group of non-practitioners.

Richard Shweder's test provides an experimental procedure whereby the cognitive capacities of traditional healers could be systematically compared with those of lay individuals partaking of the same cultural tradition (Shweder 1968). In accordance with this procedure, all six of the village *rawhaniya* and twelve non-practitioners matched for sex, age, and socio-economic status were presented with four series of photographs depicting objects and scenes which are familiar to the local population. I showed each of the respondents four series (A, B, C, D) of photographs of a *sagya* (water wheel), a field of cotton, a man ploughing, and a party of cotton pickers. Each series had been developed through six different stages of clarity ranging from a complete blur in the #1 photograph of each series to a well-focused scene in the #6 photograph. All the pictures were arranged and presented to respondents as six consecutive rounds. The first round included all #1 photographs of each of the four scenes. The second round included all the #2 photographs of each of the four series and so on, with the last round being composed of the perfectly focused photographs of each of the four scenes. For photographs of series A and C, respondents were told to describe what they saw in each photograph only if they were sure of what each of the photographs represented. They were instructed to give the answer "I don't know" in cases where they were not sure of the representations in the photograph. For series B and D, respondents were presented with alternative answers. For the *sagya* of the B series, respondents were told that the photograph might represent a stack of hay, the dome of a mosque, or a *sagya*. Similarly, in the case of series D, the scene of a man ploughing, respondents were asked to choose between the alternatives of an animal turning the *sagya*, a bridge, a man ploughing. As in the case of series A and C, respondents were asked to describe what they saw only if they were sure; they were instructed to say "I don't know" if they were not. The objective of the test was to determine which group (practitioner or non-practitioner) was more inclined to impose form and order on the blurred and ill-defined scenes illustrated in the photographs, and which group would provide the response "I don't know" more readily.

As in the case of Shweder's *h'iloletik*, the *rawhaniya* offered the response "I don't know" less frequently (see Table 5.3). For the photographs where alternative choices were offered, the *rawhaniya*, when they did not provide the right answer, showed a greater inclination for guessing rather than saying, "I don't know." Moreover, in providing such guesses, they sometimes also provided answers which were not included in the alternative choices of the experimental procedure. This greater inclination on the part of the *rawhaniya* to impose coherence on the ill-defined representations of the photographs is consistent with their expected role of imposing coherence when presented with fragmentary information surrounding an illness episode.

Cosmopolitan Medical Care

Within the village, cosmopolitan medical care is available from a sanitary barber (*halag il siha*) who has received informal training at the hands of physicians. As noted in Chapter 1, professional medical treatment is also obtained by the villagers from private physicians and the government health clinic and hospital in the nearby town and in other provincial towns.

TABLE 5.3   Practitioners' and Non-Practitioners' Responses to Shweder's Test (percent of responses)

Photograph	"I don't know"		Imposed Structure	
	P.	N.P.	P.	N.P.
Series A				
1	50	75	50	25
2	33.3	75	66.6	25
3	16.6	50	83.4	50
4	0	18.3	100	81.7
5	0	0	100	100
6	0	0	100	100
Series C				
1	50	58.4	50	41.6
2	16.6	50	83.4	50
3.	0	16.7	100	83.3
4	0	8.3	100	91.7
5	0	0	100	100
6.	0	0	100	100

	Correct Answer		Guess		"I don't know"	
	P.	N.P.	P.	N.P.	P.	N.P.
Series B						
1	16.6	8.3	50	50	33.3	41.6
2	0	16.6	83.4	25	16.6	58.3
3	50	41.5	50	8.3	0	49.8
4	66.6	48.3	33.3	25	0	16.6
5	83.4	83.4	16.6	16.6	0	0
6	100	100	0	0	0	0
Series D						
1	0	0	66.6	50	33.3	50
2	0	16.6	83.4	58.3	16.6	25
3	66.6	41.6	33.3	58.3	0	0
4	66.6	75	33.3	25	0	0
5	100	100	0	0	0	0
6	100	100	0	0	0	0

The nearby hospital has 80 beds. It is staffed by a physician/director, 2 surgeons, 2 residents, 1 endemic disease specialist, 2 dentists, and a nursing staff of graduates from the governorate school of *hakimat*. In addition to having X-ray facilities and a clinical laboratory, the hospital houses a School Health unit. A Child Health Center is located in a nearby building. This is staffed by a physician, a pharmacist, and one senior *hakima,* who is assisted by 7 juniors. Some women from Fatiha frequent this center for prenatal care, and the *hakimat* are available for assistance with birth in the village itself. The center also provides checkups for infants and informs the *cumda* of the due dates for vaccinations. After the age of five, children become the responsibility of the School Health Unit.

The most desirable form of cosmopolitan medical treatment which the peasants aspire to is that of a private physician. The most accessible cosmopolitan medical services, including those of private physicians, are located in the nearby town, about three kilometers from the village. Two private physicians and a dentist in this town are frequented by the villagers. Dr. Mikhail is by far the most popular among them.

The clientele of Dr. Mikhail is composed of approximately 25% women, 25% children, and 50% men. This distribution is largely a reflection of peasants' greater willingness to invest resources for the curing of men. It is said that men are the breadwinners and that if they are not healthy, the life of the whole family falls apart. This preferential care begins with early age, as parents are more likely to allocate scarce cash for the cure of male as opposed to female children.

According to Dr. Mikhail, among children the most common health problems in the summer are due to enteritis. Intestinal inflammations due to bacterial and protozoan sources are more prevalent in the cases of young children than is the dysentery due to parasitic worms. In winter bronchial inflammations are the most frequent afflictions. It is also estimated by the physician that 20–30% of the sick children brought to his clinic are diagnosed as suffering from malnutrition. Conjunctivitis is also prevalent among children in the summer. Among adults, approximately 20% suffer from pellagra, and bronchial asthma is widespread.

The distribution of bilharziasis reaches nearly 100% according to Dr. Mikhail. As secondary effects of bilharzia parasitosis, liver and spleen enlargement and cancer of the bladder are diagnosed frequently in males. Common among males also are a variety of renal ailments and urine disturbances which are also identified by the physician as secondary effects of bilharziasis. He reports that a large proportion of his older adult clientele suffer from arteriosclerosis, bronchitis (in winter), and diarrhea. In all age groups in the summer, nearly 70% of all cases examined by the physician are diagnosed as malaria. Around the time of insecticide spraying people visit the physician's clinic with complaints of vomiting and diarrhea.

A survey of responses to illness over a one-year period, which I conducted among the adults of the sample households population, shows that beyond the family context, the physician is by far the number one choice of the villagers (see Table 5.4). One may note with wonder such a result under the assumption of consonance between the underlying

TABLE 5.4   Utilization of Different Forms of Medical Treatment

Medical Personnel or Treatment	Order of Choice	Number of Patients
Physician	1st	69
	2nd	25
	3rd	0
Halag Siha	1st	15
	2nd	4
	3rd	0
Rawhaniya	1st	1
	2nd	12
	3rd	1
Public clinic	1st	5
	2nd	3
	3rd	0

logic of illness explanations and treatment strategies. Distanced from the social causation which the villagers themselves consider central, the physician's probing questions center around the body, with minimal, if any, consideration of interpersonal relations and psychological disposition. The physician's medical logic, which derives from a naturalistic theory of illness and an associated ontological conception of disease, certainly contrasts with villagers' medical explanatory models, which accommodate social, naturalistic, and supernaturalistic elements. Yet biomedical treatment is greatly valued. Evidently what is important for the villagers in choosing the physician's treatment, when they do, is not its underlying logic but the obvious fact that such treatment is effective.

Beyond the significance of cosmopolitan medical care as an indicator of the state-regulated program of "progress," choice of medical treatment rests on the immediate requirements of relief of suffering rather than on the conceptual compatibility of logical categories underlying different forms of treatment. Indeed, as the villagers put it, "Illness comes from a mountain and health comes from the eye of a needle."

The Hierarchy of Resort to
and Dynamics of Treatment Choice

Villagers generally utilize cosmopolitan health care facilities for symptomatic relief. Disorders which are considered directly related to socially significant ultimate causes are viewed as requiring the expertise of a traditional healer. In this regard it should also be emphasized that, unlike the physician whose domain is strictly medical, traditional healers are frequented for a variety of misfortunes ranging from loss of prized possessions to marital conflict to barrenness and sterility, along with a variety of problems involving interpersonal conflicts and tensions. These problems are not isolated from a person's state of health, which is seen as influenced by any one of such distressful events and conflicts in daily life.

Villagers do not perceive cosmopolitan medicine to be in conflict with their other forms of health care. They point to the complementarity of different health care resources. In some cases people continue to take the *migawiyat* (strengthening substances) of the physician, wear the *hijab* (charm) of the sheikh, and visit the shrine of a *wali* or even a Christian church, all in the pursuit of the reversal of a state of ill-health. Traditional healers themselves frequent physicians for symptomatic relief:

> I vomited and then they sent me the ambulance. Three doctors checked me and said that I must take injections. Dr. Ahmad [the director of the hospital] said "I'll let you stay but don't take my business from me." The sheikh Yassin [her possessing spirit] came and Dr. Ahmad asked him if I can take injections and medicine, he said "yes." They gave me hospital clothes to wear but my body could not stand them. Then they agreed to let me wear my clothes. I stayed for twelve days . . . all my loved ones from . . . [Fatiha] came to visit me.

This *rawhaniya* also claims that Dr. Ahmad believes in a division of labor between physicians and *rawhaniya* and that he recommends her services to some of his urban friends.

Villagers also distinguish between the expertise of traditional practitioners and physicians; they have different expectations from these two groups of health care specialists. This is illustrated by Dr. Isma⁽il's house call; he came to the village to examine Sabha's daughter. He did not prescribe any medication and told the mother to take her daughter to the *hadra*. Sabha became furious. Refusing the physician's advice, she said, "I am bringing a doctor, not a *sheikh*. I expect you to prescribe medicine."

The social context in which the label "sick" is to be publicized is an important consideration in the selection of healers. For example, whereas a barren woman is likely to frequent a healer to obtain such legitimization, the physician is necessarily the choice of an agricultural cooperative worker who does not show up for work. As a government employee, he is obliged to seek dispensation from role obligations by someone whose credentials are acceptable to the worker's superiors. In short, the specific form of legitimation depends on the specific power domain in which the label "sick" is to be displayed.

The valorization of biomedical specialists' technical competence does not detract from villagers' resentment of maltreatment at the hands of this group of privileged compatriots. People complain of humiliation by biomedical personnel. Ironically these specialists may well include children of peasants, whose social mobility has been underwritten by the state's program of subsidized education and training.

Unlike when villagers interact with traditional healers, they have to cope with a monumental knowledge gap when they frequent physicians. Sensitive to urban stereotypes of peasants' "ignorance," villagers are guarded in expressing beliefs which may be considered "backward." Moreover, women cite degradation at the hands of hospital personnel as a significant reason for their resistance to delivering their babies there. Even women who are willing to withstand insult themselves try to insulate their husbands. In this regard, Hanem reasoned that it is all right for her to go to the clinic but that she would rather pay for her husband to go a private physician "to preserve his dignity."

When physicians' treatments fail to bring about the desired cure, and when circumstances of interpersonal conflict or serious departure from culturally defined role prescription continue, people turn to *rawhaniya*. For example, Karima, who is barren, was operated upon by a physician to no avail. When she gave up on physicians she started frequenting a number of *rawhaniya*. In turning to the *rawhaniya*, Karima secured the diagnostician's validation of her claims of supernatural causation, which she described as beyond physicians' knowledge. Unlike the physician, whose diagnosis burdens Karima with a sense of personal failure as the owner of a dysfunctional body, making her less than womanly, the *rawhani* absolves her of such responsibility. *Rawhani* diagnosis of spirit illness "in house of child" may even be utilized to shift responsibility for Karima's childlessness to other members of her household. She may well argue that it is the emotional distress imposed upon her by a demanding husband, an unkind mother-in-law, or even a jealous neighbor that initiated the spirits' action, targeting her otherwise healthy reproductive organs.

The very fact that the services of a *rawhani* are sought is indicative of expectation of a certain type of diagnosis. Whereas physicians' efforts focus on the reconstruction of the symptomatic person's organismic integrity, *rawhani* healing lends legitimacy to deviations from social well-being, including approximation of gender role expectations, whether in relation to parenthood for females and males, providing for the family by males, or submission to the authority of members of the older generation by those of the younger one.

Far from having a clear rationale for choice of treatment, people who are desperate for relief of their loved one's suffering are willing to try any form of treatment. This is evident in Zakiya's account of her attempt to save her dying husband. He had died about three years prior to our meeting, following an illness which lasted for a year. According to Zakiya, he first vomited and defecated blood. He informed her when this happened to him for the first time. She then consulted her brother, who decided that the situation was extremely dangerous and took the ailing man to the hospital. The husband's condition improved after returning home and taking the physician's medicine. After being informed by the physician that her husband's illness was not curable, Zakiya went to a variety of traditional healers. No supernatural cause was identified. Instead, his illness was attributed to the drinking of cold water when his body was warm. On her part, Zakiya does not believe this or other explanations by traditional healers. Although she describes the diagnosis of traditional healers as "empty words" (*kalam faregh*, i.e., nonsense) and insists that they are nothing but swindlers, she admits to having frequented them. She explains this as her way of pleasing her desperate dying husband, adding, "I took him there so that I will have done all I could do."

Aside from such cases of utter desperation, villagers generally have more specific expectations from cosmopolitan health providers and spiritualists. Physicians are generally expected to attend to life-threatening acute illness involving bodily dysfunctions, regarding which neither healers nor other villagers claim any expertise. As for traditional healers, they are considered qualified to deal with illness which is principally defined in terms of psychosocial criteria. This often entails chronic disorders, which although not necessarily outwardly manifest on a sustained basis are nevertheless associated with stable interpersonal relations, including power differentials. Such states of compromised health are reflected psychologically and projected publicly through what Kleinman has referred to as "somatic masks."

Spiritualist diagnosis, although distinguishable from its biomedical counterpart, is by no means insulated from it. A physician's biomedical evaluation may well serve in the protracted process of legitimation of a psychosocially defined state of compromised health.

Healing in Social Context

Presentation of symptoms does not automatically grant a person the status "sick." Two persons may present identical symptoms and one may be denied the label "sick" while the other may have it bestowed without solicitation. Neither is the severity of the symptomatic person's condition as perceived by him/herself a guarantee of legitimation of claim to sickness and consequent pursuit of appropriate treatment.

Individuals whose social roles, and health, are highly valued may not even have to initiate the process of "making social of disease" themselves. He/she may be granted the designation "sick" on the basis of other household members' perception of signs of ill health.

Women consistently identify their husbands as ill more readily than they do themselves or other members of nuclear family households. At the slightest sign of compromised health they urge them to seek medical treatment. Women rationalize that the husband is the breadwinner and his health should be protected for the benefit of the whole family.

For the less-privileged members of village households, it is ironic that their relative powerlessness, which is itself conducive to compromised health and attendant individually perceived illness, also impedes the legitimating of their claim to the sick role. Thus women's position of relative powerlessness itself reduces their prompt access to the privileged treatment associated with the sick role.[15]

Although villagers in superordinate positions of power have the authority to deny to their subordinates validation of claims of sickness, this may eventually prove far from beneficial if neglect leads to incapacitation and attendant compromised social roles. When this happens, it undermines the authoritative person's power, which is itself contingent on subordinates' performance of culturally established roles. Alternatively, the validation of the claims of subordinates initiates treatment, a step towards social reintegration, which involves offsetting the sick person's deviation from role expectations, including subordination to the authority of superiors. In this regard social mediation of culturally established power differentials is central (cf. Robinson 1971:12).

One obvious question comes to mind: Why doesn't the powerless person present his/her significant others with behavior indicative of inability to perform according to role expectations, thereby earning a temporary dispensation from role obligation through claims to the sick role? Why does he or she not simply show functional incapacitation? To answer these questions, we must take into account elements of social status which are not immediately apparent in the study of a given illness episode in isolation of its broader social context. This is illustrated by the case of a woman called Bahana, who lives in an extended-family household.

Bahana is the mother of female children only, and her powerlessness is exploited by her mother-in-law, who works her and her female children to the point of exhaustion. Bahana's appearance indicates severe malnutrition, which is attributed by the people of her neighborhood to her mother-in-law, whose stinginess they describe by a tightened fist. In gatherings with other women of her age, Bahana complains of weakness and always refers to her chronic condition of illness. She is saddened by the continued denial of her claim of ill health by her mother-in-law.[16] She says that she has stopped complaining to her mother-in-law and has simply accepted her fate although she feels sometimes that she will simply fall and die.

When Bahana's friends advise her to defy her mother-in-law and have her own husband take her to the doctor, who would keep her in the hospital so that she would rest, she resists their advice. This is in spite of the fact that such an arrangement is well within her husband's abilities; he has access to many of the government officials in the nearby town. Bahana fears even more disastrous consequences that may result from her defiance of her mother-in-law. Specifically, she dreads her mother-in-law's suggestion to her son that he marry another woman.

The older woman herself complains of her junior subordinate's miserable appearance and her "ugly yellow face" and underscores the latter's powerlessness by reference to her devalued status as the mother of females, using vulgar language to this effect. She also says, "Will it be from all," implying that if the only useful thing that the daughter-in-law does is her work, and if even that is abandoned because of illness, she will have nothing remaining to justify the continuation of her marriage to the older woman's son. Realistic about her lack of control over culturally valued resources, Bahana continues to suffer in silence, especially in view of the fact that the mother-in-law is known to have been the direct reason for her son's earlier divorces. Bahana has therefore chosen to forego the sick role to ensure the maintenance of her role as wife. She has apparently chosen to sacrifice the short-term gain associated with sickness for the long-term, culturally significant status of married woman.

In such cases where the legitimation of the sick role is denied to symptomatic persons, he/she continues to be distressed while performing the tasks assigned by superiors with whom legitimation rests. The denial of claim to sickness is itself an additional source of distress. In Bahana's case, she feels that she is wasting away. The scorn of her senior female affine is not offset by support from her own family. She looks emaciated and remains chronically depressed.

In contrast to Bahana, persons whose self-perception of illness results in socially approved exemptions from role obligations are accorded certain privileges. These include reduced or no work, preferential treatment in the allocation of choice food, and even forgiveness of disrespect towards superiors. Familial support is expressed emotionally and accompanied by concerted efforts to attend to any apparent or signaled discomfort. Such care is not limited to household members but is also forthcoming from neighbors and relatives, as well as others in the village. At times of illness, particularly in its severe form, villagers are under obligation to console the sick person's kin, usually by paying visits to their home and bringing gifts of food. The number of visitors is proportional to the prestige of the afflicted person.

With illness made social, the initial phase of treatment is often confined to the household and the immediate social network of the sick person. Depending on the perceived severity of the illness and the resources at the disposal of the family, treatment may go beyond emotional support, privileged access to prized food, and treatment with home remedies such as herbal infusions, prayers, and other minor religious rituals.

If the sick person's condition calls for specialized treatment, and his/her family is financially capable, the physician is the first choice. The trip to the physician's office is a status symbol reflecting the importance of the person whose family privileges him/her with private biomedical treatment. The physician's diagnosis, no matter its specific content, is a significant reaffirmation of a legitimized state of ill-health. The number of medications prescribed by the physician is taken as an index of the severity of the illness and as further substantiation of the sick person's claim to discomfort. In case the explanation of illness shifts to the supernatural domain, the physician's diagnosis of "normal health" or "just strained nerves" is still maintained as a support to patients' or their significant others' claims of supernatural etiology.

The utility of a physician's failed recognition of spiritual illness (*marad rawhani*) is illustrated by the case of ʿAisha's 35-year-old daughter, who died a few months prior to my arrival in the village. Unlike the physician, who describes the daughter's condition as epilepsy (*saraʿ*), ʿAisha refers to her daughter as having been possessed by a very tough jinn, who was identified by a famous *rawhani* in Desuk as the Red Devil. In private, ʿAisha's adversaries support the physician's diagnosis, noting that the daughter had been subject to seizures accompanied by frothing at the mouth since childhood. By contrast the mother cites the doctor's identification as evidence of spiritual illness. As one friend of the family remarked, "[The doctor] is all right for colds, for intestinal illness, and for giving injections and medicines but he does not know anything about this type of illness." Out of social obligation of kindness to ʿAisha after the tragic loss of her young daughter, even those on less than friendly terms with her concur with this rationale in the presence of the grieving mother.

For some households, financial constraint requires families to bypass treatment by a private physician in favor of the alternative treatment of the public clinic a few kilometers from the village. A more accessible substitute is the service of the local sanitary barber. He may prescribe any of a number of standard drugs prescribed by physicians or administer an antibiotic by injection. Medication by injection is regarded as particularly efficacious in view of the direct introduction of the drug into the body. The sanitary barber also prescribes vitamin tonics and administers injections of calcium.

Treatment at the hands of the barber within the village is generally preferred for its friendly and neighborly character, in contrast to the formalized interaction with biomedical personnel on their turf in the public health unit. Since the sanitary barber does not dispense medication free of charge, his treatment may in fact cost more than that obtained at the public health unit. To some villagers, the cost is worthwhile.

The social power relations which inform the "making social" of a symptomatic person's claim of illness are also operative with regard to selection of differently valued forms of treatment. Conversely, types of treatment, differentiated according to the expenditure of valued resources and according to the promptness of their administration to a sick person, may themselves be utilized as an index of an afflicted person's location within specific culturally meaningful frameworks of power relations. On the basis of this logic I focused on a selected sample of village households for assessment of differential responses to members' compromised health.

To investigate the form of treatment extended to household members, differentiated according to their relation to the head of the household, I selected a group of sixteen families from the study's population sample of 100 households. Residents of the sample households were asked to describe the specific forms of treatment extended to sick members of the family, their order, and their cost during biweekly interviews over a period of nearly four months.

During the biweekly visits, reported cases of illness were described in terms of generalized and diffuse symptoms (e.g., weakness, aches all over, lack of appetite, etc.) and generally did not differ significantly from one case of illness to another. But while symptoms did not figure prominently in the evaluation of severity and related urgency of treatment, the status of the symptomatic person clearly did. The highly valued and expensive services of private physicians were systematically provided to members of the household whose health receives culturally informed valorization.

The average cost of treatment for illness cases reported for females was L.E. 1.50, while that for males was L.E. 2.20. As for the order of resort to different types of treatment (beyond home remedies), males resorted to the more expensive treatment of the physician more readily than females, with 37% of the males selecting the private physician as their first choice as opposed to 10% of the females. When persons making up the sample are differentiated according to relation to household head (HHH), of the six male HHHs who were treated for illness, four selected a private physician as their first choice. For one male HHH, the physician was the second choice, and the remaining one resorted to the physician of the public health unit. The average cost of treatment for this group of male HHHs is L.E. 3.75. Among the corresponding group of female HHHs, expenditure for treatment of illness is more modest. Among three female HHHs, none selected the physician as their first resort, and one chose him as the second resort. The average cost of treatment among this group is L.E. 1.00. Of the eight wives of HHHs who were treated for illness, only one utilized the private physician as the first form of treatment. The average cost of treatment for this group is L.E. 2.13. Mothers of married sons reported 3 cases of illness with an average cost of treatment of L.E. 2.83. Two women of this group were taken to private physicians on their initial expression of discomfort.

Comparison of treatment type and expense extended to daughters and brothers' daughters of HHH on the one hand, and sons and brothers' sons of HHH on the other, shows higher expenditure for the treatment of males than for their female counterparts. The average cost of treatment for the seven sons was L.E. 1.73, as compared to L.E. 0.92 for daughters. Among the male group, one was taken to a private physician on the first trial at treatment and two were examined by private physicians on the third trial. The remaining sons were treated with independently purchased drugs; one was taken to the public clinic in the nearby town. Among the five daughters treated for illness, only one was taken to a private physician. In this lone case, consultation of a physician represented the second attempt at treatment. The lowest average cost of treatment is associated with young female affines of the sampled households, namely sons' wives and brothers' wives. In the case of this group of three women, the average cost of treatment amounted to only L.E. 0.18, and none of them were taken to a private physician at any phase of their illness.

Informal interviews and participant observation lend further credence to the implications of the foregoing data. For example, when I inquired from Zohra about her daughter's emaciated appearance, the mother explained that the young girl's poor health resulted from neglect when her now-deceased father (Zohra's husband) was ill. She said,

He was seriously ill. Of course, I used every penny [*millim*] for his treatment. I figured his health is much more important to us than this bit of a girl. All the time that he was ill I would beg men to look after his work in the field. I would do some of the work myself, and sometimes I would even hire men to do it. I wish she [her daughter] had died instead of him. Now we wouldn't be this way and he would have kept the house opened up for us. As you see, all my children are girls. At least if I had a son he would have kept his father's house open.

The importance of the HHH's health in the maintenance of the family is also emphasized by other women. In justifying the expenditure of large sums of money for the treatment of their husbands, women make such statements as "He is our man. We had to pay to hire a laborer for three days [to do the fieldwork ordinarily carried out by the husband]." By contrast, and in view of women's relatively devalued work contributions, villagers undermine the adverse consequences to the family welfare of a woman's sickness. When the woman concerned is a junior affine, there is obvious reluctance to invest valued resources for her treatment. When a son's wife asked to consult a physician, her mother-in-law mockingly remarked, "You would think that my son married a princess. . . . She wants us to wait on her."

In addition to gender identity and relation to HHH (which varies according to the developmental cycle of the family), other variables are operative in affecting treatment of compromised health. Deterrents to the utilization of cosmopolitan health facilities include the financial burden imposed by private consultations. This becomes clear when one realizes that the average yearly income of a peasant family owning one faddan of land is L.E. 120 and that a visit to a private physician costs at least L.E. 1, not counting the cost of prescribed medication. In this regard a female villager explained, "We do not go to Dr. ᶜAmr because he writes a prescription the length of my arm. How can we afford to buy all this medicine?"

As for public health care facilities, these provide a far from satisfactory alternative. Villagers complain of the long hours of waiting in the public clinic. To them, medical professionals' work "by the clock" stands in contrast to the flexible schedule of traditional healers, who consider it their neighborly duty to respond to their "kin's" distress at any time of the day or night. Instead of having this perpetual access to medical professionals, villagers are expected to report to the clinic during its working hours, which coincide with their own working hours. Moreover, the time spent in going to the health care center is not always rewarded by a meeting with a physician. The physician may not be bound by the "work hours" imposed on the peasants.

Although matters of sickness and healing are understandable in terms of the local context of the community's organizational power relations, including those pertaining to gender differentiation, it is important to keep in mind the relation between this local context and national developments. Particularly relevant in this regard are the earlier discussions of the status of Egyptian peasants in the nation state (Chapters 1 and 2). Assertions of peasants' "ignorance" of the benefits of cosmopolitan medicine by upper class compatriots do not take into account the power differential which limits access to health resources. To the allegedly ignorant peasants themselves, partaking of these benefits involves much more than their "acceptance" of the "miracles" of modern medicine.

Notes

1. This hand is directed at the giver of the covetous glance who should have five fingers cast in his/her eye.

2. This form of protection extends to valued farm animals.

3. In 1975, in conjunction with increased discussion of the world of supernatural creatures in the mass media, some advertisements by these more famous healers appeared in the national press.

4. Midwives are not considered obstetrical specialists. See Morsy 1981 for information on the role of midwives, pregnancy, and childbirth.

5. I met and interviewed this lady in the *khalifa*'s household in Desuk, where I was hosted during the 1974 *mulid.*

6. There is no specific term which the villagers use in reference to indigenous healers. They simply use their names preceded by the title Sheikh/a and indicate their specialization.

7. I had the occasion to interview some of these practitioners, including the famous Sheikh El Barad (pseudonym). Along with his brothers and patrilateral male cousins, this man is known for his practice of natural medicine. He and his kinsmen specialize in curing "naturally caused illnesses," including rheumatism, male impotency, male and female sterility, and illness of the spleen (*tuhal*). Sheikh El Barad described his diagnosis and treatment of illness as follows: "The sick person's description of his ailment is the basis of our diagnosis. He points to the part of the body which causes him discomfort. . . . Rheumatism is caused by cold and moisture. High fever causes the illness of *tuhal* [spleen] and sterility may be caused by *tarba* [fright], so we try to relax the nerves by getting rid of the boiling [*fawaran*] of the blood by ironing. . . . We use ironing [cauterizing], it relaxes the state of excitement of the blood. It relieves headaches, eye pain, and nervousness. We also use ironing on the back [lower back] of men who are sterile. For women who are barren we give them a blessed wool [*sufa mabruka*] which they wear before uniting with their husbands. . . . We inherited the *baraka* from our grandfather and we transfer our *baraka* to the sick persons. Our inherited *baraka* comes from our bodies and our learning and training allows us to perfect the art of healing. But the *baraka* is the important basis of our healing abilities. Our grandfather ironed for a man who was separated from him by the sea. Spitting on the ironed part of the body is itself *baraka* from us. . . . The illness will never return to the person again after he has received our *baraka*, but only if he follows the special dietary routine which we prescribe. People with rheumatism should not eat eggs, fish, salty, or spicy foods. Those who suffer from sterility should eat good rich food such as meat and fish and eggs and butter and milk."

8. People come from different parts of Egypt, as well as other parts of the Muslim world, including Sudan, where the current (1974) Sheik of the *tariqa* il Burhamiya lives.

9. Traditional practitioners refer sick persons not only to other traditional practitioners but also to physicians.

10. Literally, one who knows. i.e. a seer.

11. According to the sheik, *awliya* are "people like the Sidi Ibrahim il Disuki and Sidi Ahmad il Badawi. They are good people; they are descendants of the Prophet Muhammad. They gathered together and divided their *karamat* [*baraka*] on different parts of the world. They roam their individual corners of the earth on Monday and Friday. Each has a servant [*khadim*] who has known [the *wali*'s] path [*tariga*] and these servants [*khudam*] are themselves filled with *baraka*. . . . The *awliya* and their khudam reside in the shrines [e.g., at the religious centers of Sidi Ibrahim in Disuk, Sidi il Sayid in Tanta, and Sidi Mursi Abu il ᶜAbass in Alexandria] and from there they roam the world on Mondays and Fridays. The secret [*sir*, i.e., *baraka*] of the different *awliya* is diffuse throughout [each's respective] sphere of influence. For example, if you have an illness and I make a vow [*nadr*] to Sidi Ibrahim, if for example my *nadr* is a duck, I send out a duck during the *mulid* of Sidi Ibrahim. The dervishes [*darawish*] at the shrine of Sidi Ibrahim are *khudam* [servants] to Sidi Ibrahim. . . . They include men and women. The women are not inhibited; they join the *zikr*, just like the men do and they sleep in the midst of men during the *mulid*. I am a follower of Sidi Ibrahim. In order to be a follower, one has to pray and have a special devotion to Sidi Ibrahim. When I went to Cairo, I met Sheikh Abu il Magd il Shahawi who is a descendent of Sheikh Ibrahim il Desuki and he registered me as a follower of the [Sufi] *tariga* il Burhamiya [he showed me his I.D. card with his picture, which indicated his official registration as follower of the Sheikh Ibrahim il Disuki]."

12. This group is not represented in Fatiha but found at a nearby village to which Fatiha residents travel on foot, or by automobile, depending on the condition of the sick person whom they accompany.

13. Among practitioners who have limited knowledge of the Quran, dissolution of sorcery is brought about by imitative magic. As Sheika Aziza describes, "I melt the lead in a pan of water over the head of the person for whom the ᶜ*amal* was done. This dissolves the ᶜ*amal*."

14. It is important to note that spiritual healers are not themselves the locus of supernatural power. Instead, they perceive themselves and are perceived by others as mediators between supernatural and human life. The most prestigious channel of such mediation is religious learning, which involves literacy (cf. Good & Good 1988).

15. This is not unlike another situation of power differential involving management and workers in industrial settings. Here members of the former group are easily granted social confirmation of their unsubstantiated claims of illness, in contrast to workers who are required to produce professional validation.

16. Once, in my presence, Bahana's request to take her infant to the public health clinic was refused outright by the senior woman and supported by her husband. Turning to me, the mother-in-law said, "There is nothing wrong with the child, all she needs to give her is some *hilba* to warm the stomach. She wants to go to the [health] unit [*wihda*] to waste the whole day and blabber with the women who have nothing to do."

GENDER AND MEDICAL
DISCOURSES IN CONTEXT:
A CONCLUSION

For a culture to materialize requires [appreciation of] difference [which] can be perceived and exaggerated. Anthropology cements the exaggeration. . . . We have . . . to investigate the lived space, which is the experiential counterpart of the implicational cultural space. . . . It is this world that the anthropologist must enter. (Hastrup 1990:47,48)

The world which we have entered in the foregoing historically informed ethnographic journey is one which diverges from that portrayed in the "promissory notes" of Egypt's now aborted "transition to socialism" (cf. Kruks et al. 1989). The culture which has been the focus of the foregoing "exaggeration" by an upper class urban compatriot of the villagers of Fatiha, who entered their lives with explicit political inspiration (Morsy 1988; see also Harrison 1991), represents historically specific lived experiences of Egyptian *peasants*. As such, the account of peoples' lives constructed here establishes a basis for comparison between peasant women's lived experiences and those of the primary beneficiaries of Nasserist state feminism, as well as those of today's "Open Door" society (Abaza 1987; Abdel Wahab 1988; Hatem 1992a, 1992b; Mursi 1988).

More generally, this empirically derived depiction has relevance for the theoretics of comparative studies of gender, sickness, and healing. It is to these analytical concerns that this segment of the book is devoted, beginning with a methodological note pertaining to the historical and social contextualization of gender differentiation. This is followed by consideration of gender in relation to the local imprint of state agrarian policies. Next I address the theoretical implications of the medical ethnographic data collected in Fatiha in light of sociomedical discourse on the body, diagnosis, healing, and medical pluralism.

Mirroring current anthropological concern with time and place in ethnographic research (Appadurai 1986; Fardon 1990; Roseberry 1989;

Valeri 1991), the assessment of gender power relations undertaken in this book involves historical contextualization and localization. Thus derived, this evaluation leads to the conclusion that women in the village of Fatiha of 1974–1975 are subordinated to male authority, but not without resistance and occasional defiance. Reached by way of a historical detour, this judgment of male-female power relations, and expression thereof in medical discourse, represents an alternative to *a priori* assumption of the alleged "God given" inferiority of Muslim women (Patai 1969; cf. Ahmed 1982; Rosen 1978) or variants thereof which insulate gender identity from variation in time and place, in addition to neglecting the class specificity of its construction (cf. Mohanty 1991).

Part I of the book demonstrates that the "gap" between "us" and "them" transcends the reified urban-rural binary opposition with its constituent element of cultural lag. As shown in Chapters 1 and 2, the "distance" involves a historically derived structural asymmetry which informs peasants' daily lives, extending to gender differentiation and related matters of sickness and healing.

Formulated as a historically delineated problematic, this investigation of gender differentiation in the Egyptian Nile Delta is distanced from models of universal subordination of women and from associated binary oppositions such as that between the domestic and public spheres. In the Delta, the "domestic" sphere is not only "a lively area of economic action" (Joseph 1986:4), but the peasant household "action" of production and social reproduction is intricately bound to the "public," historically different policies of the state.

Similar limitation of dualistic typologies is disclosed by the Egyptian historical experience with regard to the alleged opposition between the western/modern and non-western/traditional. The Egyptian record, and more generally Arab/Islamic history, documents the protracted encounter between the "west" and "non-west," including "a long history of productive cultural exchange" (Abaza and Stauth 1988:344; see also S. Amin 1989), not the least of which relates to medicine (Ulmann 1978). As outlined in Chapter 1, the oppositional framework is further challenged by the fact that Muhammad Ali's nineteenth century modernist development project, which "integrated" women into industrial development and lent the authority of the state to modern allopathic medicine, was aborted at the hands of none other than *Western* colonial authorities.

The methodological orientation of this study also departs from the "heritage approach to the Middle East," which undermines history as social process (P. Gran n.d. 14–15). Based on decontetuxalized and detemporalized abstractions, this approach has been rejected for its essentialist representations of Arab/Muslim societies, which extend to gender relations (Asad 1986; Aswad 1978; Fluehr-Lobban 1973; Nelson 1986). As shown in more recent studies, for these societies, as for others, women's gender identities are historically contingent and analytically inseparable from their class affiliations (Altorki 1986; Bookman and Morgen 1988; El-Messiri 1978; Fernandez-Kelley 1983; Joseph 1975, 1985; Tucker 1986). These class identities and attendant power differentials, while dialectically engaged to personal agency, are by definition collective rather than individual. Their expression is manifest in *social* relations.

In Chapter 1, where gender differentiation is located within historically specific forms of social relations of production, the class specificity of gender identity comes into focus. Under Muhammad Ali, the state's taxing of the peasantry involved, among other mechanisms, the recruitment of women to work on public projects. While some of these women arrived at the site of state projects in shackles, the surplus which they helped create not only enriched the state treasury but ensured the comfort of the women of the upper classes. Women of the families of the Pasha's employees were privileged not only with wealth but also with special hospital care for protecting their health. During colonial rule British ladies were joined by members of the indigenous upper classes in the "charitable" disbursement of health care while peasant women and children suffered the consequences of the colonial state's agrarian and public health policies. Until the declaration of health care as a state responsibility in the wake of the July 1952 Revolution, it was also the ladies of Fatiha's Turkish elite who dispensed such charitable care to their peasant subjects.

Even during the Nasserist welfare era, when some peasant women's families, for the first time ever, became land owners and some village women happily came to be cared for by physicians, even then, women's peasant status remained manifest in their health, their children's, and that of other underprivileged members of their communities. For although the post-1952 era witnessed a significant improvement in income distribution, by the mid-seventies rural per capita income amounted to no more than 60% of the urban counterpart (Nyrop et al. 1976:98). This occurred while 31% of the gross domestic product derived from agriculture and an excess of 80% of export earnings were similarly generated (Ibid:270–271).

Structurally, the agricultural surplus which was created and appropriated in the public sector expresses a basic contradiction of the Nasserist era: increased socialization of production and private appropriation of surplus value (Radwan 1975:99). This culminated in the Sadatist Open Door era (cf. Sorj 1977) and the "rolling back of Egypt's agrarian reform" (Springborg 1990), now awaiting more explicit official endorsement by President Mubarak's Peoples Assembly.

In Fatiha, the Free Officers regime did not terminate the power of the old village masters over the peasants. Although locally articulated in terms of social origin (*asl*), the significance of historically antecedent class relations continued to be manifest, albeit in a form different from earlier historical expressions. This reproduction of the ideology of social differentiation, which is partially anchored in the authoritative religious domain and which is personified by a female saint, is informed by what Annette Weiner describes as "cosmological authentication" (Weiner 1992:4). Not unlike the case of the Maori chief whose brandishing of her sacred cloak shows that "she *is* her ancestors" (Ibid:6), the ʿumda's procession on the day of the *mulid* authenticates his authority. This enables him to circumvent even the regulations of the state regarding candidacy for public office. Ironically, his derivative power originates, at least in part, with a woman whose being revered by many villagers contradicts their assertion that women are "lacking in mind and religion." Even in her life, it was her social status as a descendant of the socially privileged religious elite of Desuk that averted the dissolution of her marriage.

Concomitant with this study's emphasis on socially contextualized expression of male-female power relations, I have attempted to avoid the selective focus on human agency associated with methodological individualism, and expressed in the power-authority dichotomy ascribed to women and men respectively (Rosaldo and Lamphere 1974). Instead, the analysis of gender differentiation presented here partakes of a concept of power which focuses on context-specific "performance or evidence of power" (Adams 1967, 1975). Thus attention is accorded to the societal context of expression of gender roles, the social mediation of their cultural construction, and the social consequences of their being transgressed. Indeed, as shown with regard to diagnosis, as well as with regard to the related social processes of "making social of disease" and therapeutic interventions, the cultural construction of gender is but one element operating in a discursive network. The negotiation of meaning even extends to situations of compromised health, which are, by definition, occasions for culturally legitimated departures from role expectations.

For the peasants of Fatiha themselves, although the language of class is not part of their vocabulary, and neither is the rhetoric of equality (*musawa*) of men and women which characterizes upper class feminist discourse (cf. West 1991), the consequences of their status as peasants are anything but understated. Exemplary of their "emic" rendition of social inequality is a song which sets up a comparison between their situation of deprivation and the comforts of the rich:

The rich one is happy while misery is the share of the poor. The rich [person] drinks boiled milk sweetened with sugar for breakfast; the poor eats fava beans not fit for donkeys. If a rich [person] gives out two moans he finds at his side two doctors; if the poor one lets out two moans he finds at his side the angel of death. The rich lives in an apartment with a radio and a dog; the poor lives in a grave and pays rent with curses. For every step the rich takes a taxi; the poor's path is contrary; [he] hangs on to the tail of a donkey. . . . The rich one gets up in the morning to a garden and the hunting of birds; the poor rises to a dump [and] hunts roaches. Misery is the share of the poor.

The centrality of peasant status and its reproduction within the framework of state institutions is also elaborated by villagers in everyday conversations, whether in relation to agrarian production, formal education, or health.

As has villagers' own insights, the role of the state has formed an integral part of my analysis of organizational power relations in Fatiha. As illustrated in Part II, this conceptualization of the state as a "conditioning boundary for gender relations" (Kim 1989:34) is complemented, methodologically, by a complex of other institutionalized social relations. As Eun-Shil Kim explains,

[Constituting] discourses of gender, which create the forms of gender relations in women's lived reality, are [not] independent from each other. . . . All intersect with each of the other categories of power to produce the contradictions of women's lives. (Ibid)

In Part III attention extends further to those relations pertaining to sickness and healing, wherein gender differentiation is expressed in terms of culturally meaningful power relations.

Extension of the power-authority/public-private oppositional logic to the sphere of production has sometimes led to equating women's wage employment and their modernist "emancipation" (Smelser 1970:37 and Goode 1970:242–243, quoted in Tiano 1981:2; Patai 1969:1; cf. Bossen 1975). Egyptian women's experience as wage laborers during the nineteenth century reign of Muhammad Ali, particularly their organized revolt, seems to lend support to this assertion. On further consideration it becomes clear that women's protest "at the point of production" did not occur to the exclusion of other expressions of resistance to the authority of the modern state (cf. Sacks 1989). Aside from individual women's "everyday forms of resistance," such as the infliction of harm on their own and their children's bodies to avoid incorporation into the state's labor force, women's *collective* action found expression in the healing rituals of Sufi orders.

In Fatiha the relationship between spouses who engage in wage labor is no doubt more egalitarian than in cases where the husband is considered the "breadwinner." As one woman put it, "He is a beggar, and I am a beggar, so how can he boss me around?" Yet, in this very statement is indication of the social devaluation of the status "wage laborer," whether for men or women (cf. Kandiyoti 1989:185). Far from the desocialization of individual action, wage laborers, like other poorer villagers, are distinguished from the "children of the big people" (*awlad il akaber*). So while more egalitarian relations may well obtain in the households of "landless" villagers, their rank in the community is far from elevated.

In contrast to the supporters of state feminism (who regard as "emanicipatory" official promotion of women's "participation in development" through work outside the home), our peasant sisters consider release from such responsibility as liberating. As Fernandez-Kelley (1983) has argued for Mexicans, involvement in wage labor by the villagers of Fatiha is an element of familial strategies which are themselves analytically inseparable from macro-social influences, not the least of which are the state's agrarian policies (see also Deere and Magdalena 1987; Redclift and Mingione 1985). As in the case of Fernandez-Kelley's subjects, the women of Fatiha who engage in wage labor do not see themselves as members of the working class but as wives, mothers, daughters, and sisters who are associated with socially stratified households whose prestige rests on descent, wealth (measured in landholdings), honorable reputation, religiosity, and education.

Far from being a generalized cultural orientation of familism (Ayrout 1938:116 as cited in Mitchell 1990:135), the centrality of kin-based social units as sites for the reproduction of class and gender relations (Rapp 1982 as cited in Kim 1989:22) is better understood in light of state agrarian policies in the post-1952 era (Amer 1958; Byres 1977; Glavanis and Glavanis 1983, 1986; Hopkins 1986, 1989; Saleh 1979; Seddon 1986; Stauth 1989). Indeed, "the social production of the family system (entails) connections between the public and domestic domains" (Sayigh 1987:119), which are otherwise obscured by cultural reductionism and the public-private oppositional model.

From their earliest implementation after the expulsion of the monarch in 1952, land reform programs were *designed* to expand small family holdings (Abdel Fadil 1975:8). Consequently, peasants' labor came to be deployed simultaneously for primary and secondary reproduction, associated with household and social formation respectively (Evers et al. 1984). The taxation of the peasantry provided not only cash to the state treasury but also an agricultural surplus. This was used locally as cheap food for urban areas or, as in the case of cotton, exported in return for hard currency which helped finance industrial development.

As the Free Officers proceeded to "reorganize political and economic life *within* the framework of the established mode of production . . . , relying on the modernistic wing of the upper bourgeoisie"[1] (M. Hussein 1973:97, emphasis added), the revolution's reforms gave land ownership to some villagers in Fatiha. Others came to enjoy secure tenancy. Although both these forms of landholding have meant formal control over the means of production, the productive process itself has remained subordinated to state regulation. For although the agricultural cooperative is managed by an elected council of villagers, these members are subject to the directives of the technicians/bureaucrats of the Ministry of Agriculture. Local representatives of the state have the authority to initiate legal action against peasants who fail to comply with state directives.[2]

As peasants, villagers are minimally rewarded for their hard work. For the entire village, agricultural production yields an annual net income of L.E. 112,465. Distributed among the 3,200 inhabitants of the village, this amounts to an average per capita share of L.E. 35.145 per annum. Moreover, the very obligation to the state may well leave the producers' own food bins far from full, posing risk to their health. People complain of having no other option but to buy some of the very products which they grow themselves on the open market. Here the prices, even with state subsidy, are higher than what the producers are paid.

In response to complaints regarding the rice quota, an older villager, a vocal admirer of Nasser, reminded some of his co-villagers of a time when Gamal prevented his prime minister from raising the price of rice by one-half piaster (1/200 L.E.). Bringing us back to 1974, a female villager lamented her misfortune and that of other peasants, remarking,

> City people . . . take all [the products of] our efforts and our struggle. The agricultural cooperative charges tax for rice, even though we work very hard and we do not have enough rice for our home and children. The government takes our rice and we end up having to buy rice from the market. But buying from the market is very expensive.

Villagers' access to the very sustenance of life, and health, although less hampered than during the pre-revolution years, is nevertheless far from easy.

Burdened by a "double squeeze" of monetary taxation and appropriation of a surplus of agricultural products, the villagers of Fatiha, like other small proprietors who form the "backbone" of Egyptian agriculture, have developed appropriate strategies to retain their hold over their highly valued means of production. As shown in Chapter 2, outstanding among these mechanisms is the reliance on familial unremunerated labor. Indeed, nothing less than self-exploitation has been essential to the reproduction of the household as a productive unit (cf. Beneria and Sen 1981; Croll 1986; Glavanis 1984; Harris and Young 1984; Long 1984).

Not only is the peasant household in Fatiha a critical site for the reproduction of national class relations, it is also the context for the reproduction of patriarchal values. Aside from some older villagers' emphasis on the complementarity of male and female labor contributions, the ideology of work which prevails in the village is clearly informed by the logic of the dominant mode of production. Thus, not unlike national statistics which obscure women's contributions unless their work is performed within the framework of market relations, in Fatiha women's role in the household labor process is devalued compared to men's.

In more recent years, and specifically in relation to migration to the oil-producing countries of the Arab region, women's and children's labor has become crucial to the extended reproduction of the peasant household as a productive unit (cf. Graham-Brown 1989). This was evident to me on a return visit to the vicinity of Fatiha in the early eighties. More striking is the devaluation of the work of men whose productive activities do not approximate the new definition of "breadwinner" as a source of remittances (Morsy 1990b). Within the framework of the ODEP and associated rentier values (Beblawi 1990), devaluation extends more generally to local dealings and the productive agricultural sector, "the spheres now left to women" (Abaza 1987a:5).

The invalidity of certain binary oppositions, discussed for Fatiha's productive relations, extends to the body, a symbolic medium of social reproduction. As indicated in Chapter 3, villagers' body concepts are holistic rather than dualistic, entailing a reciprocal relationship between the individual body and its natural and social environments. Far from believing in a mind-body dualism, villagers believe in the articulation of the psychic and the somatic, expressed in terms of an "idiom of distress" (Nichter 1981; see also Early 1988; Good 1977; Kleinman and Kleinman 1986; Lock 1986, 1989; Taussig 1980b). Even men, who are believed to have stronger "nerves" than women, are not insulated from the adverse health consequences of emotional anguish. Distress among men, as among women, is expressed in terms of its embodiment and attendant discomfort.

Villagers share a tendency towards somatization, not only with their working class urban compatriots but also with those of ascendant social groups. In this regard the Egyptian case lends support to Pliskin's suggestion that we question the assumption that "people with a higher education, presumably the upper and middle classes . . . have a psychological orientation toward illness, whereas those who are less educated, "traditional," and working class or lower class somatize more" (Pliskin 1987:251; cf. Finkler 1985a:51; Scheper-Hughes 1989:12).

Villagers' ideas about the human body naturalize gender ideology. This is evident with regard to the more determinant role assigned to the male "seed" in the process of conception (cf. Delaney 1986) and extends to the emphasis of men's superior physical strength, which rationalizes male dominance in social life. Nourishment of the body also discloses gender hierarchal differentiation (cf. Raikes 1989:454). Additionally, the different rationalizations for the practice of circumcision on males and females reflect villagers' ideology of female impulsiveness in sexual behavior. Furthermore, males' practice of using stimulants for the maintenance of a healthy disposition, and its relative restriction for females, also reflects the belief in males' greater capacity for self-control. Even death, which is regarded as the "ripening" of the body and the termination of its viability by divine will, serves as occasion for the reproduction of gender ideology. A person's misfortune of not having a son is lamented by mourners.

In general, village women's own concept of the "natural" basis of male-female differences does not contradict that of the male-dominated social order. As reported for other societies around the world, the women of Fatiha share with the men of the community beliefs intended to "restrain women and to provide a surveillance of female reproductive capacity" (Turner 1987:85). Regarding genital surgery, although the same terminology, "purification" (*tahara*) refers to both female and male genital excisions, the practice of clitoridectomy in Fatiha cannot be realistically considered "an assertive symbolic act" (Boddy 1989:74; cf. Gruenbaum 1988) or a practice whereby women "declare their equality with men" (Skinner 1988:211). Neither do villagers restrict their rationalization of the practice to its import as a ritual for "beauty and cleanliness" (Assaad 1981:9). Indeed, they are explicit in noting its significance as a means of curtailment of unmarried women's sexual passion for the express purpose of ensuring their chastity. The guarding of women's virginity is not only a matter of living up to men's expectation of a chaste woman at marriage. For the women themselves, virginity is a highly valued attribute which they are generally intent on not "squandering."

Although older women may appear eager to inflict the brutality that their mothers had inflicted upon them on their own daughters, they are in fact in a position to ameliorate the pain of clitoridectomy and its adverse health effects. The result of older women's urging the gypsy who performs the operation to "go easy" may well be the minimization of "excision" to the point of scraping the prepuce of the clitoris. Bleeding is thus reduced, as is the risk of infection. Far from representing an affront to male authority, older women's call for restraint is rationalized as nothing less than concern for men. It is reasoned that husbands would otherwise be "exhausted" by sexual intercourse with a severely circumcised woman whose orgasm is impeded. Women themselves claim a right to sexual gratification, which they consider to be religiously sanctioned (cf. Rassam 1986). While they share accounts of their sexual experiences, it would be unthinkable for them to define sexuality as a basis of solidarity with other women in a "struggle for freedom" (Accad 1991:247; cf. Ahmed 1989).

Although women's collective subordination to male authority is taken for granted, with the assistance of kin, neighbors, friends, or higher-status members of the community, individual women are far from passive in dealing with established authority, but not in isolation from structural constraints. As the Indian feminist Lata Mani has argued in opposition to Eurocentric individualist feminist discourse,

> What is foresaken here is the notion of women's oppression as a multi-faceted and contradictory social process. . . . When [local] feminists speak of woman as victim it is in a complex material sense . . . , emphasizing women's systematic subordination rather than debating questions of agency. . . . If criticism is to be "worldly" or "situated" . . . or engaged, it must take account of the worlds in which it speaks. (Mani 1990:38)

In light of the historically grounded and localized conceptualization of "women's systematic subordination," presented in Parts I and II, it is not surprising to find that outlawing the practice of clitoridectomy in Egypt has not resulted in its eradication. In Fatiha an educated young woman who aspires to a university education and a professional career may secretly express revulsion at this "backward" practice, if not openly urge older women not to inflict it on a younger sister, cousin, or neighbor. In so doing she contradicts the views of the majority of village women. But she has access to an alternate path of social pursuits; the essence of her sisters' womanhood centers around their eligibility for marriage and motherhood, for which ritual genital surgery is a prerequisite.

Unlike many urban women, including female industrial workers whose politicization is congruous with state feminism (Tomiche 1968b), the women of Fatiha do not relate to this national emancipatory agenda. Neither do they assume that upper class urban women share their subordination, which is defined primarily in terms of their peasant status. Similar to the experience of their counterparts in the Upper Egyptian village of Silwa, studied by Nawal Ammar in the late eighties, the experience of the women of Fatiha negates the expectation that "an obsolete practice such as female circumcision could not persist against a new tide of [post-1950s] feminist consciousness" (Toubia 1985:156 as quoted in Ammar 1989:25).

Differences also pertain to menstrual pollution (cf. Ginsburg and Rapp 1991:319). For example, when an educated young woman in Fatiha dismisses as "nonsense" the belief in the power of menstrual blood or post-partum bleeding to inhibit the growth of plants or neutralize the action of yeast in baking, she expresses her "emancipation" from "ignorance." For her "uneducated" sister-in-law in an extended family household, there is nothing emancipatory about the consequences of being denied the privilege of a rest period in light of the logic of her educated affine. The later's "enlightment" deprives the sister-in-law of a culturally sanctioned mechanism for protecting women's own health, and that of their newborns, under circumstances of limited alternative health-enhancing resources.

In Fatiha the regulation of women's bodies is not limited to local mechanisms but involves the state. Improvement of health standards as an aspect of the expansion of citizenship rights has been accompanied by the imposition of state regulation of bodies. For the country as a whole, and in addition to the outlawing of clitoridectomy, this has included the management of the reproduction of life itself through state programs of family planning (cf. Turner 1987:218, 225).

As the encouragement of increasing production in the Nasserist era was framed in nationalistic terms, so was the state's campaign of curtailing women's reproductive capacities rationalized as a means of enhancing the national standard of living. As discussed in Chapter 1, the state's promotion of family planning precipitated a contradiction between its demand on small peasant households and its promotion of the ideal of a small family.

In Fatiha the majority of women had the support, if not the urging, of their husbands to simply ignore official pleas for limiting family size. In certain cases, however, some women were confronted with a contradictory inclination from their own "enlightened" husbands. But even under these circumstances women continued to "forget" the pill as they pursued the goal of establishing the nucleus of a primary power base through motherhood (cf. Petchesky 1984:10 as cited in Browner and Sargent 1990:220). More recently, since the early 1980s, the state's involvement in taming women's bodies has taken a more aggressive form. There is now explicit commitment to the medicalization of reproduction. Hormone-injected and -implanted women are effectively deprived of the right of "forgetfulness" (Morsy 1986a).

Following from their belief about the socially engaged human body, villagers' diagnosis of illness, discussed in Chapter 4, involves the social environment. By contrast, minimal significance attaches to anatomical structures or physiological processes associated with compromised health (cf. Rubel and Hass 1990:121; Finkler 1985b). As villagers consider their personal lives to be inextricable from their social contexts, they regard individually manifest ill-health as an extension of social relations. This is not to say that illness is explained solely in terms of social inter-actions, but diagnosis ultimately leads to the social environment of the afflicted person. When illness symptoms become manifest, their origin is traced to significant episodes of emotional distress, relative power-lessness, and/or adversary social relations.

Beyond dealing with the underlying logic of villagers' medical taxon-omy to the situational variability of interpretations of compromised health, Chapter 4 provides illustrations of context-specific explanations of illness episodes which disclose "social insight" (Kleinman 1980). Explanations of specific illness experiences also entail multiple levels of causation. As for the "making social" of compromised health (Franken-burg 1980), which culminates in the granting of the legitimacy of the sick role, this is subject to negotiations which are informed by the symp-tomatic person's social identity. While gender identity is significant in this regard, as in the differential incidence of illness, it is by no means the only relevant social variable. Documented illness episodes shed light on the social mediation of culturally established gender differentiation.

Discussion of possession illness and illustrative case studies pre-sented in Chapter 4 bring into focus the contrast between the logic which informs diagnosis by villagers, including traditional healers, and that which informs diagnosis by biomedical professionals. Certainly not distanced from the "medical paradigm" (Claus 1985), and as reported for other parts of the world, including adjacent Arab, African, and Middle Eastern societies, illness constitutes the "initiation into the spirit idiom" (Crapanzanno and Garrison 1977:14; see also Greenwood 1981; Lewis 1991:1; Safa 1988).

The presentation of possession illness as "typically feminine" (Ferchiou 1991:215), as related "almost entirely [to] women," and as "almost al-ways [associated with] the young wives of fairly wealthy older men" (Harer n.d.:3) also does not hold for Fatiha (cf. Brink 1987; Saunders 1977; Swagman 1989). In this village, the possession "role" (*dor*) is asso-ciated with women as well as men and is also imputed to children by adults (cf. Freed and Freed 1990; Davis and Low 1989). Transcending what Allan Young has described as the "fragmented . . . attributes of individuals" (1980:136), including gender status, the investigation of the "epidemiology of possession" (Lewis 1966:308; Rubel 1964) in Chapter 4 reveals that among adults the incidence of the affliction represents *social relations* wherein the possessed is in a position of relative power-lessness (cf. Dressler et al. 1986 as cited in Dressler 1990:256). This is by no means an attribute which is unique to women. At the level of household social organization, power differential varies in accordance with the developmental cycle of the family and the network of social support accessible to given members, as well as in the extent to which a given woman or man approximates culturally constructed role expectations.

Anthropological investigation of possession challenges assertions of female passivity by presenting possession as a form of resistance (Lewis 1989). Although possession may well be considered as "a thinly disguised protest against the dominant sex" (Lewis 1971:31 as cited in Ong 1988:33; cf. O'Nell and Selby 1968), it cannot be realistically considered as "permit[ting] . . . long-term increases in women's power and control" (Crapanzano and Garrison 1977). Socially sanctioned rebellion is not equivalent to women's self-empowerment.

Far from reversing structurally embedded powerlessness, the social legitimation of claims to possession in Fatiha helps reproduce the very power relations which contribute to its social production (cf. Gromm 1975). The sick role assumed by the *maᶜzour/a*, like that reported in other anthropological studies of culturally patterned disorders, "is in fact *institutionalized* by ritual and custom" (Turner 1987:56, emphasis added).

While the sick role legitimated by spiritualists provides the relatively powerless, whether male or female, with an opportunity to renegotiate social relations, it does not entail rejection of institutionalized social structure or its underlying cultural logic. As Henrietta Moore has argued,

[Such] renegotiation is an asymmetrical process through which the socially dominant becomes the socially acceptable. When women construct representations of themselves. they do so using the material which the socially dominant representations of women provide. (Moore 1983:184 as cited in Craddock 1990:24)

Such renegotiation as it pertains to possession illness in Fatiha in 1974–1975 differs from the involvement of eighteenth century Egyptian women in the activities of Sufi *turuq*. The historically antecedent organized protest represented an attempt at appropriation of what Moore describes as "the dominant social frame." The more recent form of "disguised protest" among Egyptian peasant women bears more resemblance to the case of nineteenth century U.S. women's "hysterics" as described by historian Carol Smith-Rosenberg:

The hysterical fit, for many women, must have been the only acceptable outburst—of rage, of despair, or simply of *energy*—possible. But as a form of revolt it was very limited. No matter how many women might adopt it, it remained completely individualized: hysterics don't unite and fight. As a power play, throwing a fit might give a brief psychological advantage over a husband or a doctor, but ultimately it played into the hands of the doctors by confirming their notion of women as irrational, unpredictable, and diseased. (Smith-Rosenberg 1972 as cited in Ehrenreich and English 1978:140–141)

Turning to health care in Fatiha, Chapter 5 brings into view multiple health resources and the significance of kin, friends and neighbors in the management of an illness episode. Utilization of the different preventive measures shed light on the social valorization of persons to whom they are administered, and on the significance of occasions with which they are associated.

Regarding treatment, actual illness episodes indicate its situational variability; its specific course is not predictable from interviews focusing on medical taxonomy. Illness occurrences exhibit a pattern of differential allocation of valued health resources. For the community as a whole, villagers of the more affluent households utilize the services of private physicians more frequently than do their less "capable" neighbors. In the context of the household, the relative power of a symptomatic person is significant not only in determining the form of medical treatment which is extended to him/her but also for the more fundamental process of extension of social legitimation of the sick role, upon which initiation of treatment is contingent. In general, valued resources are allocated more frequently for the treatment of males than for the treatment of females. However, gender identity is mediated by the dynamics of power relations associated with the developmental cycle of the family. Thus, beyond the preferential provision of resources for the household head/"breadwinner" (usually a male), a woman who enjoys the culturally valued status of mother of adult sons is provided with more prompt and expensive medical treatment than is a young, relatively powerless son's bride, or a male child of a not-so-favored son and daughter-in-law.

Within the framework of medical pluralism, a villager's choice of healing resource derives from diagnosis. As Libbet Crandon-Malmud (1990:203) observes in her Bolivian study, "in [this] domain the notion of medical efficacy becomes problematic, subject to cultural context . . . and social definition as well." It is indeed in light of such contextualization that we can comprehend the voluntary abandonment of the physician's otherwise valued treatment in favor of *tib rawhani* (cf. Csordas and Kleinman 1990:12; Katz and Katz 1987:397). Noteworthy in this regard is a difference between the people of Fatiha and their urban educated compatriots (the primary beneficiaries of both state feminism and biomedical services). The later are more likely to accept a physician's diagnosis uncritically. Locally, women and men may well reject the physician's diagnosis when it does not accommodate social causation, which they define as the basis of their bodily sufferings (cf. Martin 1987).

As for the medical knowledge on which traditional treatment is based, this is widely shared by members of the community. But it is women, and particularly older women, who are actively involved in both the prevention and household-centered treatment of illness, as well as in caring for the sick (cf. Ammar n.d.:5; Finerman 1989). In addition to women's being completely responsible for matters of pregnancy and birth in the village (cf. Sargent 1982) (in contrast to urban Egypt, where males dominate in obstetrical services [cf. Jordan 1983]), they are extensively involved in health care that extends to specialized traditional healing. It is women who are more likely to go, or accompany kin or friends, on visits to healers or the shrine of the local female saint. In contrast, for cosmopolitan medical care, and aside from women's accompaniment of children to the public health unit, it is usually men who play a more active role in relation to this health sector. They accompany kin and friends to physicians' clinics and generally take responsibility for purchasing pharmaceuticals.

Traditional healers do not appear to be distinguished from nonpractitioners in terms of medical knowledge (cf. Garro 1986); neither do they find it necessary to subject their ailing visitors to medical examination (cf. Finkler 1985b). This is commensurate with the underlying logic of their diagnosis and treatment of illness. Whereas the biomedical gaze targets the individual body as a focus of diagnosis and treatment, the *rawhaniya* are expected to attend to the social context of an embodied social crisis. As Brown reports for shamanistic healers among the Aguaruna Jivaro of Peru, they "shift disorder from the body human to the body politic" (M.F. Brown 1988:102).

Although biomedical and spiritualist healing represent therapeutic processes which are informed by contrasting underlying logic, it is important not to overlook certain shared social attributes of these two healing traditions. It is not only the biomedical gaze which transforms "active forms of protest . . . into passive acts of 'breakdown'" (Lock and Scheper-Hughes 1990:68). While certain forms of behavior associated with compromised health are not defined by traditional practitioners as "pathological" in the biomedical sense, these *are* nevertheless considered deviant. A *rawhani*'s diagnosis and treatment, while different from that of the biomedical professional in that it brings attention to the social production of ill-health, nevertheless shares with biomedicine its transformative role. Traditional healers help the villagers of Fatiha *cope* with their distress. Unlike the historically antecedent Sufi healing traditions noted in Chapter 1, these local healers do not provide a rallying point for solidifying and collectivizing their clients' somatized protests. In fact healing contributes to the affirmation of hegemonic cultural constructions of self and social relations (Comaroff 1981:369; see also Finkler 1986).

The observation that "stress and related lifestyle do not lend themselves to simple solutions through . . .'heroic [bio]medicine'" (Turner 1987:224) is equally applicable to *tib rawhani*. Indeed, the very tolerance of traditional healers by state authorities may be understood in light of the fact that their rituals of regulating protest are distanced from the fundamental basis of villagers' powerlessness, and the political economy of health inequities, generated by macro-structural relations. Whereas the *rawhani*-centered therapeutic process contrasts with that of the physician in that it considers extrasomatic agonies which are anchored in power differentials (cf. Young 1981), this "social insight" is limited to familial and community relations.

While spiritualists' sensitivity to local power differentials may differentiate them from physicians, they nevertheless share with biomedical professionals the role of "agents of the social consensus" (Scheper-Hughes 1989:13; see also Navarro 1986; Waitzkin 1984). Whereas many of their clients define their peasant status as an ultimate cause of compromised health, as agents of social control (Zola 1978), these healers fail to address the broader framework of national political economy, not to mention its international articulation, in which local organizational power is embedded. As the physician's diagnosis does not lead to "social engineering, economic management, or political realignment, which might be critical variables in the reestablishment of health" (Crandon-Malmud 1991:203), neither does the spiritual healer's.

As for medical pluralism, its historical specificity in terms of power relations is noteworthy:

> At the beginning of the nineteenth century, Louis Frank, a French doctor practicing in Tunis, found that he had to stay on good terms with the Muslim chief of physicians to practice European medicine without difficulties. At the end of the century, Hamda b. Kilani, a Muslim doctor and son of the former chief of physicians of Tunis, found that he had to be classed as *medecin tolere* (a second-class medical status) by the French Medical authority to practice Arabic medicine at all. (Gallagher 1983:1)

In Chapter 1 the discussion of nineteenth century developments in Egypt brought attention to how medicine "as culture, rather than the details of its practice . . . is [linked] to the outcome of larger social and cultural struggles in the various periods" (P. Gran 1979b:339; cf. Crandon-Malmud 1991:205; Mullings 1984:189). While this "outcome" has meant the ascendancy of positivist biomedicine since the nineteenth century, this has not resulted in the obliteration of Egypt's medical pluralism. In fact, as noted for other parts of Africa, Egypt continued to be a "market-place of . . . therapeutic systems and settings" (Janzen 1985).

Distanced from the social contexts in which they once dominated, and relatively constrained in their original epistemological elabora-tions, subordinated medical models in Egypt's class society remained operative within the framework of medical pluralism (cf. Frankenburg 1980:96). As in other socially stratified societies, these have not been in-sulated from the "materially founded authoritative discourse which seeks continually to preempt the space of radically opposed utterances" (Asad 1979:621; cf. Baer 1989). Beyond the initial nineteenth century resistance to the state's rural public health programs, the cultural hegem-ony of biomedicine has been sustained not through coercion but by vol-untary support through what Ibn Khaldun designated *"iltiham"* and Gramci described as acceptance of the rulers' "conception of the world" (Salame 1990:32).

Neither the nineteenth century state's promotion of positivist bio-medicine nor Nasserist support of rural health services precipitated the demise of medical pluralism. For the petty commodity production sec-tor of rural society, a variety of historically antecedent medical beliefs and practices, including spiritual medicine and the *baraka* of saints, continued to be important in health care. However, with the "etatisa-tion" of medical culture, promoted through formal education and the mass media, popular medical traditions increasingly came to be re-garded as manifestations of "backwardness" and "ignorance" (cf. Stauth and Zubaida 1985:14).

As with shared cultural models pertaining to gender differentiation (Gilmore 1987, 1990), medical beliefs and practices in Fatiha, described in Chapters 3, 4, and 5, validate Good and Good's (n.d.) observation of cultural continuity. Indeed, these beliefs and practices no doubt bear resemblance not only to those of ancient Egypt but also to their histori-cally derived counterparts in other societies of the Arab/African and Muslim worlds which are informed by earlier literate Arabic/Islamic medical traditions. Beyond the geographic contours of the civilizational area designated the Middle East, other anthropological studies also doc-ument the extension of this shared medical culture to the adjacent circum-Mediterranean region (cf. Antes 1989; Delaney 1987; B. Good 1976; M.J. Good 1980; B. Good and M.J. Good n.d.; Laderman 1987; Myntii 1988; Pliskin 1987; Rahman 1987, 1989; Von Denffer 1976).

The villagers of Fatiha, like many of their compatriots, share with their ancient Egyptian ancestors a variety of beliefs and practices related to illness causation and the therapeutic process (Blackman 1927). In

addition to believing in the harm of the evil eye and the agency of supernatural spirits, or ill winds, as well as the association between religious
knowledge and healing, villagers share certain beliefs and practices pertaining to fertility which resemble their ancient analogues. Not unlike
present-day villagers' explanation of sterile women's deviant behavior in
terms of the compromised state of the "house of child" (*bit il wild*),
resulting from spirit intrusion, a 1900 B.C. papyrus attributes "hysterical"
behavior among women to malfunctioning of the womb (Turner
1987:90).

Among the practices for the prevention of conception described in
the Petri Papyrus, which dates to the reign of Amenemhet III, the
one which relies on crocodile dung inserted as a pessary in the vagina
(Meinardus 1970:289–290) resembles a practice in Fatiha known as *arfa*
(Morsy 1981). A similar practice which is intended to regulate the acidity
of the reproductive tract through the insertion of lemon juice is known
among older villagers as having been practiced as a means of sex-selection.
Whereas these examples point to similarities of ideas pertaining to
fertility, they leave us wondering about the articulation of related
concepts and historically specific contexts (Asad 1979, 1986; Harris
1968:231; Palsson and Durrenberger 1990).

With regard to Arabic/Islamic medical traditions, including Prophetic
medicine, we find in the practice of the local healer of *tib tabi⁽i* elements of resemblance to these earlier literate traditions, including
humoral medicine. Villagers seek her out to perform such practices of
ancient origins as cautery, or on their own, they prescribe honey, noting
the Prophet's reference to its curative value. However, they do not know
of or relate to ancient traditions as coherent medical systems with distinctive logical schemes. In fact it is only among the relatively few educated villagers that Ibn Sina's or Ibn Rushd's names are recognized.

The anthropologist may well detect similarities between the underlying logic of ancient humoral traditions and villagers' (as well as other
Egyptians') descriptions of personality types in terms of "light" or
"heavy" blood. One may also note a similarity between villagers' refer-
ences to innate energy levels and the extent of differential volatility in
the face of insult as "hot" or "cold" (high or low, respectively). Such linkage has no significance for the villagers themselves. Similarly, one may
interpret villagers' positive reference to the cooling effect of watermelon
in the summer as indicative of the survival of the classical humoral tradition. For the villagers themselves, the consumption of this food item
means nothing more than changing body temperature, an effect also
believed to be precipitated by the consumption of Coca-Cola. More fundamentally, to the villagers, both watermelon, like other fruits, and
Coca-Cola are significant as symbols of relative affluence with

associated implications of "good eating" and attendant enjoyment of health.

My experience in Fatiha resembles that of Swagman in Yemen, where he found that "there was not nearly as much evidence of the classical humoral theories as [he] was led to expect from the western literature." As observed for Fatiha, many of the practices documented in classical medical works, such as cautery, are still found in Yemen, "but not within the context of highly elaborated humoral theory" (Swagman 1988:1; see also Early 1988:72; cf. Foster 1987; Kay 1977:162 as cited in Rubel and Hass 1990:120).

As described in Chapter 3, villagers' body concepts partake of historically antecedent Arab/Islamic medical traditions such as the unity of soma and psyche and the articulation between the body-self and its social environment (Devisch and Vervaeck 1986). Villagers also share with these traditions common beliefs surrounding the reproduction of gender ideology within the framework of medical discourse, exemplified by the assignment of a determinate role of the male seed in the process of conception.

It is important to bring attention not only to the similarities but to the heterogeneity of discursive traditions during any given historical period (Asad 1986:16–17), whether these relate to women's bodies in medieval times (Ahmed 1989) or to the risks to health of bereavement in contemporary Muslim societies (Wikan 1988). Fundamental to this reasoning is the issue of social contextualization in sociomedical analysis (Lewis 1986; Van der Geest 1987; Young 1982:270). Christine Delphie's remarks on patriarchy are relevant in this regard:

> An institution that exists today cannot be explained by the fact that it existed in the past. . . . I do not deny that certain elements of patriarchy today resemble elements of the patriarchy of one or two hundred years ago; what I deny is that this *continuance*—in so far as it really concerns the same thing—in itself constitutes an explanation. . . . [I]t is as illegitimate to seek keys to the present situation in the nineteenth century as in the Stone Age. (Delphie 1988:260–261)

The importance of historical contextualization is well illustrated by the variable forms of expression of spirit illness, which has been linked to ancient Egypt, Prophetic medicine, the Ottoman conquest, and the intensification of Egyptian-Sudanese contacts during the nineteenth century, among other significant historical developments (Al-Masri 1975; Gallagher 1983:9; Oweiss 1986). Elsewhere, in a comparative study of the possession illness variant known as ᶜ*uzr*, discussed in Chapter 4, I have shown a shift in the differential incidence of this affliction in association with local manifestations of Egypt's current economic liberalization policies and with its regional petro-economy (Morsy 1991). Fieldwork in the early eighties in a village in the region of Fatiha (to which I have assigned the pseudonym Bahiya) documents the regular participation of some mothers-in-law in the weekly *hadra*. Also in contrast to the Fatiha of 1974–1975 is the regular participation at this weekly event of men whose continued work as local agricultural producers does not approximate the new definition of "breadwinner" as depeasantized international laborer.

While possession illness continues to represent a culturally meaningful "idiom of distress" in the Delta (as well as in other parts of rural and urban Egypt), the specific negotiation of meaning is subject to new forces, expressed as changes in local organizational power relations, which are themselves inextricable from national and international developments of a specific historical moment.

The historical specificity and local particularity of expressions of medical traditions extends to biomedicine (V. Adams 1988; Low 1985; Navarro 1989; Singer 1990:184; Tsalikis 1988; Starr 1982). For Egypt, the contrast between Nasserist and Sadatist state policies as these relate to biomedically informed health care in rural society illustrates this variability (El-Gawadi 1987; Naseer 1987; H. Nassar 1987). Noteworthy in this regard is Raymond Baker's comparison of the two regimes:

> [O]n the eve of the [1952] revolution . . . the vast majority of the rural population was deprived of the benefits of modern medicine. Set against such a background, the record of the new regime is impressive, especially in the period up to 1965 before Nasser's revolution stalled. The degree of improvement is registered in the fact that the total amount spent in the seventy years prior to the revolution for health care was matched by the Nasser regime in just the years 1961–1964. . . . [During] the Nasser era, [expenditure] . . . increased an average of 11 percent per year. . . . [I]t [is] hard to be optimistic for any great improvement in rural health care in the near future . . . [in relation to] . . . Sadat's liberalization measures. (1979:219–220, 232, 233)

Within the framework of the state's ODEP, Egypt witnessed a number of changes reminiscent of those described in Chapter 1 for the period of British colonial rule which followed the defeat of Muhammad Ali's etatist development project. As I have noted elsewhere (Morsy 1988b), prominent among these is state promotion of private health care, including "touristic health care," which draws many customers from the oil-enriched societies of the Gulf. The later part of the seventies to the present has also witnessed a decline in the state's budgetary allocations to public health services and the growing influence of international development agencies in defining the country's health development priorities. Accordingly, health programming may well be reduced to population control. Women's bodies are now targeted for experimental trials of new contraceptive technologies (Morsy 1986a) as "population explosion" continues to be a rationalization for Egypt's economic problems and unprecedented level of food importation, as well as for the malnourishment of its people (Mitchell 1991b).

Biomedicine as charity has also regained some of its former significance. In addition to the so-called Islamic clinics and their Coptic counterparts, "society ladies" have resumed an earlier role. Replacing the past prominence of Western ladies in the delivery of charitable colonial health care are indigenous affiliates of Western institutions such as the Lions and Rotary clubs of the urban areas. According to announcements in the society section of the national press, these new forms of voluntary associations appear to constitute an important framework for the charitable endeavors of their respective women's groups. Even fashion shows at luxury hotels now provide the setting for the practice of health charity.

The "openness" of the Egyptian market in health is not limited to increasing commoditization of biomedical health services, as was the case during the period of colonial rule, or to the allocation of international aid funds for the importation of western high technology medical equipment. With the present regime's continued commitment to market principles, supply and demand logic is manifest in the unprecedented sale of body parts. Surpassing by far the "ritual dismemberment" associated with the biomedical gaze (Clark 1989), this trade in human spare parts has reached such magnitude that the *New York Times* saw it as "news fit to print" in a January 1992 issue.

As Egyptian body parts are exported in the human cavities of the materially endowed, Western physicians and nurses have once again found their way into the Egyptian medical arena, but not without protest from the political opposition, and attempts at regulation by the Physicians' Syndicate (El-Wafd, December 29, 1988). In medical education, the timing of the attempt at making it more "society oriented" (Baker 1979:233) is reminiscent of Bryan Turner's discussion of such efforts in conjunction with the commercialization of medical knowledge and professional practice, with the resulting production of "a fragmentary pastiche of disciplines rather than intellectual integration" (Turner 1990:1; see also Morsy 1986b).

In the Fatiha of 1974–1975, the "hierarchy of resort," as discussed in Chapter 5 (cf. Romanucci-Ross 1969; Lane and Inhorn Millar 1987), is also informed by state policies and attendant social relations of production. In this Egyptian peasant community the subordination of peasant household production to the requirements of national industrial development has a counterpart in the realm of reproduction, as manifest in the domain of health care.

The state's incapacity in providing essential conditions of health, notably quality food, sanitation, as well as adequate health services, is consistent with its tolerance of what *it* defines as the illegal practices of traditional healers. By no means restricted to the medical domain, such convenient oversight also pertains to child welfare. The state's own legal codes regulating child labor are violated on a daily basis, and from a very early age, as families struggle to meet their obligation of subsidizing national development programs. As the significance of peasants' legislated control over means of production is undermined by the state's imposed burden on the peasantry, the once greatly appreciated provision of public health services is undermined by inadequate support in terms of personnel, equipment, and medication.

In considering peasants' resort to traditional healers as an alternative to state-sanctioned biomedicine, which insulates diagnosis from social causation, we should not undermine the high esteem in which peasants hold cosmopolitan care, including its public form, in spite of its outstanding limitations. Far from joining the vocal opponents of Arab "Socialism" in the now familiar blasting of the Nasserist era of "closing up" (*inghilaq*), Fatiha's older villagers generally express great appreciation of the state's programs of public health. These represent a vast improvement over what was available to them prior to the 1952 Revolution. Along with other villagers they express their valorization of hegemonic biomedicine in spite of the fact that their existential conditions are excluded from the concerns of this medical culture. With the notable exception of contraceptive pills, appreciation generally extends to the efficacy of pharmaceuticals (cf. Van Der Geest and Whyte; Nichter 1988: 204–210), which became readily available through public sector industries. This is not to say that villagers' reactions towards the state's health care program do not include reproach, and particularly from younger adult villagers. These are people who grew up in a community which is in many ways different from that of their parents' childhood. They are the ones who laugh about how older villagers used to dread going to the hospital.[3]

The younger people of Fatiha are similar in attitude to those of Saad's (1988) account of land reform in another Delta village. They take biomedical health care for granted and are more critical of the limitations of health services than are the now aged earlier beneficiaries of the state's public health reforms. Far from aspiring to the services of traditional healers as an alternative, younger villagers wish to transcend the entire framework of peasant social life. For this they continue to expect state programs, whether for education, vocational training, or employment.

No longer using the *ancien regime* as a reference point, villagers point to their status as peasants in their complaints of misfortune, including ill-health. To many villagers, reducing the distress of daily life requires nothing less than distancing from peasant status. As Fat'heya, a young married woman in her twenties put it,

> I wish we could live like the city. I wish we could live there [with] all the electricity and water. . . . People in the city have more money; they buy meat at least once a week, not like us. I wish I was born in the city; I would have gone to school and learned to read and write.

Although desiring the material comforts and health-promoting practices of urban life, this young woman, like the majority in her village, remains partial to her own community's standards of women's appropriate conduct. Bypassing other criteria of "emancipation" associated with state feminism, she adds, "But there are better things here, for example our women are modest in dress [*mithashimin*] but in the city women go around naked."

In sum, although programs initiated by the Nasserist state went a long way towards improving the lives of peasants, due to a complex of internal and external developments, these did not succeed in fulfilling the aspirations of many of us who belong to the generation of the revolution and recall promises to eradicate "ignorance, poverty, and disease." As in the case of formal education, the state's efforts at reduction of peasants' poverty and improvement of their health have been undermined by its very demands on rural society. Indeed, implementation of the state's development agenda, including official feminism, has been underwritten by the laboring and sacrifices of rural communities, personified by men, women, and children of peasant households. It was people such as these who hosted, tolerated, and shared many of their experiences, and often their affection, with me, an upper class compatriot turned anthropologist.

Notes

1. Sayed Mar^ci, a member of this "modernistic wing" played a prominent role in the formulation of the land reform program in the early days of the revolution.

2. Villagers' subservience to the authority of the state is not without challenge. Although they do not engage in open revolt, they find occasions to resist

compliance. Examples include retaining a larger portion of their crop yield than permitted, selling part of their cotton crop to private traders, or engaging in illegal sharecropping.

3. The *ʿumda* recalls an incident in 1938 when his head guard became cross at his suggestion that he go to the hospital for treatment of a chronic illness.

REFERENCES

Abaza, Mona. 1987a. The Changing Image of Women in Rural Egypt. Cairo Papers in Social Science Vol. 10, Monograph 3.

———. 1987b. Feminist Debates and "Traditional Feminism" of the Fellaha in Rural Egypt. Working Paper #93, Sociology of Development Research Center, University of Bielefeld.

Abaza, Mona, and Georg Stauth. 1988. Occidental Reason, Orientalism, Islamic Fundamentalism: A Critique. International Journal of Sociology 3(4):343–364.

Abdel Fadil, Mahmoud. 1975. Development, Income Distribution and Social Change in Rural Egypt. London: Cambridge University Press.

Abdel Khader, Soha. 1987. Egyptian Women in a Changing Society, 1899–1985. Boulder: Lynne Rienner Publishers.

Abdel Khalek, Gouda. 1982a. The Open Door Policy: The Roots, the Harvest and the Future. Cairo: Arab Center for Research and Publication (in Arabic).

———. 1982b The Open Door Economic Policy in Egypt: Its Contribution to Investiment and Its Equity Implications. In Rich and Poor States in the Middle East. M.H. Kerr and S. Yassin, eds. Boulder: Westview Press. Pp. 259–283.

Abdel Malek, Anwar. 1968. Egypt: Military Society. New York: Random House.

Abdel Wahab, Laila. 1988. Social Participation of Egyptian Women. Paper presented at the Conference on the Impact of Petro-Economy on the Conditions of Arab Women. Cairo, A.R.E.: Egyptian Committee for Afro-Asian Peoples Solidarity (in Arabic).

Abu-Lughod, Lila. 1989. Zones of Theory in the Anthropology of the Arab World. Annual Review of Anthropology 18:267–306.

Abu-Zahra, Nadia. 1970. On the Modesty of Women in Arab Muslim Villages: A Reply. American Anthropologist 72:1079–1088.

Accad, Evelynne. 1991. Sexuality and Sexual Politics: Conflicts and Contradictions for Contemporary Women in the Middle East. In Third World Women and the Politics of Feminism. Chandra Talpade Mohanty, Ann Russo, and Lourdes Torres, eds. Bloomington: Indiana University Press. Pp. 237–250.

Adams, R.N. 1967. The Second Sowing: Power and Development in Latin America. California: Chandler Publishing Company.

———. 1975. Energy and Structure: A Theory of Social Power. Austin: University of Texas Press.

Adams, Richard H. 1985. Development and Structural Change. World Development Vol. 13(6):705–723.

———. 1986a. Taxation, Control, and Agrarian Transition in Rural Egypt: A Local-Level View. *In* Food, States, and Peasants: Analyses of the Agrarian Question in the Middle East. Alan Richards, ed. Boulder: Westview Press. Pp. 159–182.

———. 1986b. Development and Social Change in Rural Egypt. Syracuse, N.Y.: Syracuse University Press.

Adams, Vincanne. 1988. Modes of Production and Medicine: An Examination of the Theory in Light of Sherpa Medical Traditionalism. Social Science and Medicine 27(5):505–13.

Ahmed, Leila. 1982. Feminism and Feminist Movements in the Middle East. *In* Women and Islam. Aziza Al-Hibri, ed. Oxford: Pergamon. Pp. 153–168.

———. 1989. Arab Culture and Writing Women's Bodies. Feminist Issues 9(1):41–55.

Akhavi, Shahrough. 1975. Egypt's Socialism and Marxist Thought: Some Preliminary Observations on Social Theory and Metaphysics. Comparative Studies in Society and History 17:190–211.

Al-Azhary Sonbol, Amira. 1981. The Creation of the Medical Profession in Egypt During the Nineteenth Century: A Study in Modernization. PhD Dissertation, Georgetown University.

Al-Hibri, Aziza, ed. 1982. Women in Islam. Oxford: Pergamon.

Al-Masri, F. 1975. The Zar: A Pshychological and Anthropological Study. Cairo: Al Hay'a Al Masriya Al-ᶜama lil Kitab (in Arabic).

Alavi, H. 1973. Peasant Classes and Primordial Loyalties. Journal of Peasant Studies 1:23–62.

Altorki, Soraya. 1986. Women in Saudi Arabia: Ideology and Behavior Among the Elite. New York: Columbia University Press.

Amer, Ibrahim. 1958. Land and Peasant. Cairo: al-Dar al-Misriya (in Arabic).

Amin, Galal. 1982. External Factors in the Reorientations of Egypt's Economic Policy. *In* Rich and Poor States in the Middle East. M.H. Kerr and S. Yassin, eds. Boulder: Westview Press. Pp. 285–315.

Amin, Samir. 1976. Unequal Development. New York: Monthly Review Press.

———. 1978. The Arab Nation. London: Zed Press.

———. 1989. Eurocentrism. New York: Monthly Review Press.

Ammar, Hamed. 1961. Growing Up in an Egyptian Village. New York: Octagon Books.

Ammar, Nawal. 1989. Children's Health in a Changing World: A Case Study from Upper Egypt. Paper presented at the Annual Meeting of the American Anthropological Association, Washington, D.C. November 14–20.

———. n.d. The Co-existence of Indigenous and Western Medicine: A Case Study from Silwa, An Upper Egyptian Village Community. Unpublished Paper.

Anonymous. 1976. The Worries of the Fallah Fat'hi Hamada. Al-Taliᶜa 4:24–53 (in Arabic).

Ansari, Hamied. 1986. Egypt: The Stalled Society. Albany: State University of New York Press.

Antes, Peter. 1989. Medicine and the Living Tradition of Islam. *In* Healing and Restoring Health: Health and Medicine in the World's Religious Traditions. Lawrence E. Sullivan, ed. New York: Macmillan. Pp. 173–202.

Antoun, Richard. 1968. On the Modesty of Women in Arab Muslim Villages: A Study in the Accommodation of Tradition. American Anthropologist 70:671–697.

Appadurai, Arjun. 1986. Theory in Anthropology: Center and Periphery. Comparative Studies in Society and History 28:356–361.

Arnold, David. 1988. Introduction: Disease, Medicine and Empire. *In* Imperial Medicine and Indigenous Societies. David Arnold, ed. Manchester: Manchester University Press. Pp. 1–25.

Asad, Talal. 1979. Anthropology and the Analysis of Ideology. Man 14:607–627.

———. 1986. The Idea of an Anthroplogy of Islam. Occasional Papers Series, Center for Contemporary Arab Studies. Washington, D.C.: Georgetown University.

Assaad, Marie. 1980. Female Circumcision in Egypt: Social Implications, Current Research, and Prospects for Change. Studies in Family Planning 11(1):3–16.

———. 1981. A Communication Gap Regarding Female Circumcision. *In* Health Needs of the World's Poor Women. P. Blair, ed. Washington, D.C.: Equity Policy Center.

Aswad, Barbara. 1978. Women, Class, and Power: Examples from the Hatay, Turkey. *In* Women in the Muslim World. L. Beck and N. Keddie, eds. Cambridge: Harvard University Press. Pp. 473–81.

Ayrout, Father. 1963 (1938). The Egyptian Peasant. Boston: Beacon Press.

Badran, Margot. 1987. Harem Years: The Memoirs of an Egyptian Feminist by Huda Sharawi. London: Virago Press.

———. 1988. Dual Liberation: Feminism and Nationalism in Egypt 1870s–1925.

Baer, Hans. 1989. The American Dominative Medical System as a Reflection of Social Relations in the Larger Society. Social Science and Medicine 28(11):1103–1112.

Baer, Gabriel. 1969. Studies in the Social History of Modern Egypt. Chicago: The University of Chicago Press.

Baker, Raymond. 1979. Egypt's Uncertain Revolution Under Nasser and Sadat. Cambridge: Harvard University Press.

Bates, Daniel, and Amal Rassam. 1983. Peoples and Cultures of the Middle East. Englewood Cliffs: Prentice-Hall.

Beblawi, Hazem. 1990. The Rentier State in the Arab World. *In* The Arab State. Ciacomo Luciani, ed. London: Routledge. Pp. 85–98.

Behman, F. 1953. The Zar in Egypt. BA Project, American University in Cairo.

Beneria, Lourdes, ed. 1982. Women and Development: The Sexual Division of Labor in Rural Societies. New York: Praeger.

Bennoune, Mahfoud, and Imane Hayef. 1986. Class Structuration and Economic Development in the Arab World. Journal of Asian and African Studies XXI(1–2):45–65.

Blackman, W.S. 1927. The Fellahin of Upper Egypt. London: George C. Harrap.

Boddy, Janice. 1989. Women, Men, and the Zar Cult in Northern Sudan. Madison: The University of Wisconsin Press.

Bookman, Ann, and Sandra Morgen. 1988. Women and the Politics of Empowerment. Philadelphia: Temple University Press.

Bossen, Laurel. 1975. Women in Modernizing Societies. American Ethnologist 2(4):587–601.

Brink, Judy. 1987. Western Capitalism and Zar Possession. Paper presented at the Annual Meeting of the American Anthropological Association. Chicago, Illinois, November 18–22.

Broadman, K., Albert J. Erdmann, Jr., Irving Longe, and H.G. Wolff. 1951. CMI Health Questionnaire II: As a Diagnostic Instrument. Journal of the American Medical Association CXLV:152–157.

Brown, Michael Fobes. 1988. Shamanism and Its Discontents. Medical Anthropology Quarterly 2(2):102–120.

Brown, Nathan J. 1990. Peasant Politics in Modern Egypt: The Struggle Against the State. New Haven: Yale University Press.

———. 1991. The Ignorance and the Inscrutability of the Egyptian Peasantry. In Peasants and Politics in the Modern Middle East. Farhad Kazemi and John Waterbury, eds. Miami: Florida International University Press. Pp. 203–221.

Brown, Peter. 1987. Microparasites and Macroparasites. Cultural Anthropology 2(1):155–171.

Browner, Carol. 1989. Women, Household and Health in Latin America. Social Science and Medicine 28(5):461–473.

Browner, Carole, and Carolyn Sargent. 1990. Anthropology and Studies of Human Reproduction. In Medical Anthropology: Contemporary Theory and Method. Thomas Johnson and Carolyn Sargent, eds. New York: Praeger. Pp. 215–229.

Bybee, Dorothy Ann. 1978. Muslim Peasant Women of the Middle East: Their Sources and Uses of Power. Ph.D. Dissertation, Department of Anthropology, Indiana University.

Byres, T.J. 1977. Agrarian Transition and the Agrarian Question. Journal of Peasant Studies 4(3):258–274.

CAPMAS (Central Agency for Mobilization and Statistics). 1972. The Egyptian Woman in Twenty Years: 1952–1972. Cairo: Markaz al-Abhath wa al-Dirasat al-Sykaniya (in Arabic).

Caudill, W. 1953. Applied Anthropology in Medicine. In Anthropology Today. A.L. Kroeber, ed. Chicago: University of Chicago Press.

Cherif, Khadija. 1989. L'Aspect du Travail des Femmes sur les Changements des Structures Familiales et Sociales dans les Bourgeoisies Urbaines: Example de la Ville de Tunis. Paper presented at the UNESCO Division of Human Rights and Peace International Symposium on "The Access of Women to Salaried Employment as a Source of Social Change." Ankara, Turkey, September 4–9.

Clark, M. 1989. The Body as a Commodity: Ritual Dismemberment in Contemporary Biomedicine. Paper presented at the Annual Meeting of the American Anthropological Association. Washington, D.C. November 15–19.

Claus, P. 1984. Medical Anthropology and the Ethnography of Spirit Possession. Contributions to Asian Studies XVII:60–72.

Clot, Antoine Barthelemy. 1840. Apercu General Sur L'Egypte. Paris: Fortin,
Masson et Cie.

Comaroff, J. 1981. Healing and Cultural Transformation: The Tswana of Southern Africa. Social Science and Medicine 15B:367–378.

Cooper, Mark. 1982. The Transformation of Egypt. Baltimore: Johns Hopkins
Universtiy Press.

Craddock, Susan. 1990. Getting Left Out and Left Behind: An Inquiry into the
Health of Wives of Migrant Laborers in East and Southern Africa. Unpublished Manuscript.

Crandon-Malamud, Libbet. 1991. From the Fat of Our Souls: Social Change,
Political Process, and Medical Pluralism in Bolivia. Berkeley: University of
California Press.

Crapanzano, V., and V. Garrison, eds. 1977. Case Studies in Spirit Possession.
New York: John Wiley.

Croll, Elizabeth. 1986. Rural Production and Reproduction: Socialist Devel-
opment Experiences. *In* Women's Work: Development and the Division of
Labor by Gender. E. Leacock and H. Safa, eds. Massachussetts: Bergin and
Garvey Publishers. Pp. 224–252.

Csordas, Thomas J. and Arthur Kleinman. 1990. The Therapeutic Process. *In*
Medical Anthropology: Contemporary Theory and Method. Thomas M.
Johnson and Carolyn F. Sargent, eds. New York: Praeger. Pp. 11–25.

Davis, Eric. 1975. Political Development or Political Economy? Political Theory
and the Study of Social Change in Egypt and the Third World. Review of
Middle East Studies 1:41–62

Davis, Dona L., and Setha M. Low, eds. 1989. Gender, Health, and Illness: The
Case of Nerves. New York: Hemisphere Publishing Corporation.

Dawson, W.R. 1930. The Beginnings, Egypt and Assyria. New York: Hafner
Publishing Company.

DeClerque, J., A.O. Tsu, M.F. Abul-Ata, and D. Barcelona. 1986. Rumor, Misin-
formation and Oral Contraceptive Use in Egypt. Social Science and Med-
ince 23 (1): 83–93.

Deere, Carmen Diana, and Magdalena Leon. 1987. Rural Women and State
Policy: Feminist Perspectives on Latin American Agricultural Development.
Boulder, Colorado: Westview Press.

Delaney, Carol. 1986. The Meaning of Paternity and the Virgin Birth Debate.
Man 21:495–513.

―――. 1987. Seeds of Honor, Fields of Shame. *In* Honor and Shame and the
Unity of the Mediterranean. David Gilmore, ed. Washington,D.C.: American Anthropolgical Association.

―――. 1988. Mortal Flow: Menstruation in Turkish Village Society. *In* Blood
Magic: The Anthropology of Menstruation. T. Buckley and A. Gottlieb, eds.
Berkeley: University of California Press. Pp. 75–93.

Delphy, Christin. 1988. Patriarchy, Domestic Mode of Production, Gender and
Class. *In* Marxism and the Interpretation of Culture. Chicago: University of
Illinois Press. Pp. 259–271.

Devisch, Renaat, and Bart Vervaeck. 1986. Doors and Thresholds: Jeddi's Approach to Psychiatric Disorders. Social Science and Medicine 22(5):541–551.

Devons, E., and Max Gluckman. 1964. Conclusion: Modes and Consequences of Limiting a Field of Study. *In* Closed Systems and Open Minds. Max Gluckman, ed. Chicago: Aldine.

Dewalt, R.R., and P.J. Pelto. 1985. Micro and Macro Levels of Analysis in Anthropology. Boulder: Westview Press.

Dressler, William. 1990. Culture, Stress, and Disease. *In* Medical Anthropology: Contemporary Theory and Method. Thomas Johnson and Carolyn Sargent, eds. New York: Praeger. Pp. 248–268.

Dressler, W., A. Mata, A. Chavez, F.E. Viteri, and P.N. Gallagher. 1986. Social Support and Arterial Blood Pressure in a Central Mexican Community. Psychosomatic Medicine 48:338–350.

Dwyer, Daisy. 1978. Images and Self Images: Male and Female in Morocco. New York: Columbia University Press.

Early, Evelyn. 1988. The Baladi Curative System of Cairo, Egypt. Culture, Medicine and Psychiatry 12:65–83.

Edholm, Felicity, Olivia Harris, and Kate Young. 1977. Conceptualizing Women. Critique of Anthropology 3(9–10):101–130.

Ehrenreich, Barbara, and Deirdre English. 1973. Complaints and Disorders: The Sexual Politics of Sickness. Glass Mountain Pamphlet no. 2. Old Westbury, N.Y.: The Feminist Press.

———. 1978. The "Sick" Woman of the Upper Classes. *In* The Cultural Crisis of Modern Medicine. John Ehrenreich, ed. New York: Monthly Review Press. 123–143.

Eickelman, Dale F. 1989. The Middle East: An Anthropological Approach. Englewood Cliffs: Prentice-Hall.

El-Gawadi, Muhammad Muhammad. 1987. Health and Medicine in Egypt. Zagazig: Zagazig University Publications (in Arabic).

El-Gindi, M.S. 1978. Urban and Rural Expenditure Patterns in Egypt Based on Cross-Sectional Data, 1958/59–1964/65. *In* The Egyptian Economy in a Quarter Century, 1952–1977: Research and Discussions of the Third Annual Scientific Conference of Egyptian Economists, Cairo, March 23–25. Ismail Sabri Abdallah, Ibrahim El-Essawi, and Gouda Abdel Khalek, eds. Cairo: Al-Hay'a Al-Misriya Al-ᶜAma Lil-Kitab. Pp. 474–495.

El-Islam, M.F. 1967. The Psychotherapeutic Basis of Some Arab Rituals. International Journal of Social Psychiatry 13:265–268.

———. 1975. Culture Bound Neurosis in Qatari Women. Social Psychiatry 10:25–30.

El-Mehairy, Theresa. 1984. Medical Doctors: A Study of Role Concept and Job Satisfaction, The Egyptian Case. Leiden: E.J. Brill.

El-Messiry Nadim, Nawal. 1977. Family Relationships in a 'Harah' in Cairo. *In* Arab Society. Nicholas S. Hopkins and Saad Eddin Ibrahim, eds. Cairo: The American University in Cairo Press. Pp. 212–222.

El-Rafᶜi, ᶜAbdel Rahman. 1968. The 1919 Revolution. Cairo: Dar Al-Shaᶜb (in Arabic).

El-Sanabary, Nagat. 1989. Determinants of Women's Education in the Middle East and North Africa: Illustrations from Seven Countries. PHREE Background Paper Series 89/14, Washington, D.C.: The World Bank.

El-Sendiony, M.F. 1972. Sociocultural Influences Upon Psychiatric Disorders in Egypt: A Stress Model. Unpublished Ph.D. Dissertation, University of Alberta.

El-Solh, Camillia. 1985. Migration and the Selectivity of Change: Egyptian Peasant Women in Iraq. Peuples Mediterranees 31/32: 243–258.

―――. 1988. Gender, Class, and Origin: Aspects of Role During Fieldwork in Arab Society. In Arab Women in the Field: Studying Your Own Society. Syracuse: Syracuse University Press.

Esfahani, Hadi S. 1987. Growth, Employment and Income Distribution in Egyptian Agriculture, 1964–1979. World Development 15(9):1201–1217.

Evers, Hans-Dieter, Wolfgang Class, and Diana Wong. 1984. Subsistence Reproduction: A Framework for Analysis. In Households and the World Economy. Joan Smith et al., eds. Beverly Hills: Sage Publications. Pp. 23–36.

Fabian, J. 1983. Time and the Other: How Anthropology Makes Its Object. New York: Columbia University Press.

Fabrega, Horacio. 1970. Dynamics of Medical Practice in a Folk Community. Milbank Memorial Fund Quarterly 48:391–412.

―――. 1972. Medical Anthropology. Biennial Review of Anthropology, 1971.

―――. 1974. Disease and Social Behavior: An Interdisciplinary Perspective. Cambridge: MIT Press.

―――. 1976. The Biological Significance of Taxonomies of Disease. Journal of Theoretical Biology 63:191–216.

―――. 1990. A Plea for a Broader Ethnomedicine. Culture, Medicine and Psychiatry 14(1):129–132.

Fabrega, H., and D.B. Silver. 1973. Illness and Shamanistic Curing in Zinacantan. Stanford: Stanford University Press.

Fardon, Richard, ed. 1990. Localizing Strategies: Regional Traditions of Ethnographic Writing. Edinburgh: Scottish Academic Press.

Faithorn, E. 1975. The Concept of Pollution Among the Kafe of the Papua New Guinea Highlands. In Toward an Anthropology of Women. Rayna [Rapp] Reiter, ed. Pp. 127–140.

Fakhouri, Hani. 1968. The Zar Cult in an Egyptian Village. Anthropological Quarterly 41:49–56.

Farley, John. 1988. Bilharzia: A Problem of 'Native Health,' 1900–1950. In Imperial Medicine and Indigenous Societies. David Arnold, ed. Manchester: Manchester University Press. Pp.189–207.

Farsoun, Samih K. 1988. Class Structure and Social Change in the Arab World: 1995. In The Next Arab Decade. Hisham Sharabi, ed. Boulder: Westview Press.

Farsoun, Samih K., and Walter F. Carroll. 1978. State Capitalism and Counterrevolution in the Middle East: A Thesis. In Social Change in the Capitalist World Economy. Barbara Kaplan, ed. Beverly Hills: Sage.

Ferchiou, Sophie. 1991. The Possession Cults of Tunisia: A Religious System Functioning as a System of Reference and a Social Field for Performing

Actions. *In* Women's Medicine: The Zar-Bori Cults in Africa and Beyond. I.M. Lewis, Ahmed Al-Safi, and Sayyid Hurreiz, eds. Edinburgh: University Press for the International African Institute. Pp. 209–218.

Ferguson, Anne. 1986. Class Differences in Women's Roles as Health Care Managers: A Case Study from El Salvador. Paper presented at the National Women's Studies Association Meetings, Champaign-Urbana, Illinois, June 11–15.

Fernandez-Kelley, Maria Patricia. 1983. For We Are Sold, I and My People: Women and Industry in Mexico's Frontier. Albany: State University of New York Press.

Fields, A. Belden. 1988. In Defence of Political Economy and Systemic Analysis: A Critique of Prevailing Theoretical Approaches to the New Social Movements. *In* Marxism and the Interpretation of Culture. Cary Nelson and Lauren Grossberg, eds. Chicago: University of Illinois Press. Pp. 141–158.

Finerman, Ruthbeth. 1989. The Forgotten Healers: Women as Family Healers in an Andean Indian Community. *In* Women Healers. Carol McClain, ed. New Brunswick: Rutgers University Press. Pp. 24–41.

Finkler, Kaja. 1985a. Symptomatic Differences Between the Sexes in Rural Mexico. Culture, Medicine and Psychiatry 9(1):27–57.

———. 1985b. Spiritualist Healers in Mexico: Success and Failure in Alternative Theapeutics. South Hadley, Mass: Bergin and Garvey Publishers.

———. 1986. The Social Consequences of Wellness: A View of Healing Outcomes from Micro and Macro Perspectives. International Journal of Health Services 16(4):627–642.

Fluehr-Lobban, Carol. 1973. Sudanese Women's Struggle. *In* Women in the Middle East. Cambridge, Mass: Women's Middle East Collective. Pp. 5–7.

Foster, George. 1972. The Anatomy of Envy: A Study in Symbolic Behavior. Current Anthropology 13:165–202.

———. 1987. On the Origin of Humoral Medicine in Latin America. Medical Anthroplogy Quarterly 1(4):355–393.

Frankenberg, Ronald. 1980. Medical Anthropology and Development: A Theoretical Perspective. Social Science and Medicine 14b(4):197–207.

Freed, Ruth S., and Stanley A. 1990. Ghost Illness in a North Indian Village. Social Science and Medicine 30(5): 617–623.

Gadalla, Saad M. 1978. Is There Hope?: Fertility & Family Planning in a Rural Egyptian Community. Cairo: The Social Research Center and the American University in Cairo Press; Chapel Hill: The Carolina Population Center, The University of North Carolina.

Galal, Essam E. 1983. National Production of Drugs: Egypt. World Development 11(3):237–241.

Gallagher, Nancy Elizabeth. 1983. Medicine and Power in Tunisia: 1790–1900. Cambridge: Cambridge University Press.

———. 1985. What Happened to Islamic Medicine? *In* African Healing Strategies. B.M. du Toit and I.H. Abdalla, eds. Owerri: Trado-Medic Books. Pp. 47–57.

———. 1990. Egypt's Other Wars. Syracuse: Syracuse University Press.

Galul, Feisal. 1984. Elitist Ideas in the Writings of Nawal Saadawi. Al Fikr Al ᶜArabi 2(17/18): 142–157

Garro, Linda. 1986. Intracultural Variation in Folk Medical Knowledge: A Comparison Between Curers and Noncurers. American Anthropologist 88:351–70.

Ghalioungui, P., and Z.E. Dawakhly. 1965. Health and Healing in Ancient Egypt. Cairo: Dar Al-Maᶜaref.

Gilmore, David. 1990. Performative Excellence: Circum-Mediterranean. *In* Manhood in the Making. New Haven and London: Yale University Press. Pp. 30–55.

Gilmore, David, ed. 1987. Honor and Shame and the Unity of the Mediterranean. Washington, D.C.: American Anthropological Association.

Gilsenan, Michael. 1973. Saint and Sufi in Modern Egypt: An Essay in the Sociology of Religion. Oxford: The Clarendon Press.

———. 1982. Recognizing Islam: Religion and Society in the Modern Arab World. New York: Pantheon Books.

Ginsburg, Faye, and Rayna Rapp. 1991. The Politics of Reproduction. Annual Review of Anthroplogy 20:311–343.

Glavanis, Kathy. 1984. Aspect of Non-Capitalist Social Relations in Rural Egypt: The Small Peasant Household in an Egyptian Delta Village. *In* Family and Work in Rural Societies. Norman Long, ed. London: Tavistock. Pp. 30–60.

Glavanis, Kathy and Pandeli. 1983. The Sociology of Agrarian Relations in the Middle East. The Persistence of Household Production. Current Sociology 31(2):1–109.

———. 1986. Historical Materialism or Marxist Halography? A Response to a Positivist Critique. Current Sociology 34(2):172–198.

———. 1989. The Rural Middle East. London/New Jersey: Birzeit University Zed Books Ltd.

Glick, Leonard. 1963. Foundations of a Primitive Medical System: The Gimi of the New Guinea Highlands. Unpublished PhD Dissertation, University of Pennsylvania.

———. 1967. Medicine as an Ethnographic Category. Ethnology 6:31–56.

Gomm, R. 1975. Bargaining from Weakness: Spirit Possession on the South Kenya Coast. Man 10(4):530–43.

Good, Byron. 1977. The Heart of What's the Matter: Semantics and Illness in Iran. Culture, Medicine and Psychiatry 1:25–58.

Good, Mary-Jo Delvecchio. 1980. Of Blood and Babies: The Relationship of Popular Islamic Physiology to Fertility. Social Science and Medicine 14B: 147–156.

Good, Mary-Jo Delvecchio, and Byron J. Good. 1988. Ritual, the State, and the Transformation of Emotional Discourse in Iranian Society. Culture, Medicine and Psychiatry 12:43–63.

———. n.d. The Comparative Study of Islamic Medicine as Symbolic System. Manuscript.

Goode, W. 1970. Industrialization and Family Change. *In* Industrialization and Society. B.F. Hoselitz and W.E. Moore, eds. The Hague: Mouton. Pp. 237–259.

Graham-Brown, Sarah. 1989. Agriculture and Labor Transformation in Palestine. *In* The Rural Middle East: Peasant Lives and Modes of Production. Kathy and Pandeli Glavanis, eds. London: Zed Press/Birzeit: Birzeit University. Pp. 53–69.

Gran, Judith. 1977. The Impact of the World Market on Egyptian Women. MERIP 58:3–7.

Gran, Peter. 1979a. Medical Pluralism in Arab and Egyptian History: An Overview of Class Structures and Philosophies of the Main Phases. Social Science and Medicine 13B: 339–348.

———. 1979b. Islamic Roots of Capitalism. Austin: University of Texas Press.

———. 1987. Reflection on Contemporary Arab Society: The Political Economy School of the 1970s. Arab Studies Quarterly 9(1):76–97.

———. n.d. Readings from the Text: Political Economy in Anglo-American Middle Eastern Studies. Manuscript.

Granqvist, Hilma. 1947. Birth and Childhood Among the Arabs: Studies in a Muhamadan Village in Palestine. Helsingfors: Soderstrom.

Greenwood, Bernard. 1981. Cold or Spirits? Choice and Ambiguity in Morocco's Pluralistic Medical System. Social Science and Medicine 15B:219–235.

Greyghton, M.L. 1977. Communication Between Peasant and Doctor in Tunisia. Social Science and Medicine 11:319–325.

Gruenbaum, Ellen. 1988. Reproductive Ritual and Social Reproduction: Female Circumcision and the Subordination of Women in Sudan. *In* Economy and Class in Sudan. Norman O'Neill and Jay O'Brien, eds. Brookfield: Avebury.

Haddad, Yvonne. 1985. Islam, Women and Revolution in Twentieth-Century Arab Thought. *In* Women, Religion and Social Change. Yvonne Yazbeck Haddad and Ellison Banks Findly, eds. Albany: State University of New York. Pp. 275–306.

Hakky, Ulfat. 1974. The Hakky Personality Test. Cairo: Ein Shams University.

Hale, Sondra. 1989. The Politics of Gender in the Middle East. *In* Gender and Anthropology: Critical Reviews for Research and Teaching. Sandra Morgen, ed. Washington, D.C.: American Anthropological Association. Pp. 246–267.

Hammam, Mona. 1977. Women Workers and the Practice of Freedom as Education: The Egyptian Experience. PhD Dissertation, University of Kansas.

———. 1980. The Continuum of Economic Activities in Middle Eastern Social Formations, Family Division of Labour and Migration. Paper presented at the Burg Wartenstein Symposium on "The Sex Division of Labor, Development and Women's Status," August 2–10.

Hammami, Reza and Martina Rieker. 1988. Feminist Orientalism and Orientalist Marxism. New Left Review 170:93–106.

Hammarneh, Sami. 1967. History of Arabic Medicine and Pharmacy. Cairo: Dar il Kutub.

Handousa, Heba A. 1978. The Public Sector in Egyptian Industry 1952–1977. *In* The Egyptian Economy in a Quarter Century, 1952–1977: Research and Discussions of the Third Annual Scientific Conference of Egyptian Economists,

Cairo, March 23–25. Ismail Sabri Abdallah, Ibrahim El-Essawi, and Gouda Abdel Khalek, eds. Cairo: Al-Hay'a Al-Misriya Al-ᶜAma Lil-Kitab. pp. 497–518.

Harer, W.B., Jr. n.d. Azar—A Spirit of Women's Liberation Rural Egyptian Style. Unpublished paper.

Harris, Marvin. 1968. The Rise of Anthropological Theory. New York: Thomas Y. Crowell Company.

Harris, Olivia, and Kate Young. 1984. Engendered Structures: Some Problems in the Analysis of Reproduction. *In* The Anthropology of Pre-Capitalist Societies. J. Khan and L. Lobera, eds. London: Macmillan. Pp. 109–147.

Hastrup, Kirsten. 1990. The Ethnographic Present: A Reinvention. Cultural Anthropology 5(1):45–61.

Hatata, Sherif. 1968. Health and Development. Cairo: Dar Al-Maᶜarif (in Arabic).

Hatem, Mervat. 1986. The Enduring Alliance of Nationalism and Patriarchy in Muslim Personal Status Laws: The Case of Modern Egypt. Feminist Issues 6(1):19–43.

———. 1987. Class and Patriarchy as Competing Paradigms for the Study of Middle Eastern Women. Comparative Studies in Society and History 29(4):811–818.

———. 1992a. Privatization and the Demise of State Feminism in Egypt (1977–1990). *In* Structural Adjustment and Women in the Third World. Pamela Sparr, ed. Vienna: NGLS

———. 1992b. Economic and Political Liberalization in Egypt and the Demise of State Feminism. Forthcoming in International Journal of Middle East Studies.

Hijab, Nadia. 1988. Womanpower: The Arab Debate on Women at Work. Cambridge: Cambridge University Press.

Hobsbawn, E.J. 1962. The Age of Revolution 1789–1848. New York: Mentor Books.

Hopkins, Nicholas, and Sohair Mehanna. 1981. Egyptian Village Studies. Economics Working Papers #42. Giza: Agricultural Development Systems Project. Arab Republic of Egypt-University of California.

Hopkins, Nicholas. 1986. Class Consciousness and Political Action in Testour. Dialectical Anthropology 11(1):73–92.

———. 1977. The Emergence of Class in an Tunisian Town. International Journal of Middle East Studies 8:453–491.

———. 1987. Agrarian Transformation in Egypt. Boulder: Westview Press.

———. 1989. The Agrarian Transition and the Household in Rural Egypt. *In* Household Economies and Their Transformaitons. Morgan D. Maclachlan, ed. University Press of America/Society for Economic Anthropology. Pp. 155–172.

———. 1991. Clan and Class in Two Arab Villages. *In* Peasants and Politics in the Modern Middle East. Farhad Kazemi and John Waterbury, eds. Miami: Florida International University Press. Pp. 252–276.

Hopper, Kim. 1975. On Language and the Sorcerer's Appendix: A Critical Appraisal of Horacio Fabrega's Disease and Social Behavior. Medical Anthropology Newsletter 19(3):9–14.

Hosseinzadeh, Esmail. 1988. How Egyptian State Capitalism Reverted to Market Capitalism. Arab Studies Quarterly 10(3):299–318.

Hussein, Adel. 1981. The Egyptian Economy from Independence to Dependency, 1974–1979. Beirut: Dar al-Kalimah lil Nashr (in Arabic).

Hussein, Mahmoud. 1973. Class Conflict in Egypt: 1945–1971. New York: Monthly Review Press.

Inhorn Millar, Marcia, and Sandra D. Lane. 1988. Ethno-Ophthalmology in the Egyptian Delta: An Historical Systems Approach to Ethnomedicine in the Middle East. Social Science and Medicine 26(6):651–657.

Isselbacher, K.J., R.D. Adams, E. Braunwald, R.G. Petersdorf, and J.D. Wilson. 1980. Harrison's Principles of Internal Medicine. New York: McGraw-Hill Book Company.

Janzen, John. 1978. The Quest for Therapy in Lower Zaire. Berkeley: University of California Press.

———. 1985. Changing Concepts of African Therapeutics: An Historical Perspective. In African Healing Strategies. Brian M. du Toit and Ismail H. Abdalla, eds. New York: Trado-Medic Books. Pp. 61–81.

Jordan, Brigitte. 1983. Birth in Four Cultures. Montreal: Eden Press.

Joseph, Suad. 1975. Urban Poor Women in Lebanon: Does Poverty Have Public and Private Domains? Paper presented at the Annual Meeting of the Association of Arab-American University Graduates, Chicago.

———. 1986. Women and Politics in the Middle East. MERIP Reports 138:3–8.

Kandiyoti, Deniz. 1989. Women and Household Production: The Impact of Rural Transformation in Turkey. In The Rural Middle East: Peasant Lives and Modes of Production. Kathy and Pandeli Glavanis, eds. London: Zed Press/Birzeit: Birzeit University. Pp. 183–194.

———. 1990. Women, Islam and the State: A Comparative Approach. Manuscript.

Katz, Sydney S., and Selig H. Katz. 1987. An Evaluation of Traditional Therapy for Barrenness. Medical Anthropology Quarterly 1(4):394–405.

Keesing, Roger M. 1981. Cultural Anthropology: A Contemporary Perspective. New York: CBS Publishing Asia Ltd.

Kehoe, A., and H. Giletti. 1981. Women's Preponderance in Possession Cults: The Calcium Deficiency Hypothesis Extended. American Anthropologist 83:549–561.

Kelley, Allen, Atef M. Khalifa, and M. Nabil El-Khorazaty. 1982. Population and Development in Rural Egypt. Durham: Duke University Press.

Khalaf, ᶜAbdel Ghaffar. 1987. Egypt's Health Policies. Unpublished Manuscript.

Khater, Akram, and Cynthia Nelson. 1988. Al-Harakah Al-Nissa'iyah: The Women's Movement and Political Participation in Modern Egypt. Women's Studies International Forum 11(5):465–483.

Kim, Eun-Shil. 1989. The Anthropology of Gender and Feminism. Unpublished Manuscript.

Kleinman, Arthur. 1977. Lessons from a Clinical Approach to Medical Anthropological Research. Medical Anthropology Newsletter 8(4):11–15.

———. 1980. Patients and Healers in the Context of Culture. Berkeley: University of California Press.

Kleinman, Arthur, and Joan Kleinman. 1985. The Interconnections Among Culture, Depressive Experiences, and the Meanings of Pain. *In* Culture and Depression. Arthur Kleinman and Byron Good, eds. Berkeley: University of California Press.

Koptiuch, Kristin. 1985. Fieldwork in the Postmodern World: Notes on Ethnography in an Expanded Field. Paper presented at the Annual Meeting of the American Anthropological Association, Washington, D.C.

Korayem, Karima. 1978. Income Distribution Between Urban and Rural Egypt. *In* The Egyptian Economy in a Quarter Century, 1952–1977: Research and Discussions of the Third Annual Scientific Conference of Egyptian Economists, Cairo, March 23–25. Ismail Sabri Abdallah, Ibrahim El-Essawi, and Gouda Abdel Khalek, eds. Cairo: Al-Hay'a Al-Misriya Al-ᶜAma Lil Kitab. Pp. 65–111 (in Arabic).

———. 1981a. Women and the New International Economic Order in the Arab World. Cairo Papers in Social Science 4(4):45–79.

———. 1981b. The Rural-Urban Income Gap in Egypt and Biased Agricultural Pricing Policy. Social Problems 28(4):417–429.

Kruks, Sonia, Rayna Rapp, and Marilyn B. Young. 1989. Promissory Notes: Women in the Transition to Socialism. New York: Monthly Review Press.

Kuhnke, Laverne. 1974. The 'Doctress' on a Donkey: Women Health Officers in Nineteenth Century Egypt. Clio Medica 9(3).

———. 1990. Lives at Risk: Public Health in Nineteenth-Century Egypt. Berkeley: University of California Press.

Kunstadter, Peter. 1975. Do Cultural Differences Make Any Difference? Choice Points in Medical Systems Available in North-Western Thailand. *In* Medicine in Chinese Culture. A. Kleinman et al., eds. Washington, D.C.: U.S. Government Printing Office for Fogarty International Center. Pp. 351–383.

Laderman, Carol. 1987. Destructive Heat and Cooling Prayers: Malay Humoralism in Pregnancy, Childbirth and the Postpartum Period. Social Science and Medicine 25(4):357–365.

Lakhdar, Lafif. 1978. The Development of Class Struggle in Egypt. Khamsin 5:47–80.

Lane, Sandra. 1987. A Biocultural Study of Trachoma in an Egyptian Hamlet. Ph.D. Dissertation, University of California, San Francisco.

Lapidus, Ira. 1988. A History of Islamic Societies. Cambridge: Cambridge University Press.

Leacock, Eleanor. 1977. Women in Egalitarian Societies. *In* Becoming Visible: Women in European History. R. Bridenthal, ed. New York: Houghton Mifflin. Pp. 11–35.

Lewis, Bernard. 1990. Race and Slavery in the Middle East. New York: Oxford University Press.

Lewis, I.M. 1966. Spirit Possession and Deprivation Cults. Man 1:307–29.

———. 1971. Ecstatic Religion: An Anthropological Study in Spirit Possession and Shamanism. Harmondsworth: Penguin.

———. 1983. Spirit Possession and Biological Reductionism: A Rejoinder to Kehoe and Giletti. American Anthropologist 412–413.

———. 1986. Religion in Context: Cults and Charisma. Cambridge: University Press.

———. 1989. Ecstatic Religion, 2nd edition. London: Routledge.

———. 1991. Introduction. *In* Women's Medicine: The Zar-Bori Cult in Africa and Beyond. I.M. Lewis, Ahmed A.-Safi, and Sayyid Hurreiz, eds. Edinburgh: University Press for the International African Institute. Pp. 1–16.

Lewis, I.M., Ahmed A.-Safi, and Sayyid Hurreiz, eds. Women's Medicine: The Zar-Bori Cult in Africa and Beyond. Edinburgh: University Press for the International African Institute.

Lock, Margaret. 1986. Plea for Acceptance: School Refusal Syndrome in Japan. Social Science and Medicine 23:99–112.

———. 1989. Words of Fear, Words of Power: Nerves and the Awakening of Political Consciousness. Medical Anthropology 11(1):79–90.

Long, Norman, ed. 1984. Family and Work in Rural Societies: Perspectives on Non-Wage Labor. London: Tavistock.

Low, Setha M. 1985. Culture, Politics and Medicine in Costa Rica. Bedford Hills: Redgrave Publishing.

Lutsky, V. 1969. Modern History of the Arab Countries. Moscow: Progress Publishers.

Mani, Lata. 1990. Multiple Mediations: Feminist Scholarship in the Age of Multinational Reception. Feminist Review 35:24–41.

Marcus, George, and Michael Fischer. 1986. Anthropology as Cultural Critique. Chicago: University of Chicago Press.

Marsot, Afaf Lutfi Al-Sayyid. 1978. The Revolutionary Gentlewomen in Egypt. *In* Women in the Muslim World. Lois Beck and Nikki Keddie, ed. Cambridge: Harvard University Press. Pp. 261–276.

———. 1984. Egypt in the Reign of Muchammad Ali. Cambridge: Cambridge University Press.

———. 1989. Women and Social Change. *In* The Modern Economic and Social History of the Middle East in Its World Context. Georges Sabagh, ed. Cambridge: Cambridge University Press. Pp. 112–129.

Martin, Emily. 1987. The Woman in the Body. Boston: Beacon Press.

Mayfield, J.B. 1974. Local Institutions and Egyptian Rural Development. Ithaca: Center for International Studies, Cornell University.

McClain, Carol, ed. 1989. Women Healers. New Brunswick: Rutgers University Press.

McNeill, William. 1977. Plagues and Peoples. New York: Anchor Books

Mechanic, David. 1961. Stress, Illness, and the Sick Role. American Sociological Review 26:51–58.

Meinardus, Otto F.A. 1970. Christian Egypt: Faith and Life. Cairo: The American University in Cairo Press.

Mernissi, Fatima. 1982a. Women and the Impact of Capitalist Development in Morocco, Part I. Feminist Issues 2(2):69–104.

———. 1982b. Women and the Impact of Capitalist Development in Morocco, Part II. Feminist Issues 2(3): 61–112.

————. 1988. Doing Daily Battle: Interviews with Moroccan Women. London: The Women's Press.

Millar, Marcia Inhorn, and Sandra D. Lane. 1988. Ethno-Ophthalmology in the Egyptian Delta: An Historical Systems Approach to Ethnomedicine in the Middle East. Social Science and Medicine 26:651–657.

Mitchell, Timothy. 1990. The Invention and Reinvention of the Egyptian Peasant. International Journal of Middle East Studies 22(2):129–150.

————. 1991a. The Representation of Rural Violence in Writings on Political Development in Nasserist Egypt. *In* Peasants and Politics in the Modern Middle East. Farhad Kazemi and John Waterbury, eds. Pp. 222–251.

————. 1991b. America's Egypt: Discourse of the Development Industry. MERIP Reports 169:18–34.

Mohanty, Chandra Talpade. 1991. Under Western Eyes: Feminist Scholarship and Colonial Discourse. *In* Third World Women and the Politics of Feminism. Chandra Talpade Mohanty, Ann Russo, and Lourdes Torres, eds. Bloomington: Indiana University Press. Pp. 51–80.

Mohsen, Safia. 1985. New Images, Old Reflections: Working Middle-Class Women in Egypt. *In* Women and the Family in the Middle East. Elizabeth Fernea, ed.

Moore, Henrietta L. 1986. Space, Text, and Gender: An Anthropological Study of the Marakwet of Kenya. Cambridge: Cambridge University Press.

————. 1988. Feminism and Anthropology. Minneapolis: University of Minnesota Press.

Moors, Analiese. 1989. Gender Hierarchy in a Palestinian Village: The Case of Al-Balad. *In* The Rural Middle East. K. Glavanis and P. Glavanis, eds. London: Zed Press/Birzeit: Birzeit University. Pp. 195–209.

Morgan, Lynn. 1987. Dependency Theory in the Political Economy of Health: An Anthropological Critique. Medical Anthropology Quarterly 1(2):131–155.

Morsi, Fuad. 1976. This Economic Opening. Cairo: Dar al-Thaqafa al-Jadida (in Arabic).

Morsy, Soheir A. 1972. The Changing Role and Status of Arab Women. MA Thesis, Department of Anthropology, Michigan State University, E. Lansing, Michigan.

————. 1978. Sex Roles, Power and Illness in an Egyptian Village. American Ethnologist 5(1):137–150.

————. 1979. The Missing Link in Medical Anthropology: The Political Economy of Health. Reviews in Anthropology 6:349–363.

————. 1980. Reorientation in Capitalist Development: A Note on Sadat's *Infitah*. Paper presented at the Central States Meetings of the American Anthropological Association, Ann Arbor, Michigan, April 9–12.

————. 1981a. Towards a Political Economy of Health: A Critical Note on the Medical Anthropology of the Middle East. Social Science and Medicine 15(B):159–163.

————. 1981b. Childbirth in an Egyptian Village. *In* An Anthroplogy of Human Birth. M. Kay, ed. Philadelphia: F.A. Davis Company. Pp. 147–174.

————. 1985. Familial Adaptation to the Internationalization of Egyptian Labor. WID Working Papers #94. East Lansing, Michigan: Michigan State University.

————. 1986a. Implant Contraception and Family Planning: Between Propaganda and Serious Evaluation. Al-Maraa-Al Gadida [The New Woman], July (in Arabic).

————. 1986b. Reflections on the Politics of Health. Al-Tali^ca February. Pp. 49–59 (in Arabic).

————. 1988a. Field Work in My Egyptian Homeland: Towards the Demise of Anthropology's Distinctive-Other Hegemonic Tradition. *In* Studying Your Own Society: Arab Women in the Field. Soraya Altorki and Camilia El-Solh, eds. New York: Syracuse University Press. Pp. 69–90.

————. 1988b. Islamic Clinics in Egypt: The Cultural Elaboration of Biomedical Hegemony. Medical Anthropology Quarterly 2(4):355–369.

————. 1989. Introduction and Discussant's Commentary on "Medical Anthropology in the Arab World." Invited Session, Society for Medical Anthropology. Annual Meeting of the American Anthropological Association. Washington, D.C., November 14–20.

————. 1990a. Political Economy in Medical Anthropology. *In* Medical Anthropology: Contemporary Theory and Method. T.M.Johnson and C. Sargent, eds. New York: Praeger. Pp. 26–46.

————. 1990b. Rural Women, Work and Ideology: A Study in Egyptian Political Economic Transformation. *In* Women in Arab Society: Work Patterns and Gender Relations in Egypt, Jordan and Sudan. Oxford/Paris: Berg/UNESCO. Pp. 87–159.

————. 1991. Spirit Possession in Egyptian Ethnomedicine: Origins, Comparison and Historical Specificity. *In* Women's Medicine: The Zar-Bori Cult in Africa and Beyond. I.M. Lewis, Ahmed Al-Safi and Sayyid Hureiz, eds. Edinburgh: Edinburgh University Press for the International African Institute. Pp. 189–208.

Mullings, Leith. 1984. Therapy, Ideology, and Social Change: Mental Healing in Urban Ghana. Berkeley: University of California Press.

Murphy, Robert. 1971. The Dialectics of Social Life. New York: Basic Books.

Myntti, Cynthia. 1988. The Social, Economic and Cultural Context of Women's Health and Fertility in Rural North Yemen. *In* Micro Approaches to Demographic Research. V. Hill and A. Hill,eds. London: Routledge Paul International.

Nader, Laura. 1989. Orientalism, Occidentalism and the Control of Women. Cultural Dynamics II(3): 323–355.

Naseer, ^cEmad El-Din. 1987. Medicine Is Sick . . . How? People and Medicine 1:26–31 (in Arabic).

Nash, June. 1981. Ethnographic Aspects of the World Capitalist System. Annual Review of Anthropology 10:393–423.

Nash, June, and M.P. Fernandez-Kelley, eds. 1983. Women, Men, and the International Division of Labor. Albany: State University of New York Press.

Nassar, Heba. 1987. Critical Evaluation of Previous Studies on Health Policies in Egypt. Paper presented at the symposium on Analysis of Public Policies, Center for Political Research and Studies, Faculty of Economics and Political Science, Cairo University, December 23–26.

Nassar, Mohamed Nabil. 1986. Development of Rural Health Service System. Unpublished paper, Cairo: Ministry of Health, General Administration for Basic Rural Health Care.

Natvig, Richard. 1991. Some Notes on the History of the Zar Cult in Egypt. *In* Women's Medicine: The Zar-Bori Cult in Africa and Beyond. I.M. Lewis, Ahmed Al-Safi and Sayyid Hurreiz, eds. Edinburgh: Edinburgh University Press for the International African Institute. Pp. 178–188.

Navarro, Vicente. 1986. Crisis, Health, and Medicine: A Social Critique. New York: Tavistock Publishers.

Nelson, Cynthia. 1971. Self, Spirit Possession and World View: An Illustration from Egypt. International Journal of Psychiatry XVII(3):194–209.

———. 1983. Reconceptualizing Health Care. Cairo Papers in Social Science Vol. 1(1):13–24.

———. 1986. Old Wine, New Bottles: Reflections and Projections Concerning Research on 'Women in the Middle East.' Paper presented at the Conference on the State of the Art of Middle Eastern Studies. University of Calgary, Canada, August 1–4.

Nichter, Mark. 1981. Idioms of Distress. Culture, Medicine and Psychiatry 5:379–408.

———. 1989. Anthropology and International Health: South Asian Case Studies. Dordrecht: Kluwer Academic Publishers.

Noble Tesh, Sylvia. 1988. Hidden Arguments: Political Ideology and Disease Prevention Policy. New Brunswick: Rutgers University Press.

Nyrop, F.R., B.L. Benderly, W. Cover, D.R. Eglin, R.A. Kirchner. 1976. Area Handbook for Egypt, Third Edition. Washington, D.C.: U.S. Government Printing Office.

Ohnuki-Tierney, Emiko. 1990. Culture Through Time: Anthropological Approaches. Stanford: Stanford University Press.

Okasha, A. 1966. A Cultural Psychiatric Study of El-Zar in UAR. British Journal of Psychiatry 112:1217.

O'Nell, C.W., and H.A. Selby. 1968. Sex Differences in the Incidence of Susto in Two Zapotec Pueblos: An Analysis of the Relationship Between Sex Role Expectations and a Folk Illness. Ethnology 7:95–105.

Ong, Aihwa. 1988. The Production of Posssession: Spirits and Multinational Corporations in Malaysia. American Ethnologist 15(1): 28–42.

———. 1990. Status Versus Islam: Malay Families, Women's Bodies, and the Body Politic in Malaysia. American Ethnologist 17(2):258–276.

Onoge, Omafume. 1975. Capitalism and Public Health: A Neglected Theme in the Medical Anthropology of Africa. *In* Topias and Utopia in Health. S.R. Ingman and A.E. Thomas, eds. The Hague: Mouton. pp. 21–232.

Ortner, Sherry. 1974. Is Male to Female as Nature is to Culture? *In* Women, Culture and Society. M.Z. Rosaldo and L. Lamphere,eds. Stanford: Stanford University Press. Pp. 67–88.

Palson, Gisli, and E. Paul Durrenberger. 1990. Systems of Production and Social Discourse: The Skipper Effect Revisited. American Anthroplogist 92:130–141.

Patai, Raphael. 1969. Golden River to Golden Road. Philadelphia: University of Pennsylvania Press.

Petchesky, Rosalyn Pollack. 1984. Abortion and Woman's Choice: The State, Sexuality, and Reproductive Freedom. New York: Longman.

Pliskin, Karen. 1987. Silent Boundaries: Cultural Constraints on Sickness and Diagnosis of Iranians in Israel. New Haven: Yale University Press.

Radwan, Samir. 1975. Towards a Political Economy of Egypt: A Critical Note on the Egyptian Economy. Review of Middle Eastern Studies 1:95–110.

———. 1977. Agrarian Reform and Rural Poverty in Egypt, 1952–1975. Geneva: ILO.

Rahman, Faslur. 1987. Health and Medicine in the Islamic Tradition. New York: Crossroad.

———. 1989. Islam and Health/Medicine: A Historical Perspective. In Healing and Restoring Health: Health and Medicine in the World's Religious Traditions. Lawrence E. Sullivan, ed. New York: Macmillan. Pp. 149–172.

Raikes, Alanagh. 1989. Women's Health in East Africa. Social Science and Medicine 28(5):447–459.

Rapp, Rayna. 1977. Gender and Class: An Archaeology of Knowledge Concerning the Origin of the State. Dialectical Anthropology 2:309–316.

———. 1982. Family and Class in Contemporary America: Notes Toward an Understanding of Ideology. In Rethinking the Family: Some Feminist Questions. B. Thorne and M. Yalon, ed. New York: Longman.

Rassam, Amal. 1986. Review of "Sexuality in Islam" by Abdelwahab Bouhdiba. American Anthroplogist 13(3):577.

Redclift, N., and E. Mingione, eds. 1985. Beyond Employment: Household, Gender and Subsistence. Oxford: Basil Blackwell.

Richards, Allan. 1980. Egypt's Agricultural Development in Trouble. MERIP Reports 84:3–13.

———. 1982. Egypt's Agricultural Development 1800–1980. Boulder: Westview Press.

Richards, Alan, and John Waterbury. 1990. A Political Economy of the Middle East: State, Class, and Economic Development. Boulder: Westview Press.

Robinson, D. 1971. The Process of Being Ill. London: Routledge and Kegan Paul.

Romanucci-Ross, Lola. 1969. The Hierarchy of Resort in Curative Practice: The Admirality Islands, Melanesia. Journal of Health and Social Behavior 10: 201–209.

Rosaldo, M.Z., and L. Lamphere, eds. 1974. Woman, Culture, and Society. Stanford: Stanford University Press.

Roseberry, William. 1988. Political Economy. Annual Review of Anthropology 17:161–85.

———. 1989. Anthropologies and Histories: Essays in Culture, History, and Political Economy. New Brunswick: Rutgers University Press.

Rosen, Lawrence. 1978. The Negotiation of Reality: Male-Female Relations in Sefrou, Morocco. In Women in the Muslim World, L. Beck and N. Keddie, eds. Cambridge: Harvard University Press. Pp. 561–584.

Rubel, Arthur. 1964. The Epidemiology of a Folk Illness: Susto in Hispanic America. Ethnology 3:268–283.

————. 1966. Across the Tracks: Mexican Americans in a Texas City. Austin: University of Texas Press.

Rubel, Arthur, and Michael Hass. 1991. Ethnomedicine. *In* Medical Anthropology: Contemporary Theory and Method. Thomas Johnson and Carolyn Sargent, eds. New York: Praeger. Pp. 115–131.

Saad, Reem. 1988. Social History of an Agrarian Reform Community in Egypt. Cairo Papers in Social Science Vol. 10, Monograph 4.

Sabea, Hanan. 1987. Paths of Rural Transformation: Stratification and Differentiation Processes in a New Lands Village. MA Thesis, Department of Sociology-Anthropology, American University in Cairo.

Sacks, Karen Brodkin. 1989. Toward a Unified Theory of Class, Race, and Gender. American Ethnologist 16(3):535–551.

Safa, Kaveh. 1988. Reading Saedi's *Ahl-e Hava*: Pattern and Significance in Spirit Possession Beliefs on the Southern Coast of Iran. Culture, Medicine and Psychiatry 12:85–111.

Salame, Ghassan. 1990. 'Strong' and 'Weak' States: A Qualified Return to the *Muqaddimah. In* The Arab State. Giacomo Luciani, ed. Berkeley, University of California Press. Pp. 29–64.

Saleh, M. S. 1979. Feudalism and Agrarian Capitalism in Egypt: From the Period of Muhammad Ali to Abdel Nasser. Beirut: Dar Ibn Khaldun (in Arabic).

Sargent, Carolyn F. 1982. The Cultural Context of Therapeutic Choice: Obstetrical Decisions Among the Bariba of Benin. Dordrecht: Reidel.

Saunder, Lucie. 1977. Variants in Zar Experience in an Egyptian Village. In Possession. V. Crapanzano and V. Garrison, eds. N.Y. John Wiley and Sons. Pp. 177–192.

Saunders, Lucie W., and Sohair Mehanna. 1988. Smallholders in a Changing Economy: An Egyptian Village Case. Journal of Peasant Studies 16(1):5–29.

Sayigh, Rosemary. 1987. Moral Familism: The Egyptian Model. Reviews in Anthropology 14(2):115–122.

Scheper-Hughes, Nancy. 1984. Infant Mortality and Infant Care: Cultural and Economic Constraints on Nurturing in Northeast Brazil. Social Science and Medicine 19:535–546.

————. 1989. Embodied Knowledge: The Message in the Bottle. Draft of paper prepared for the Annual Meeting of the American Anthropological Association. Washington, D.C. November 15–19.

Scheper-Hughes, Nancy, and Margaret Lock. 1987. The Mindful Body: A Prolegomenon to Future Work in Medical Anthropology. Medical Anthropology Quarterly 1:6–41.

————. 1990. A Critical-Interpretive Approach in Medical Anthropology: Rituals and Routines of Discipline and Dissent. *In* Medical Anthropology: Contemporary Theory and Method. Thomas Johnson and Carolyn Sargent, eds. New York: Praeger. Pp. 47–72.

Schulze, Reinhard. 1987. Mass Culture and Islamic Cultural Production in 19th Century Middle East. *In* Mass Culture, Popular Culture, and Social Life in the Middle East. Frankfurt am Main: Campus Verlag/Boulder: Westview Press.

————. 1991. Colonization and Resistance: The Egyptian Peasant Rebellion, 1919. *In* Peasants and Politics in the Modern Middle East. Farhad Kazemi and John Waterbury, eds. Miami: Florida International University Press. Pp. 171–202.

Scotch, N.A., and H.J. Geiger. 1963. An Index of Symptoms and Disease in Zulu Culture. Human Organization. 22:304–311.

Scott, James. 1976. The Moral Economy of the Peasant. New Haven: Yale University Press.

————. 1986. Weapons of the Weak: Everyday Forms of Peasant Resistance. New Haven: Yale University Press.

Seddon, David. 1986. Commentary on Agrarian Relations in the Middle East: A New Paradigm? Current Sociology 34(2):151–72.

Shafᶜi Bey. 1862. Nubtha fi al-Tibb al-Tajribi. Memoires ou Travaux Originaux presente et lus a L'Institut Egyptien. Paris. Pp. 505–512.

Shehata, Samer. 1990. Notes on Social Class in Egypt. Honors Thesis, University of California Berkeley.

Shetla, Abdel Moneim. 1976. Commentary on the "Worries" of Fathi Hamada. Al-Taliᶜa 4:55–58 (in Arabic).

Shiloh, A. 1961. The System of Medicine in the Middle East Culture. Middle East Journal 15:277–288.

————. 1968. The Interaction Between the Middle Eastern and Western Systems of Medicine 2:235–248.

Shweder, R.A. 1968. Aspects of Cognition in Zinacanteco Shamans: Experimental Results. *In* Reader in Comparative Religion, 3rd, ed. W.A. Lessa and E.Z. Vogt, eds. New York: Harper and Row.

Singer, Merrill. 1989. The Limitations of Medical Ecology: The Concept of Adaptation in the Context of Social Stratification. Medical Anthropology 10(4): 218–229.

————. 1990. Reinventing Medical Anthropology: Towards a Critical Realignment. Social Science and Medicine 30(2):179–187.

Singer, Merrill, Lani Davison, and Gina Gerdes. 1988. Culture, Critical Theory, and Reproductive Illness Behavior in Haiti. Medical Anthropology Quarterly 2(4):370–385.

Skinner, Elliot. 1988. Female Circumcision in Africa: The Dialectics of Equality. *In* Dialectics and Gender. R.R. Randolph, D.M. Schneider, and M.N. Diaz, eds. Boulder, Colorado: Westview Press. Pp. 195–210.

Smelser, Neil. 1970. Mechanisms of Change and Adjustment to Change. *In* Industrialization and Society. Hoselits and Moore, eds. The Hague: Mouton. Pp. 32–54.

Smith-Rosenberg, Carrol. 1972. The Hysterical Woman: Sex Roles in Nineteenth Century America. Social Research 39(4):652–78.

Smith-Rosenberg, C., and C.E. Rosenberg. 1973. The Female Animal: Medical and Biological Views of Woman and Her Role in Nineteenth Century America. Journal of American History 21:332–356.

Sorj, Bernardo. 1977. The Dialectics of Class and State Apparatus: The Peruvian Case. Dialectical Anthropology 2:285–300.

Spooner, B. 1970. The Evil Eye in the Middle East. *In* Witchcraft Confessions and Accusations. Mary Douglas, ed. London: Tavistock.

Springborg, Robert. 1989. Mubarak's Egypt: Fragmentation of the Political Order. Boulder: Westview Press.

———. 1990. Rolling Back Egypt's Agrarian Reform. MERIP Reports 166:28–30, 38.

Starr, P. 1982. The Social Transformation of American Medicine. New York: Basic Books.

Stauth, Georg. 1989. Capitalist Farming and Small Peasant Housholds in Egypt. *In* The Rural Middle East: Peasant Lives and Modes of Production. Kathy and Pandeli Glavanis, eds. London/Birzeit: Zed Press/Birzeit University. Pp. 122–141.

Stauth, Georg, and Sami Zubaida. 1985. Introduction. *In* Mass Culture, Popular Culture, and Social Life in the Middle East. Frankfurt am Main: Campus Verlag/Boulder: Westview Press. Pp. 11–14.

Stein, H.F. 1976. A Dialectical Model of Health and Illness Attitudes and Behavior Among Slovak-Americans. International Journal of Mental Health 5(2):117–137.

Swagman, Charles. 1988. Letter to Charles Leslie, Chair, IASTAM.

———. 1989. Fija: Fright and Illness in Highland Yemen. Social Science and Medicine 28:381–88.

Taussig, Michael. 1980a. The Devil and Commodity Fetishism in South America. Chapel Hill: University of North Carolina Press.

———. 1980b. Reification and the Consciousness of the Patient. Social Science and Medicine 14B:3–13.

Tiano, Suzan. 1981. The Seperation of Women's Remunerated and Household Work: Theoretical Perspectives on "Women in Development." Women in International Development Working Paper #2. E. Lansing, Michigan: Michigan State University, WID Office.

Tibi, Bassam. 1990. Islam and the Cultural Accommodation of Social Change. Boulder: Westview Press.

Tignor, Robert. 1966. Modernization and British Colonial Rule in Egypt, 1882–1914.

Tomiche, Nada. 1957. Changing Status of Egyptian Women. New Outlook 1:39–43.

———. 1968a. Egyptian Women in the First Half of the Nineteenth Century. *In* Beginnings of Modernization in the Middle East. W.R. Polk and R.L. Chambers, eds. Chicago: University of Illinois Press. Pp. 171–184.

———. 1968b. The Position of Women in the UAR. The Middle East 3(3):129–144.

Toubia, Nahed. 1985. The Social and Political Implications of Female Circumcision: The Case of the Sudan. *In* Women and the Family in the Middle East: New Voices of Change. Elizabeth Fernea, ed. Austin: University of Texas Press. Pp. 148–159.

Tsalikis, George. 1988. Evaluation of the Socialist Health Policy in Greece. International Journal of Health Services 18(4):543–661.

Tucker, Judith. 1976. Egyptian Women in the Work Force. MERIP 50:3–9.
――――. 1983. Problems in the Historiography of Women in the Middle East. International Journal of Middle East Studies 15:321–326.
――――. 1986. Women in Nineteenth Century Egypt. Cairo: American University in Cairo Press.
Turner, Bryan S. 1987. Medical Power and Social Knowledge. London: Sage Publications.
――――. 1990. The Interdisciplinary Curriculum: From Social Medicine to Postmodernism. Sociology of Health and Illness 12(1):1–23.
Ullmann, Manfred. 1978. Islamic Medicine. Edinburgh: University Press.
UNICEF. 1985. Review of the Daya's Training in Egypt. Unpublished Report, Cairo.
Uzzell, D. 1974. Susto Revisited: Illness as Strategic Role. American Ethnologist 1(2):369–377.
Valaoras, V.G., and Mahgoub M. Farag. 1972. Population Analysis of Egypt (1935–1990). Cairo: Cairo Demographic Center.
Valeri, Valerio. 1991. Toward a Historically Informed Anthropology. Current Anthropology 32(1):90–93.
Van Der Geest, Sjaak. 1989. The Charm of Medicines: Metaphors and Metonyms. Medical Anthropology Quarterly 3(4): 345–367.
Von Denffer, Dietrich. 1976. Baraka. Islamic Studies 15(3): 167–186.
Waitzkin, Howard. 1984. The Micropolitics of Medicine: A Contextual Analysis. International Journal of Health Services 14:339–378.
Waterbury, John. 1991. Peasants Defy Categorization (As Well as Landlords and the State). In Peasants and Politics in the Modern Middle East. Farhad Kazemi and John Waterbury, eds. Miami: Florida International University Press. pp. 1–23.
――――. 1983. The Egypt of Nasser and Sadat: The Political Economy of Two Regimes. Princeton, N.J.: Princeton University Press.
Weir, John M. 1948. Report on the Medical Services and Public Health Facilities of Egypt. Unpublished report submitted to the International Health Division, The Rockefeller Foundation.
Wellin, E. 1977. Theoretical Orientations in Medical Anthropology: Continuity and Change Over the Past Half-Century. In Culture, Disease, and Healing. David Landy, ed. New York: Macmillan. Pp. 47–54.
West, Cheryl L. 1991. I Ain't the Right Kind of Feminist. In Third World Women and the Politics of Feminism. Chandra Talpade Mohanty, Ann Russo, and Lourdes Torres, eds. Bloomington: Indiana University Press. Pp. xii–xiii.
Wikan, Unni. 1988. Bereavement and Loss in Two Muslim Communities: Egypt and Bali Compared. Social Science and Medicine 27(5):451–460.
Wolf, Eric. 1990. Distinguished Lecture: Facing Power—Old Insights, New Questions. American Anthropologist 92:586–596.
Worsley, Peter. 1984. The Three Worlds: Culture and World Development. Chicago: University of Chicago Press.
Worthington, E.B. 1946. Middle East Science: A Survey of Subjects Other Than Agriculture. London: His Majesty's Stationery Office.

Young, Allen. 1980. The Discourse on Stress and the Reproduction of Conventional Knowledge. Social Science and Medicine 14B:133–146.

———. 1982. The Anthropology of Illness and Sickness. Annual Review of Anthropology 11:257–285.

Youssef, Nadia. 1974. Women and Work in Developing Societies. Westport, Connecticut: Greenwood Press.

Zaalouk, Malak. 1989. Power, Class and Foreign Capital in Egypt: The Rise of the New Bourgeoisie. London/New Jersey: Zed Books Limited.

Zola, Kenneth Irving. 1978. Medicine as an Institution of Social Control. *In* The Cultural Crisis of Modern Medicine. John Ehrenreich, ed. New York: Monthly Review Press. Pp. 80–100.

ABOUT THE BOOK
AND AUTHOR

The dynamics of sickness and healing are examined in terms of male-female power relations in this study of an Egyptian village. Dr. Morsy goes beyond an account of gender dynamics in a culturally embedded medical discourse by putting her cases of "compromised" health in the context of the local social structure and ideology and linking them with state policies since the Nasser era. *Gender, Sickness, and Healing in Rural Egypt* gives us a unique glimpse into an Arab construction of illness and gender in a period of tremendous change.

Soheir A. Morsy, a medical anthropologist, has held academic appointments at Michigan State University, the American University in Cairo, and, most recently, University of California–Berkeley.